With the Hoods

With the Hoods

The Letters of an Officer with the Royal Naval
Division at Gallipoli during the First World War
ILLUSTRATED EDITION

Charles Lister

With an Extract of the Gallipoli Campaign
from 'The Royal Naval Division'
by Douglas Jerrold

LEONAUR

With the Hoods
The Letters of an Officer with the Royal Naval Division at Gallipoli during the First World War
by Charles Lister
With an Extract of the Gallipoli Campaign from 'The Royal Naval Division'
by Douglas Jerrold

FIRST EDITION

ILLUSTRATED

Leonaur is an imprint of Oakpast Ltd

Copyright in this form © 2017 Oakpast Ltd

ISBN: 978-1-78282-650-7 (hardcover)
ISBN: 978-1-78282-651-4 (softcover)

http://www.leonaur.com

Publisher's Notes

Contents

The Soldier

If I should die, think only this of me:
That there's some corner of a foreign field
That is for ever England. There shall be
In that rich earth a richer dust concealed;
A dust whom England bore, shaped, made aware,
Gave, once, her flowers to love, her ways to roam,
A body of England's, breathing English air,
Washed by the rivers, blest by suns of home.

And think, this heart, all evil shed away,
A pulse in the eternal mind, no less
Gives somewhere back the thoughts by England given;
Her sights and sounds; dreams happy as her day;
And laughter, learnt of friends; and gentleness,
In hearts at peace, under an English heaven.

Ruper Brooke

Introduction

The war had taken possession of Charles Lister with all the intensity of the Crusades of his younger days. Perhaps even with some of their glamour—not much of this, though. This war was a very different affair and occasion. In Hooker's phrase, he looked upon our going into it as "the strong and invincible remonstrance of sound reason." He was no longer a boy liable to the Tolstois and the Gapons and the Fabians. The Call had come upon him as the Holy Ghost came down upon the apostles—as a sudden great sound in the likeness of fiery tongues.

In his last letter to me, written from the hospital ship *Gascon* on August 26th—he died on the 28th—his only complaint is of this third and tiresome interruption of the business in hand. From the nature of the wound I think he must have been in suffering, or anyhow in discomfort equivalent to suffering, but this letter is as clearly and freely written in respect of point and clearness as any he ever wrote me, and the envelope is addressed with unusual distinctness and vigour of pencil. He speaks of the hours going slowly and of his not feeling up to much reading—though he stuck to his books throughout—owing to the monotony of the fixed supine position enforced by his surgeon, but beyond that there is no word of complaint, only regret that this last wound may prove a longer job than the others.

This is what Mr. Mayne, the chaplain of the *Gascon*, wrote me at the time; it is dated August 29, 1915. Charles had died at 7 o'clock in the evening on the 28th, after being taken aboard from Cape Helles somewhere about midnight on the 25th.

He had very skilled attention and very careful nursing while on board, and was, I know, a wonderful patient. He never complained or even spoke of his wound, and if he had pain he bore it very bravely and patiently. But I believe that he did not have too much pain. We talked together sometimes, but he was easily

7

tired, and one could not stay with him long. My great regret is that I did not know yesterday that he was so much worse until rather late and when I went to see him he was unconscious. It is seldom comparatively that one sees a man in such command of himself, and so controlled. The books at his bedside spoke for his literary taste, and the day before he died I lent him a copy of the poems of Rupert Brooke whom we both knew, and who was in the Howe Battalion with your son. (*Author's error was in fact the Hood Battalion*). As I write we are waiting for the boat to take his body ashore at Mudros, where the burial will take place tomorrow. He will lie almost within sound of the heavy guns.

It is very difficult to hit on the seemly balance of anything of the kind I am trying to write, especially having regard to our close relationship and to our always having been great friends and a good deal together. Memory takes me tightly by the hand and leads me back to all kinds of scenes and incidents and places in his company: to the flat horizons and the tulips and the picture galleries of Holland; to charming Munich, its opera and its Bach-abends, its overheated but excellent hotel, its superlative caviar and beer; to the grey-green sweep of the Roman Campagna and hounds running over the *stationatas*; to Milan and to Bergamo; to the steep hills and stones above Helmsdale; to Ross's Hotel and our symposia with Mr. Ross himself—lovely August weather; liver-and-white pointers of beauty and staunchness; to many talks and rides and walks; to London theatres and pavements; to the uplands and rough pastures of Wigglesworth and Bowland.

But I am exceeding and straying outside the confines of my task, and I must let his letters speak for themselves, and rely upon some of his friends to deal with other things outside my own experiences and knowledge of Charles. It would not be possible, and I do not think it would be becoming, for me to attempt any estimate of the higher quality and value of the few years of his mortal life.

So may it be, that so dead yesterday, No sad-eyed ghost, but generous and gay, May serve your memories like almighty wine.

I know not where these lines come from or whose they are; their grammar is certainly not unimpeachable. Years ago, I copied them on to a foreign envelope, and came across it again the other day. As far as a few words can assert that the memories of Life dispute with success the supremacy of Death they seem to manage a good deal.

Ribblesdale. October 1916.

Pre-War Letters from Constantinople

To the Hon. Irene Lawley.

British Embassy, Constantinople,

March 28, 1914.

These are stirring times in which we live. I quite agree that a general election would do no good to any one now. If the Liberals come in again they won't find Ulster any more amenable. If the Tories come in they'll find the rest of Ireland in a similar condition of unrest. I don't understand how they failed to reach an agreement having got so near one unless the whole idea of compromise was impossible from the beginning. The whole Irish business discredits party politics altogether, and the only people at all in a heroic light are the Ulster people, however local their point of view has been.

In this part of the world, too, we have our Ulster; the Greeks on the southern frontier of Albania whom the Powers have decided to assign to Albania have taken matters into their own hands and are having the time of their lives. They'll see themselves damned before they become Albanians, and wish to be independent or Greek.

I can't help liking people who really want a thing. Of course of our present troubles it may be said that the Prime Minister wanted to stop in office, or that Bonar Law wanted to get into office, but I'm old-fashioned enough to think these things don't matter so much as what the Ulster people are fighting for.

I went out a grand walk since writing, up on the down country above the Bosphorus. It is very treeless round here, windswept downs with occasional wooded valleys and sheltered bits where the peach-trees grow, and one can see little clouds of pink blossom. Then occasionally there is a dip in the ground, and there appears a bit of blue sea and a glimpse of the Asiatic coast and the road to Bagdad. There are some fine castles on the Bosphorus, great walled enclosures—walls sloping up and down hill in conformity with the ground, with round high towers at the corner and broken-down little Turkish houses in the middle with the same matchwood walls and red roofs. (The Crusaders—the Christians—built castles wherever they went, much finer castles than any in Europe.—B. W. C.)

The peasants use the buffalo as in India. The Turk is a hopeless mongrel here; one can distinguish no "type," only occasionally one comes across the snub-nosed, slit-eyed, high-cheek-boned, highly coloured Mongolian, and one thinks of the original hordes that came into Europe and swarmed into India under Genghis Khan and Timur. There is a great deal of Circassian blood in the modern Turk, as all the chosen women of the *sultan* and the *pasha* were Circassians, uprooted from the ends of the Black Sea and as white as snow.

The Turks one meets in society have most agreeable manners and conversation. Sir Louis thinks the present sort are really anxious about getting things more into shape. The poverty of the State chest is appalling. Some weeks ago none of the officials were paid, and they couldn't go to their offices because they couldn't afford the tram fare and the price of the lunch. They could have got credit at the Greek shops, but the *mot d'ordre* had gone round that those were to be boycotted by good Ottomans owing to political differences. So you can imagine their suffering. Things are rather better now.

I'm afraid the new government will commit a serious crime, for they have just condemned one Aziz Ali to death on quite frivolous charges. This was the man who did all the fighting in Cyrenaica against the Italians. He is a hero, and looks like becoming a martyr. They may commute the sentence to one of life imprisonment, which is virtually equivalent. Aziz will probably "get ill in jail." The real reason seems to be that Enver, who is trying to be the Napoleon of Turkey, fears him as a possible rival. It will make a very bad impression in Egypt, which is seething with interest in Aziz Ali's fate.

To the Same.

British Embassy, Constantinople,
April 5, 1914.

I've had a very jolly time lately, take it all in all. Lots of work, Harold Nicolson having fallen ill, but some very good rides and walks. The down country from the city up to the Forest of Belgrade is really glorious; white heather and scrub all over the downs, then little valleys up which one rides and which end in woodland paths. There are everywhere violets and scarlet and purple anemones. The occasional villages with their wooden houses, a little mosque with its minaret and orchards in blossom, are most fascinating. Then below there are green hill meadows, and streams very much covered in with trees and scrub.

Yesterday I went to Santa Sofia. From some distance off one thinks it quite small; as one gets nearer one thinks it quite big, and once inside one is really staggered by the size of it. It is immense. Great porphyry and grey marble columns, and great dabs of red and grey marble covering the walls like panels—a perfect Greek-cross shape. The Turks, when they came in, painted over all the mosaics on the ceiling with gold to obliterate the Christian pictures and crosses, and put up their "*merab*" out of line with the orientation of the eastern window.

Also all the prayer-carpets which cover every inch of the floor are skew-eyed. This is because Christian churches are orientated towards Jerusalem, mosques towards Mecca. The nave of the church is covered with vulgar green plaques with gold Arabic lettering of huge size which look like patent-medicine advertisements. These are the names of the first few *Caliphs*, I think. Also, the roof is covered with a sort of silly design of no worth superimposed with the gold paint to hide the Christian symbols. The side aisles, where it is darker and where one is left with the marble walls and pillars, are most impressive. Here one sees less of the defacements of the *infidel*.

These are distressful countries; ever since the war there has been a continual *va et vient* of refugees from one state to another. Greeks had found life impossible under Bulgar rule, Bulgars under Greek rule, and so on, and they all seemed to seek soil under the flag of their own particular nation.

It is a gloomy vision, and one can picture the arrival of these unfortunate victims of a racial hatred equally awake in time of peace as in time of war, and their homelessness. Mussulmans are now pouring into Eastern Thrace from Bulgaria and Greek territories.

And what of social Constantinople? I went on the night of April 1st—a fool indeed—to two parties at the Italian and French Embassies respectively. *Such* nice parties. You would have loved them. It is extraordinary how much politics are talked of an evening in the houses of the rich and the great, when you compare it with Rome. Sir Louis never leaves the side of Talaat Bey at social functions. The French Ambassadress is giving an 1830 ball shortly. I suppose the fancy-dress ball habit would follow one to Honolulu.

To the Same.

British Embassy, Constantinople,
April 12, 1914.

Here we are, still much concerned about Aziz Ali; it is a bad business—on a par with the murder of the Duc d'Enghien by Napoleon, and Maréchal Ney by Louis XVIII—and I wish I could do something. I fear they mean to have his blood—Ugh—one has to meet these red-handed ruffians at parties.

Then we have had Easter, and I sang in the choir. The ambassador went out to Broussa in the yacht and took all the sailors with him, on whom we mostly depend for our musical talent; so, Jones (the butler) and I had to support the "virtuous females," as Mr. Jorrocks would call them, in the choir.

★★★★★★

In a letter dated Alexandria, July 1915, Charles wrote: "Jones is longing to fight, and regretting his over-age"; and in other letters he often alludes to his efficiency and merits.—R.

★★★★★★

It is tiring work, and I nearly burst a blood-vessel. However, the service rattled on very merrily, like an Irish jaunting-car. I gave the women *no* support in the "Alleluias"—a vulgar exclamation the Almighty must really resent—and always on a cracklingly high note. I don't believe you can sing as well as I do. Not as loud, anyway.

I am very happy here and pleased with most things, except that I've lamed Gerry Wellesley's pony; don't tell him. And I've furnished my bedroom at dirt-cheap price—only £16, and that includes a bookcase. But it will be difficult to make my room at all nice. I have also to buy a pony.

I have been to bazaars and looked at carpets—what a complicated hobby. I feel I'll *never* know anything about them. But the really good ones are like great sheets of deep, glowing gems—a sea of them—and the shops here have stacks of them.

And loot! think of it—think of the breach in those walls, white and brilliant against the blue skies, and the rush down the roughly cobbled streets with the dark *bazaar* arcades, and the trembling Greeks and Armenians on their knees, their faces pale and their lips quivering as they beg that something may be spared them. And the ride home with the spoils, each to his mistress, to lay the choicest at her feet.

To A. F. Lascelles.

Constantinople,
April 13, 1914.

L. Mallet is a most agreeable chief. He thinks George Lloyd will be Parliamentary Under-Secretary for Foreign Affairs in the next Tory Government. I think it is very difficult to make up one's mind which has behaved worst, during recent bothers, of the two parties. My impression is the government did want to launch troops on a perfectly orderly part of the Empire, as if it were an enemy's territory. It is quite true that the Ulster people were potentially disorderly. But the point is that they have given no provocation for such measures. In the case of strikes, troops are never sent till riots actually take place, and then on the distinct understanding that they are to defend property, etc. This cry of the army *versus* the people is quite absurd and won't catch on.

I cannot think the Prime Minister's plan of letting things rip until the Ulster movement got such purchase that he could turn to his supporters and Redmond and say that he must grant concessions has answered. This, I suppose, was his idea. However, the other alternative policy of preventing Ulster from arming might have had worse results, and made his own followers even less amenable to some settlement than they are now. Since you wrote things look rather better. A General Election now will do very little good as a solution. The parties should agree on a Federal solution—a very un-ideal one, in my view—and have all vital points settled in advance before they go to the electors. Besides, *rebus sic stantibus*, whichever party gets in, the situation remains revolutionary.

To my mind the question, on its merits, has long been settled—no incorporation of Ulster into a Home Rule Ireland; Home Rule for the rest of Ireland.

I think A. J. B.'s estimates are unduly pessimistic. After all, the thing remains "*much ado about nothing*," considering the relative smallness of the interests involved.

To the Hon. Irene Lawley.

British Embassy, Constantinople,
April i6, 1914.

One approaches the "amusements" with high expectations, and one leaves them with a feeling of pleasant surprise that it wasn't worse. London amusements, with few exceptions, are not so. Expectations generally run high and fall short. Not in my mind, because I always

13

liked the moment—*plus ou moins*. But one feels one would like other moments much better.

Here we had a *cotillon* at the French Ambassadress's: I sat unwisely in a rather prominent place, loosely attached to a pillar of the British colony. I was continually pulled up from my seat by charming and unknown damsels, and made to dance. You, who know how well I dance, can picture what this must have been. Generally I got through all right, and lasted out the figure—but not always. Dreadful having greatness thrust on me.

After a rather unusual number of collisions I retired to a back seat. It was a jolly party, and I got out well at 1 a.m.; not so a poor colleague, who was collared by our formidable hostess and made to partner a *jeune fille* for the rest of the evening. The French Ambassadress said, "*On est Ambassadrice mais on est pourtant femme*"; and that at moments of great crisis, "*On cesse d'être Ambassadrice, on redevient femme.*" Wednesday next I shall confront this social potentate in 1830 costume. I like fancy balls to see other people's dresses for one moment, and one's own in the glass. But the idea of not being in one's ordinary clothes for a whole evening makes me shudder. I should like to get my fancy clothes off *at once*. My 1830 costume will be (1) whiskers, (2) Lord R.'s riding trousers, (3) hunting coat and waistcoat, (4) special jabot stock, (5) hunting top-hat.

I have lamed Gerry Wellesley's horse; sent his dog to the vet. for a little visit (in my charge she insisted on being sick every morning); hired a horse who is estimable if inelegant, and furnished my bedroom and much of my sitting-room.

I feel no courage about buying things in a *bazaar*. They are all such experts here, from the ambassador downwards, and I feel that for such a short time as I'll have here it's no use. I suppose I haven't the real collector's spirit. My Turkish goes on badly. The work has a compelling charm. I am pining to travel, but can't get away as we're so short, so I shall come home by a wonderful detour in the autumn late, or winter.

Aziz has got fifteen years, equivalent to a death sentence. He is bronchial.

To Mrs. Graham Smith.
British Embassy, Constantinople,
April 26, 1914.

Many thanks for your charming letter, which I should have answered before now.

I have been very pleased with life here, and I am sure I shall like this place very much. The work is, of course, very much more interesting than at Rome, and one has every sort of thing to do, what with *bazaar* riding and sight-seeing.

The chief political interest just now is Turco-Greek relations. They are very strained. An exchange of population is in progress between Macedonia and Thrace at present, and every sort of hardship is involved in the migration. Then there is the question of the islands. The Turks have a very active Minister of Marine, and the confidence inspired by his reforms in the fleet may tend to make the Turkish Government rather unyielding on the Mitylene and Scios question.

Otherwise things are pretty quiet. The hunting here is quite amusing. A drag pursued by some twelve rather measly dog hounds over rather rough hill and heather country. The master wears a pink coat and hunting cap of velvet—not hard. It is very comic. The Germans are very keen, and some Turkish officers come out, who are very agreeable. They talk French, and don't like talking German, which is the lingo one would think they would naturally know.

The Turks generally are more accessible now. The ministers give dinner-parties of great splendour. Enver gave a very magnificent feast, I heard, with a band playing Wagner. He has married a royal princess, and plays the grand *seigneur* with great assiduity.

The society here is very official and political. Ministers and ambassadors on every sofa talking high politics, very unlike Rome, which was frivolous and where the politicians never went out in the *monde*.

★★★★★★

Mrs. Graham Smith was Charles's Aunt Lucy, third daughter of the late Sir Charles Tennant and sister of Lady Ribblesdale. Easton Grey, near Malmesbury, was a second home to Charles in the holidays.—B. W. C.

★★★★★★

To the Hon. Irene Law ley.
British Embassy, Constantinople,
May 9, 1914.

How I envy your Spain and your drives to Sierra, and so on. . . . I've never been to Cameldoli—several places called that, one near Genoa, one near Naples—I never went to either. We were so d——d busy at Naples that we could never get out for expeditions. I think I rather misspent my time in Italy and didn't travel enough, being so much taken up with the hunting. Worst of life is one can't do everything at once, and that's what one finds to be very much the case here. The gun-running adventure must have been thrilling; but it looks now as if the crisis, as far as any real danger of civilians goes, was passed. I do not personally approve of "Federal" systems, but it seems that there is no way out except to give all turbulent persons (or potentially turbulent) exactly what they want and be done with it. I haven't read any speeches lately but I heard Mr. Birrell's was very good. The government are very lucky not to have been hounded out of office with ignominy. I can't help thinking a more efficient Opposition would have got them out.

We had a delicious day—Harold, H.E., and me—at Therapia, about twelve miles up Bosphorus—it is the Posillipo of this place and lovely. It has a terraced garden, chock full of roses and stocks and irises and every sort of flower. Embassy has just been burnt down, but See's house is standing, a jolly old wooden house, whitewashed but generally Turkish style. The sea is at the door, we went up in the *mouche* and picked roses. Opposite Therapia is the bleak coast of Asia Minor, red soil, rock, bare scrub hills. It has a great charm for me, more so than the European side. Up and down the Bosphorus there are continual flights of little birds like petrels, little lost souls going up into the gloomy, windswept expanses of the Black Sea. There is always wind at Therapia and *always* colleagues, which makes it less nice than P. But there are always lovely flowers and garden ponds.

We have had one or two jolly hunts, the last of them graced by the "flirt" of an important personage, a lady who is not received in polite society here. His lady was also at the meet. So His E. had to steer a clear course. My poor little horse had a swollen knee as a result of the chase. I'd a jolly ride as soon as the "flirt" had left me with a broken heart. And now I can't ride.

Then there has been a great *festa* here, St. George's Day, Elias's day for the Mohammedans. The whole people go out if the weather is warm, and have a picnic off roast lamb. This time there were not many as the wind was cold. But a good many people came over. It is an extraordinary thing to see them all squatting on the ground, perfectly happy doing nothing, and one is reminded of the women and children sitting round the camp-fires of Genghis Khan, the real nomad spirit still alive. Perhaps they are still tired and quite happy simply to rest after their long marches. It is a becoming dress this black sort of nun's habit they all wear, but rather *triste* in this *ambiente* of cypresses. I doubt if I've yet seen a single real Turkish woman. On St. George's

Day, we saw a number of Imperial princesses and Circassians—in broughams—very pink and white but with black hair, dressed in light blue sort of bridesmaids' dresses and caps.

We have all suffered bitterly from the cold, but it is now at last lovely, and I am writing this in the garden, so forgive pencil. It has great possibilities, this garden, and it absolutely overlooks the Golden Horn with the row of mosques beyond. There is an upper terrace lined with orange-trees, fine, but then lawns with dreary Russian-salad-like-sort-of-beds and no Cyprus avenue or jolly perspective of an avenue.

To the Same.

British Embassy, Constantinople,
May 15, 1914.

So, you too are fired with the *wanderlust*. It is simply burning in me as the result of the presence of Miss Gertrude Bell, fresh from the heart of Arabia. She has been to a place called Hazzil, where you still find the East of the Middle Ages. It is ruled by the Amir Bim Rashid. He is a boy of sixteen, but he lives in the old-fashioned style. When Miss Bell arrived, he was away raiding, leaving behind him his grandmother—Fatima by name; fairy story at once—and his wives, concubines, and *eunuchs*. It is an entirely women-run show, Fatima being *absolutely* supreme.

The only other "European" in the place when Miss B. was there was a Circassian concubine sent to a former Bim Rashid by Abdul Hamid and passing from one head of the family to the next. The whole place smells of blood. They massacre each other in the traditional way, and the common people look with horror at the palace code of morals, and the wives pass from one stage to another as the wives of David passed to his rebel son Absalom. Miss B. was lodged in a magnificent Arabian Nights colonnaded hall. She went to audiences given by the regent, a cypher in Fatima's hands, and by the ladies of the *harem*; the ladies asked her what was the difference between Islam and Christianity, and she told them the words of the prophet Isa (Jesus).

There was a real Mogul atmosphere of gems and brocades, all come from India, and burning spices, and outside a silent town. Not a footfall can be heard, for all the streets are sand, and the camel's footfall is noiseless. The little Circassians sighed for the tramways of Constantinople. The Bim Rashid's are on the downward grade; the "man" of Arabia is one Bim Sand, Sheikh of El Hassa on the Gulf. He it was who was expelled from his city by a Bim Rashid, and reconquered it at the head of eleven men. He came by night to his wife, and she said as he knocked, "Who are you?" and he answered, "This is no time for love and kisses"; and then he went with his eleven men into every house where there were men of Bim Rashid's and killed them, and by the morning was master of the city. And to hear all this second-hand. It's *maddening*.

The Turkish provinces are in an appalling condition; in the most administered parts of the country the disorder is worst. There is not even the tribal sense of honour. Every single Arab has a rifle, and the Turks can do nothing. They have no troops; what they have are riddled with typhus. This is the great recruiting ground for the Turkish army, Asia Minor proper; there are *no* men for the wars in the Yemen, and the Balkans have thinned the population to an incredible extent. The poverty is abject.

Things are shaping for war with Greece. The Greeks will come to no arrangement not based on the *status quo post bellum*; and the Turks can offer them nothing in exchange for the islands now in Greek occupation, except the islands in Italian occupation, which in Greek views are a very bad egg, as it is doubtful if the Italians will ever turn out (I think they will, but the Greeks don't). The Greeks, if they fight now, can by a single declaration of war stop the Turks getting the Dreadnoughts due to arrive this summer. If they temporise and let the Turks get these Dreadnoughts they will have to fight at a disadvantage. They *can't* get a Dreadnought for a long time. The only thing that may deter them is the fact that the Turks can bully Greeks living in Turkey. Even at this moment massacres of Greeks are feared at Smyrna, so incensed is the Moslem population against the Greek.

It is a tragic country, and we may have to play a big role in Arabia, where the *Sheikhs* are already virtually independent, and where it would be very easy for us to establish a loosely knit protectorate and keep them to some extent from each other's throats. The Turks have failed to do this. At this moment I suppose we should give the present Turkish Government a chance of getting things right; they are the only possible government. The alternative is chaos leading to European occupation; and we are spectators at a distance—such a distance.

Turkish homes? I've been able to see very, very little of them. The Sultan Abdul, you will be glad to hear, has just got in another wife— one of his former second strings. He seems full of beans. It appears he had two children during the time of his exile—from 1909 to 1911—

one white and one jet black.

This last wife has given us a lot of trouble, as the Turkish Government had given us assurances she should live in peace with her son, after she was chucked out from the palace at the time of Abdul Hamid's exile; and the fact that she has been made to rejoin her former husband, has considerably inconvenienced her present "domestic" arrangements, consisting apparently in a life of unbridled orgies. The Imperial wives are recruited from any and every class, generally the lowest of the low, by sort of spies. The same applies to the wives of the big swells. Result: you get the blood quite spoiled, and the rise of any kind of aristocracy is rendered impossible. This must have had very harmful results, and now that the Turks are directing the Greeks and Armenians, they cannot find administration among their own subjects. Hence the progressive increase of foreign officials, etc., etc.

To the Same.
British Embassy, Constantinople,
June 8, 1914.

At a time when you write me long political letters, the crisis must be serious, and all things are possible. Write me another when you get home. We have not had much politics lately: mostly concerned with petty wrangles as to the size of the ship in which our admiral is to visit the *Sultan*. This is a very material point; bigger ships have more officers, and this entails larger banquets for the *grand vizier* and *Sultan* and more expense. The former's face fell perceptibly when he was told that the British admiral was coming to see the *Sultan*.

We hear less about war between Greece and Turkey, but things are shaping very badly. The Turks have a strong hand. If they fight they have nothing to lose. If the Greeks win the thing is not settled; either they fight before the big Turkish ships come out, in which case the Turks skulk in the Bosphorus where they can't be got at, and as soon as they have got their ships out press their demands again, or the Greeks fight while the ships are on the way or later, in which case they may destroy the Turkish fleet, and any way temporarily secure the islands; but the Turks won't give up the idea of *revanche*, and they always have in their hand so many Greek subjects whose lives they can make quite unbearable. The only way out is an exchange of islands. But this the Greeks will never consent to: they hold the Turkish naval power in utter contempt and don't care if their nationals in Turkey suffer. However, perhaps if the issue is postponed things may

19

straighten themselves out.

On Wednesday, we had the king's birthday garden party. The Ambassador stood on a carpet under a tree, and the Secretaries and Dragoman led down notable after notable into the radiant presence and then conducted them to a superb buffet—Turks, English, Armenians, Greeks, and so on. Men in cowls like lamp extinguishers, in chimney-pot *berettes*, in turbans and flowing robes, came up and fired off little speeches at him.

★★★★★★

Charles's long-standing interest in the perplexed affairs of the Near East suggested the ride through Macedonia and Albania described in the following letters. The "Durazzo crisis" discussed in the spring in the chanceries of Constantinople, and news of fighting in Albania—over a perennial Epirote grievance—added possibly the charm and invitation of a lost cause to the excursion.

First we touch the history of Serbia in its year of triumph over Bulgaria after the Second War. The first Balkan war of the Christian States against the Turks ended with the Peace of Adrianople 1912. In the Second War, Bulgaria attacked Serbia and Greece after they had formed an alliance to resist the claims of Bulgaria, discontented with the provisions of the peace.

The scene of battle visited at Kilkitsch is the field of Bregalnika, where the Bulgarian general fell on the Serbians suddenly, and where after two days' fighting the Serbs were victorious on July 1, 1913. Kilkitsch, burnt by their Greek allies, remained Serbian by the Peace of Bucharest, August 10, 1913. The scene at Kilkitsch described is typical of Serbia in the process of consolidating her new territories and moving her populations. On the other hand, the linguistic and political Babel of Albania is represented by Durazzo, the capital, too much agitated at the moment by a Greek revolt for the wise English traveller to enter.

Koritza in Albania, which was reached, is a city of great antiquity. It is the centre of much Anglo-Hellenism today. The Epirotes' cause summarized elsewhere by Charles as "the protest that they are Greeks and not Turks," was the supposed motive for the fighting which had recently dyed its streets red and that was still going on as Charles approached the scene which all along had been his goal.

But whatever passing sympathy towards an Epirote cause inspired his start, his journey in Albania was marked with prudence and moderation, even detachment towards "the revolt of Tchukes." Charles's description of the nature of the cause at issue draws a picture of a cause obscure enough to discourage active partisanship.

The Greek monastery visited on the way is near Karies, on Mount Athos. The Russian monks described belong probably to the great religious houses above the landing-places named Russovnik or Laura, on the Ionian Sea.— B. W. C.

★★★★★★

To the Same.

Salonica,
June 14, 1914.

I am very flourishing; off to Monastir tomorrow. I began my travels Monday and went to Mount Athos. Mount A. is like this, a long broken ridge running into this marvellous peak, the side of the ridge; its innumerable ravines are thickly wooded scrub and heather with wild holly on the lower slopes and chestnuts and oaks and pines on the higher. The convents are mostly within two or three hours at nearest of each other, and are only approachable by mule or boat. I expected a sort of huge monastic building, cloister on cloister, didn't you?—rather like S. Marco at Florence ten times over: or, perhaps more frowning and castellated.

They are, as a matter of fact, great rambling country houses built in sometimes an English country house style, Lutyens, or the Stamboul style, round a sort of central court, most of which is taken up by a Byzantine church formed like the Greek cross and the dome in the centre. Inside there is a sort of covered *loggia* at first, then the church. The *iconostasis* dividing the inmost shrine (or sanctuary) from the rest. The *iconostasis* is a rood screen covered with icons, curious painted faces peeping out of an armour plating of gold and jewels, and an occasional brown hand visible.

The gold and silver work is very wonderful, mostly tenth and eleventh century. Then the cups are things of wonderful workmanship, presented as a rule by some Byzantine emperor or his particular community. One I saw was in silver with little figures in gorgeous enamel worked all round, and another was of some sort of opalescent marble with gold setting and handles. Then there was a fine silver crucifix with the Emperor Constantine's seal on it which the abbot told me he was going to take back to Constantinople. There are also marvellous relics, not so much the dirty old bones themselves as the gold cases in which they are shelled.

Through a chink in a wonderful gold and jewelled gauntlet you see the hand of St. Luke or St. John, a withered brown substance, rather like Lady ——'s personality, I should think, seen through her glowing outward form. The Greek Church have a strange tendency for "angelification." St. John Baptist is always represented with wings of an angel, and the angels who visited Abraham at Mamre and were chaffed by Sarah are supposed to have been the Holy Trinity. The Byzantine Church spent much energy in discussions on the sex of angels. I don't know what would happen if they came to Mount Athos, or if this question was ever settled.

The monks were very hospitable and charming people; only one did I find who could talk French, and they did not seem to have any great cultivation. They were feverishly interested in politics. The ritual of a call was rather complex; on arrival one was ushered into a room— Axminster carpets and maple armchairs of inferior quality, walls hung with portraits of all crowned heads, oleographs and photographs. One of them brought a tray with jam, liqueurs, and glasses of water; and the proper procedure was to take a spoonful of jam, then a glass of water, then a liqueur. I made several mistakes.

I tried to combine the jam and the water as a sort of *sirop*. I had to talk Turkish to them, my Albanian servant interpreting in Greek, so you can imagine what a brilliant standard conversation reached. They often took me to their libraries where there are lovely manuscripts and little golden-backgrounded angels and evangelists every twenty pages or so, and occasionally one comes across an emperor's handwriting in purple, *i.e.* scarlet ink always; not many fine bindings. I didn't stay at a monastery; I was only there (Mount Athos) two days, and the headquarters, a place called Karies, is the most central. The scarcity which reigns there is remarkable; one evening our host could only find three eggs.

The monks seem to absorb all the eatables. My last day I went to see a Russian monastery, Moslem and organised on sort of Selfridge lines, almost two thousand people dependent on it. I saw the dinner the monks were going to have—one piece of salt fish with sauerkraut, not up to sample. Monasticism must be a vegetable sort of life tinged with discomforts no sensible man would accept.

From Mount Athos to this place (Salonica) on a dirty old boat, where the whole of the third class was taken up by Moslem refugees going to Salonica to get a boat for Turkey. They lay in the hold on their beds and mattresses, a heap of human beings one on top of the other, occasionally lit up by flashes of lightning from behind the mountains. The women wore black Turkish dresses and palest veils and head-dress in one. While they slept their troubled sleep a couple of Greek soldiers were dancing on the bridge, singing curious songs and rather drunk. You saw the whole discomfort of life here in one flash. This is the coveted city, which has been fought for and will be fought for yet again.

There is a magnificent semi-circular sweep of harbour, and from the harbour rise red roof after red roof up to the Venetian castellated walls and the fort beyond, Genoese towers by the sea close up by the walls, and in the fort, there are old Mussulman houses almost up to Stamboul, but in plaster instead of wood. The country around is barren down lands, cleared of vegetation, and a great plain on one side. The Jews are the real feature of Salonica. There are about 80,000 of them out of a population of 150,000. Most of the Salonica Jews are descended from Spanish Jews expelled by Ferdinand and Isabella. There is nothing else like it in this part of the world. There is no other town where the Jews are so much a community by themselves; they keep their old names intact also.

Politics, I need not say, are the chief interest here, and, as connected with them, refugees; and I have seen heaps and heaps of them all saying more or less the same thing.

They are just put into vast camps here, the arrivals from Turkish territory, till they can be settled, and they are given a loaf of bread a day per head by the Greek Government. Then there are Greeks from the Caucasus who have come here hoping to find the streets paved with gold, sitting on their baggage in the harbour; and there are Mussulmen leaving Christian territory, huddled into mosques, houses, anywhere till they get their boat.

Today we went out to the battlefield of Kilki, where the Serbs beat the Bulgars in the Allies War, and we saw the trenches and stood where the Bulgar General Staff directed the action, and went over the burnt ruins of the tower fired by the Greeks after the battle in very cold blood. Nearby, an enormous camp of Serb refugees from Asia and Thrace; the little boys tried to sell us bullets and shells, and the old women begged from us, and the calm of the whole scene was very impressive.

23

To the Same.

After Salonica we got off to Monastir. It is a nice little Turkish country town in the middle of a large plain with mountains all round. I stayed there one day only, and in the morning went to see the battle-field. It is a very good sight, and the most of the fighting took place on a very high hill, wooded in its lower reaches and bare on the top. The Turks had nearly trenched it, and were driven from position to position by the Serbs. It is curious to see the trenches dug while the Serbs advanced. Sometimes they are little scrapings with the bayonet simply and just dug up by a man to protect himself for the moment, sometimes rather more elaborate. The fighting went on for about three days. Below in the plain there are very heavy marshes across which the Serb army had to advance. Some of them stayed there about twenty-six hours, in winter too. They are tough devils.

From Monastir I headed my descent into Albania, This has so far consisted of two days' ride to a place called Koritza and two days' ride from Koritza on the way to a place called El Bassan, which I don't suppose I shall ever get to as the road is closed. The first day I had to make in a carriage with an attendant Serbian official who was to sort of bear-lead me—a rather tiresome little man. I don't like their jacks in office. The man of these parts if once he is educated is inclined to go downhill in character and more still in charm. He gets into the slouch-hat stage of civilization and loses his interest for the European sentimentalist busybody and also some real qualities

We went to a place called Stenia on a lovely crystal blue lake, Lake Presbra, with beautiful brown rocky hills all round except on the Monastir side, where there is a plain full of poplars like all the flat country here, and rather reminding one of France. We were met by a Serbian officer, in command of the little detachment there, and he made the soldiers do their little dances for us. They consisted in little crab-like steps with the men in a ring all round a gentleman who played bagpipes in the middle, and were very racy of the soil. The Serbian peasant seems a genial and very gay individual, always smiling and friendly. He is said to be capable of great latent cruelty.

We had a very friendly meal. The Serbs do not, happily, try to commit one to political opinions. The next day I went on along the side of the lake through even more pretty country, first great oak woods, then rocky hills covered with a lot of scrub and sort of wild box shrub, which is very pretty, and occasional great carpets of flowers. This day we had to ride practically all the time. I left my Serb friend on the Greco-Serb frontier, for we had to go through a little bit of Greece before entering the promised land. He wanted to come with me into Albania, but I knocked that on the head, saying that he would compromise me, which he would have done. I then, when it was a question of going through Greece, told him that he had better not, as he might compromise me there also. He was not a bad little fellow, but I had had enough of him.

At the frontier it was rather exciting. I wondered very much if I was going to get through. They sat me down in a little tent on a sort of floor of boxwood, and there I drank coffee and smoked cigarettes in suspense, while they had to go and find their officer, which seemed to be ages. It looked as if I would have to beat a humiliating retreat, which would have much pleased my Serbian friends, for they all said that I should be stopped for sure; they want to make out that this country is in high disorder and cannot run itself. After about half an hour I was let through amid tremendous demonstrations of Anglo-Albanian fraternisation. They told me about "Sultan Wild," and what blighters the Greeks were, and how much they liked the English.

I rode into Koritza very happy, and stayed with a missionary there, a nice man full of politics with a jolly little wife. My head reels with all they told me about the linguistic question in Epirus and the state of mind of those unfortunate people who didn't want to be Albanians and thought they were Greeks, and so on. The next morning, I saw the prefect, the bishop, the President of the Court of Appeal, and a curious old monk who had been at Mount Athos, a singular example of the unfertile type of intellect produced by monasticism combined with that diseased nationalism which is a feature of every one's mentality out here. He also breakfasted with us next morning.

The church at Koritza is lovely—built about 1707, but at first sight one would take it for a twelfth-century church. This is a real sign how far back this jolly country is. At first sight one wouldn't think so at Koritza. The country is flat; from the rock which forms the frontier into new Greece one sees a huge expanse of very well-cultivated plain. There are a number of very educated French- and English-speaking Albanians, full of modern notions; clever men, I should think. Then one sees lots of people unarmed, and the first impression is of a very quiet countryside. One can hardly believe that the Greeks were street-fighting in the town as lately as April; it is almost disappointing—one expects mountains rugged as one has never seen before, and so on.

From Koritza it was a jolly ride to a little place called Pogratetch, at the top of Lake Ochrida, which is a huge bit of water where they pull out very good trout, through the same quiet sort of country—oak-woods on all the hills, or rather oak scrub. They never let a tree grow here, it is always cut down for firewood. Today another lovely ride along the side of Lake Ochrida. Our escort passed the time shooting the fishes from their horses, which we could see in the jolly limpid water as we went along.

After about three hours along the lake, the wildest hills, rock and boxwood, with herons sitting on the tops of the "crags" in suitable attitudes, we went up and over a sort of pass into the plain of the Shumbi Valley. The Shumbi is a jolly river—rapid, with banks steep down into the water, red soil. We crossed the Shumbi, and are now in a little sort of rest-house. I am in a room like a prison and lying on matting, my bed for tonight. I am afraid I shall have to go back from here. There are insurgents within a few hours of us. I wanted to go on and made a scene. They said that I did so on my own responsibility and they will give me no escort. I think I shall funk it. They expect definite information tomorrow, and I shall act accordingly.

I am sorry for this unfortunate country, still more so for those who love it. It has too many neighbours and too few friends. The hero of a Henty novel would no doubt at once take command of these people and lead them against the enemy's positions. But I shan't, and I am sure it is the last thing they would like. Letra and the rest of them wish to make out a case for the view that Albania should in the first instance have been partitioned between herself and Greece. Well, we will see.

Later.—They (*i.e.* the authorities) *begged* me not to go beyond Tchukes. My *kavass*, after kicking a good deal, expressed great hesitation, so I funked it. Twenty hours' travelling yesterday finds me back here. Yesterday I started at four, got to the Serb frontier on horseback by 6.30, and to Straga about nine; carriage there to Monastir; two breakdowns and a walk or two, to and from places where fresh carriages available. It's the strenuous life. All over now. I am sorry. I am quite Albanoman, though I doubt their vaunted fighting qualities. These people at Tchukes and the insurgents opposed to them will sit opposite each other indefinitely. Then the authorities will bring a gun up and the rebels will scatter.

The men I talk to of the Tchukes "force" said they meant to impress the rebels by superior strength but not to fight them! The drilled peasant is really the best fighter, I should think, not the "wild man."

British Embassy, Therapia,
July 5, 1914.

Our life here has been very agreeable, with a lot of riding and not too much work. I nearly had one nasty jar: my horse, whom I was taking up a little bank, swerved into the fence, and I got my head entangled in brambles right round my neck. I was nearly pulled off, but not quite, and came back home with a line of blood round the neck as if someone had cut the head off and replaced it. The people I passed on the way home turned pale at this ghoulish sight.

The admiral has now left us; his visit was a success, I think, and the heir-apparent went on board his ship. This was a score over the Germans, whom he did not visit. He was nearly drowned in endeavouring to get on board, as the sea was very rough, and his launch captain very incompetent. I unhappily missed the *Sultan* at dinner; they did not know when I should be back from the "wilds." *Sultey* was in great form; he guffawed loudly when the ambassador remarked the dining-room was very large, and a second time when the ambassador asked him if he ever dined alone there. The food and wines were, I am told, mediocre. The admiral got a 150-guinea watch for his pains and a portrait of the heir-apparent in a silver frame. *Sultey* is very interested in King George's health, and always asks for it.

The Gerrys last night gave a very notable *festa* in their wonderful garden. We went up through a beautifully lit tunnel on to a terrace high up, and sat on carpets under pine-trees by the light of Japanese lanterns, and listened to wonderful Greek singers, who sang songs in which they had to bleat like sheep; occasionally a *basso* very *profondo* gave tongue in fine style. Very like a scene from the Decameron, if not so lascivious, with nice little boys to play with. I think this was a sort of house warming.

The new adviser to the Ministry of Justice is staying with us—a young barrister. Eton and Oxford, a high mind, and a profound knowledge of the Insurance Bill. What other qualifications could you want for inspiring respect in the Turkish mind? He is a very nice fellow.

We have given dinner to the ambassador. The German Ambassadress, who is a great friend of my housemate, Hugh Thomas, was the chief *clou*, and everything went very well.

I think this is all the Therapia news. I am afraid it is hardly scandalous enough for the jaded palate of the Londoner. I am principally kept informed of the London news by the "Letters of Eve" which appear in the *Tatler* weekly. I am much interested to hear that political feeling is running high.

To the Same.

Therapia,
July 12, 1914.

There is a writing paper famine in this house, so I shall have to keep a very straight line across the page. There is also a famine in events, as this place is very much the "cool sequestered vale of life," and the summer doings of a small, intimate, and not very interesting society require the subtle handling of a Jane Austen.

I have to sell my pony. There is no help for it. I am so full of work, as I have to know all about Kurds and Armenia, things which are at present the merest names to me; and I am also taking on *proprio motu*(?) an endeavour to get hold of what anthropological information our Consuls possess. I am writing them a circular which they will, I am afraid, think a monument of insolence, and probably throw into the wastepaper basket, if such things exist in Kurdistan. So I won't ride enough to keep my dear pony, and as I rather want cash he will have to go.

I am reading Sir C. Eliot's work on Turkey. It is an extraordinary work, and the lucidity with which he deals with the various heresies in the Eastern Church, and the migration of the Turkish tribes is quite amazing. The riddle to me of the history of the East is the ethnical kinship, quite indisputable, of the Sultans of Stamboul and the Mogul of India. In things like appreciation of the arts they are as far apart as—say—the Southend-on-Sea Town Council of today and the Signory of Florence of the Middle Ages. However, they were both nomads and dwellers in tents, as can be seen from the Mogul buildings. Here they were such copy-cats, and simply added the minaret to the Byzantine church.

It is extraordinary to see their women-folk out on a day's pleasure, quite happy just sitting in the grounds in the shade resting from the long day's march over the hot desert in their subconscious selves, I suppose nomads still in spirit—a curious contrast to the English who on the occasion I'm thinking of were out also for a day's pleasure, and getting themselves hot and thirsty playing cricket in the glaring sun. I like the looks of the Turkish women with their soft darkling eyes and neat little features, and clean, clear complexions. They look so full of inward peace, and so cherished and cared for; they have also the charm of great seriousness—at least in appearance—and of that certain knowledge of what their part is in life. I don't believe you, any of you, have.

They are a contrast to the Slav woman. The Slav looks on his womenfolk simply as drudges; they mayn't marry before they've given so many years of work in the fields. When they do marry they are wizen-like old crab-apples and haven't a trace of looks. The Turk, who is a gentleman, does look after his women, and if he isn't chivalrous at least, in a mild way, invests them with some kind of glamour. I'm not sure women aren't really happier if they live in the Oriental way. I doubt if the West is really much of a gainer from the freedom its women enjoy. However, I don't suppose you'd always like to be dressed like the women on that postcard sitting by the tombs.

We have been much thrilled by an hour spent at one of the *Sultan's* mosques on the opposite shore, a glorious building of pink marble and stone, with great palatial rooms built on a little eminence by the sea covered with trees, with a wonderful view down the Bosphorus. It is about a hundred years old, built at the time of the treaty of (illegible) with the Russians. We are at present very *bien* with the German Ambassadress, who has twice dined with us. She is a charming woman, a master at tennis, and a tall, queenly, "perfect lady" type, which I rather like—a lot to say for herself. What an awful tragedy about dear Denny Anson. That rugged charm and Viking spirit and glorious laugh. I liked him because I also felt he was doing the sort of things I should have liked to have done, but hadn't the nerve and will to do—and he was such a powerful swimmer. One's circle grows constantly narrower.

To the Same.

Therapia,
July 20, 1914.

How curious it is that deaths nowadays always cause *embêtements* among the survivors. At least three recent ones that I know of have done so and been the cause of the breaking up of life-long friendships. I believe we have subconsciously harked back to the point of view of the witchdoctor, and that we also think if anyone dies someone of his neighbours is personally responsible. If we accepted S. G.'s views on life and death, it would never be so. We, however, are an irreligious crowd, and have not even the fine fatalism of the Moslem. I am sure it is this want of religion which makes people so often squabble like ghouls at the grave-head.

Let us leave these sad subjects and get back to the wooded heights and brilliant blue of the Bosphorus. We all went a swimming party one day with the Germans, the Ambassador and Ambassadress. Some of us rode and the others went by *mouche*. It was a jolly day, and my first bathe since here. The Bosphorus itself is always agitated into tiresome little waves which fall into one's mouth, so one has to go out practically to the Black Sea for real pleasure. Also the current is so strong that it is impossible to swim up; one must go down. I have had several bathes since, and on one occasion nearly left my Chancery keys—*vital* to the Empire—at the place where I was undressing. As much as my place was worth. I should have then had to bury myself in Gisburne and to become a master of hounds.

I have dined with the American Ambassador, a spread of about fourteen courses, the aerated waters *coulaient à flots*, but the wine was less facile. Brotherly love was, howbeit, much in the ascendant. I sat next the Danish Minister, the fortunate husband of a lovely lady. He is like all Scandinavians, but we have identical views as to the value of exercise, and are both confirmed opponents of the cold bath: that is the type who has produced Ibsen. We have nothing so obvious to revolt against. After dinner I talked to his wife.

I must get up now, as I have to buy a cowboy hat for the *bal costumé*—it's the same world all over, and no far cry from the Tiber to the Bosphorus.

★★★★★★

Charles Buxton mentioned in the following letter was the eldest son of Lord Buxton. At nineteen he inclined so strongly to Socialism as to be claimed as a convert. After devoted work for the working men's college alluded to he put his theories into practice on a small holding. He was farming at Wye when he died at twenty-two. To Mrs. Hamlyn Charles Lister confided at Constantinople his hope that his own experience of Socialism would bear fruit in his life, expanded as it was by life abroad.
—B. W. C.

★★★★★★

To Mrs. Hamlyn.

Therapia,
July 25, 1914.

Many thanks for your charming letter. I was very much attached to

Charles Buxton, but had no idea he was so devoted to the simple life. He was always serious-minded, of course. I fancy his handling of the Ruskin College difficulties was very able and inspired great respect.

"We" in my letter was myself and my Albanian *kavass*—a jolly old fellow who had been with Aubrey Herbert,

Our life here has gone on very peacefully. We give occasional dinner parties, which have generally been fairly successful, and by dint of frequent *embêtements* we manage to keep our cook pretty well up to the mark. Lobster and lamb are rather frequent features in the bill of fare. But Therapia is not in itself a land of great plenty: and its lobsters are certainly almost, I should think, the equals of the Clovelly patriarchs,

I am now installed in my own rooms, with my books round me, but little more done: I feel a real nomad nowadays, and never think it worthwhile to do more than get the most hurried traces of myself into my surroundings. After all, "the world is a bridge, pass over it but build no house there"; much more so Therapia. I am in a state of continual dissatisfaction at the little I manage to get read and the little I get to know about this fascinatingly perplexing country, which I never want to leave, but am otherwise very happy and interested.

We are, by the time you get this, probably in the thick of a most difficult time abroad, Serbia and Austria *aux prises,* and a conflict raging which it will be most difficult to localise. Everyone here seems to think war is certain. The Austrian Note is worded in such a way as to make its acceptance by Servia impossible. It is a very strong order. This moment, from Austria's point of view, is a good one. The longer she waits the worse it will be for her.

No more for the present, dear Mrs. Hamlyn. Write me some more gossip. I wish I had some here for you, but we are all so well behaved.

To the Hon. Irene Lawley.

Therapia,
July 27, 1914.

Here our excitements have been principally political. It is a good moment for the Austrians. If they wait, Serbia will have time to consolidate herself in her new territories; Russia will be more ready for war than she is now; Serbia may manage to patch up an agreement with Bulgaria; their own internal difficulties may increase in other directions. It is the first time the Austrians have taken a really strong line since the beginning of the Balkan War. The Russians here were very much surprised. The Germans think the war will be localised, *i.e.* the Russians will accept their slap in the face and do very little for their Serbian friends. The Russian Ambassador's language has been so far very mild. I confess I do not see how the Russians can take it lying down, and if they once come in, the possibilities are endless. It will be curious to see whether the Germans will make use of these events as an opportunity for aggressive war against Russia.

Anti-Russian feeling is at present very strong in Germany. The Austrians have got their tails up, and the Secretaries here seem very happy at the turn events have taken. I saw the Austrian Ambassadress yesterday. She is English and charming; she will have three sons at the war. It is curious to see all our newspapers taking the side of Austria. I don't think the Austrians could have taken any other course, and on the merits of the case I am for the Austrians. We shall, however, look rather foolish if we have ultimately to range ourselves either diplomatically or otherwise, against Austria, and this is not unlikely, considering our general orientation, so our Press should have been more non-committal.

Otherwise life has been much as usual. We are now in *Ramadan*, the great fasting month. Moslems don't eat or drink all day, then at sunset they fall to and feast all the night. I fancy they sleep most of the day. I don't think this rule is very generally observed; but people like the *caiquejev*, the men who row one's boat, are inclined to be pious, and it is a bad thing to work them very much.

The *grand vizier* gave a party to celebrate an anniversary of the Constitution a little while ago. It was a very remarkable show. The American Ambassador rubbing shoulders with the Emirs of Mecca, and the villa by the Bosphorus, with its Western exterior, its pseudo-Arabesque Alhambra-like reception-rooms and its garden arranged like an open-air *café* concert. Nowhere else do you get these contrasts and this meeting of East and West.

I played cricket the other day, and made one run in the first innings and three in the second, four more than I expected to make, I can tell you. Even cricket, when little children in those delightful baggy trousers and their *fezzes* stroll across the ground, and you see the peasants working at the haystacks with their great red cummerbunds round their stomachs, and there are real buffaloes, like the Indian ones, cropping the grass hard by or cooling themselves in the water with only their shiny black flat backs showing over the surface, or perhaps the point of a curved horn, has a charm of its own.

Tennis with the Germans is the great Sunday afternoon occupation; then the German colony is seen in all its glory. It largely consists of the daughters of former dragomans, fine wenches with a powerful drive down the court and honest *mädchen* features and colouring. One can imagine their seduction *seriatim* by Goethe. I wonder if he would have had such success in any other country. They have a lovely garden with little grass valleys and lily-covered ponds.

Letters from Constantinople

Charles was too ardent and energetic to endure patiently what he describes elsewhere as the "leaden calm of Therapia" during the fateful days of early August. War was a Fact. The sight of others leaving Constantinople to take an active part in the struggle was too much for him, and whilst seeing some friends off, homeward bound, he could not resist the impulse to remain on board. He regretted the rash step as soon as he had taken it, and returned by the quickest route to his post. His longing to get to England and into the fighting line was only strengthened by this escapade, and he did not relax his efforts till he had obtained the consent of the Foreign Office to his request for leave to join the Army.—B. W. C.

To the Hon. Irene Lawley,

Therapia,
August 4, 1914.

I wish I was you in the thick of it; we are very newsless and postless here, and have very little idea of what England is going to do. So far we seem to have sat on the fence rather, and to be very much offering pills for the earthquake when we put forward our little mediation proposals, etc.

Why this paper, you will ask? I am doing an enforced trip on this old boat, not having been nippy enough while seeing people off. It is rather a bore, but I shall see Smyrna and get back to Constantinople without loss of time. It is also nice resting, doing the journey third-class. Here they simply put up an awning over the bows and let the people shift for themselves then. The people have their luggage with them, consisting of bed-clothes and a little trunk, and they put them out anywhere. I, who did not take any clothes with me, find myself at a disadvantage and rather like the Son of Man; but I lead quite a pleasant pillar-to-post existence in this glorious sunshine looking at the coasts of the Ægean islands and the coasts of Asia opposite. It is an extraordinary mixed crowd, mostly Ottoman Greeks who are trying to escape the Turkish mobilisation. They sing in a weary sing-song nasal tone all the day. They have some of them got gramophones which coin the same sort of sounds.

A more picturesque element is provided by the numerous (*illegible*) who appear in a long voile sort of dressing-gown and with sashes, or striped white and yellow, white and red tunics, and then little head capes with great knotted strings round the top, in black and gold. Then there are Central Asians with their little flower-embroidered skull-caps and snub-noses and Mongolian eyes; and the sea and sun reconcile me to almost anything, even to sitting about in dirty little corners of a third-class. You should see the state of my white ducks after these adventures—discreditable in the main but with their lighter side. Don't retail them, because I feel culpably vague about the whole thing and shall get into hot water on return.

The people on this boat are most incorruptible without exception, and will do nothing for anyone or anything. I have talked nearly all my languages today, including Turkish, with great fluency. The calm of all these people is very wonderful, and their cheerful submission to discomforts of many kinds; also their ability to sleep in almost impossible positions.

Therapia life has been peculiar; nothing to do all day, and a few little telegrams morning and evening which are very unsatisfactory and give us no real news. Food is very scarce and gold more so. I fancy a temporary accommodation is being made by the issue of bank-notes. Those who, like myself, have overdrafts will be in a jolly position, paying 11 *per cent*, on them.

I wonder what the next of the chapter of accidents will be. No one feels very happy about the situation just now except our American colleague, a fine old German Jew, who declares that the Germans will be in Paris in a month's time. In that case, it will be rather late for us to do anything by land. We should by rights have already begun landing.

I can write no more—I am depressed. Our position is, and always has been, unassailable, but we have not made the most of it.

To the Same.

British Embassy, Constantinople.

(No date.)

I am much relieved that we have come in; and our state of suspense as to whether we were going to do the right thing or not was very acute. I believe the Germans thought we were for peace at any price and would never dream of chipping in, even if they violated Belgian neutrality, which we had always told them would constitute a *casus belli*.

I feel we are in a very strong position, and even if the Germans get to Paris, we and the Russians can continue the war till we have crushed Germany.

The Turks are very cross with us now, and we may all have to come home—if the Germans manage to rush them (the Turks) into war with Russia. That is now the game; a dirty one and played with characteristic cynicism.

It is manifest Turkey is faced with certain disaster if she makes war on the Triple Entente.

To the Same.

British Embassy, Constantinople,
August 18, 1914.

I was glad to get your letter. You will, I think, regret going to America; the homing instinct is very strong if one's country is in danger, and you will be anxious and newsless over there. You can't imagine what a state of suspense we are in here—and how wretched we should be if we hadn't plenty of work.

You have no idea of what they have been doing here to compromise the Turks. They have got their warships in; *Goeben* and *Breslau* crews and German officers have been harassing our shipping in every possible way.

★★★★★★

Charles held strongly the view that our government should not have recognised the transfer of the *Goeben* and the *Breslau* to Turkey. Once we had allowed the purchase of the German ships we could only work for a much-to-be-desired rupture between Turkey and the Central Powers.—R.

★★★★★★

Destroying our wireless apparatus, while their own are left intact by the Turks, who might by right destroy *all* wireless in this, a neutral port; requisitioning British cargo for supplies for their army; putting difficulties in the way of our telegraphy or of our getting news favourable to us published in the Press, and exciting public opinion against the Triple Entente and all Christians to such a pitch that the next phase, unless the tide turns, will be the preaching of a Holy War against all "*infidels*."

Sir Louis is just back. He gives an interesting account of things at home before ministers finally decided to do the right thing, and of Kuhlmann's intrigues and suggestions that we should be content with an assurance that the Germans would not bombard Calais and Boulogne. I think no Germans are at this moment worth English tears, which I hear were so liberally shed by some over the Lichnowskys. Ever since the 1st of July Germany had decided on aggressive war against France and Russia, and the feigned innocence of the Lichnowskys should not find any believers.

The Germans here seemed to calculate on our neutrality. They were equally confident the Italians would go in, and that there would be no difficulty with the Belgians. Three big mistakes. You can't imagine our feelings those days when it was doubtful what we were going to do. I believe the Italians will join us soon; here they talk as if they were at war with Germany already. Then the Roumanians will move. What a triumph for Rodd if this happens. We may have bad news for the next fortnight or more, as the big battles on the Rhine will soon begin, but later on, when the Russian steam-roller gets moving, our stock will be up again. The morale of the French is at this moment very high, but one must at least be prepared for their failure for the moment. We have already gained a fortnight and no German soldiers on French territory, and the Russian mobilisation has gone on quicker than was expected.

To the Same.

British Embassy, Constantinople,

August 20, 1914.

You will have all our bad news long before you get this: I was personally never very sanguine as to the French resistance, but I hoped that with ourselves to help them, and after the Belgian resistance, that the German advance would at any rate have been more delayed than appears to have been the case. I fear our part in the big battle has been fine but tragic, and I can hear the "beating of the wings" of the Angel of Death very near. We have had black weeks before, and lived through them, and, as in the days of Napoleon, there is our fleet between us and a rapid fall to the status of a second-class power, so we can still hold our heads high, and I think we are rather at our best in this kind of situation. We are much where we were after Austerlitz, though the

37

débâcle of our Continental allies is not nearly so complete: and we can look with faith to our Trafalgar.

Things here have naturally gone from bad to worse; German sailors arrive by scores, and German merchantmen are being fitted out from the German Embassy as auxiliary cruisers to have a go at the Russians in the Black Sea, it is thought. We are simply powerless, and expect to have to pack up any day. The Turks are quite *tête montée*. The ministers say that they know nothing of these batches of German sailors arriving, and are in any case wholly impotent. The Bulgarian attitude is hitherto doubtful, but likely to incline to Germans after their successes. If we stay here we are likely to be faced by a serious shortage of foodstuffs. We are all, however, very cheerful and busy.

We have, I fear, missed the chance of getting Italy in to join us. If the French had made a firm offer of Tunis at the outset we might have got them. The French, however, thought they were going to win, and made evasive promises, and the Italians are now going to get all they want from their past allies without stirring a finger—simply as the price of neutrality. However, "Come the whole world in arms."

It is a good thing that one hasn't much time to think and wonder what the tranquil existence of the subject of a second-class Power would be like. I shouldn't like it myself, because I feel my life very much bound up with my flag.

I am very anxious for Diana, whom I love second best in the world—what she must be suffering now. However, she's not the only one.

I wonder about the future—I do not feel this war will make any one better friends afterwards. We shall take the German colonies, I suppose, and as the Germans cannot forgive us for the colonies we have already got, it is doubtful if they will forgive us the more for having collared theirs. Then there is the embittering role that the Press plays in all mix-ups with its polemics as to atrocities and so on. I fancy no peace will be of a very lasting character. We shall go on fighting, and finally sicken the working classes of the whole performance.

The Germans now take the line that they will make peace with the French, conduct a "platonic" war with ourselves, and then unite us all against the Russians; this is very fanciful.

Europe an armed camp for years, broken up, dissolved in final ruin and revolution by those who have long suffered; it isn't a cheerful picture. But love seems for the moment to have fled the world.

To the Same.

British Embassy, Constantinople,
August 24, 1914.

One rapid line amid the hurry of these days, just before the mail goes in the middle of all this trouble—we never know when we have a post out and so on. . . .

The reports of a French reverse in the neighbourhood of Metz are, I fear, correct, but the French say it is an incident de guerre, and will not make any substantial difference to their plan of campaign. The Germans are happy and drinking champagne, but the Russians have begun their offensive and have invaded Eastern Prussia and will soon get the blighters on the run.

Yesterday I went to my first *Baisans*, the month of feasting after the fasting month of *Ramadan*, It is a great reception held by the *Sultan* in the big hall at the palace, an enormous high room, with a colossal chandelier hanging from the centre point of the dome all hideously painted with still life and perspective effects with great plaster pilasters. The *Sultan* sits on a large sort of seat like the woolsack, covered with cloth of gold, and the notables come up; some of them kiss a sort of stole with tassels held by the Master of Ceremonies; others, more distinguished, such as the Sheriff of Mecca's representatives and the Sheik al Islam, actually kiss his coat.

As the *Sultan* comes in and goes out a shout is raised which means "Long life to our *Sultan*; yet there is God greater than him": it is now quite undistinguishable and all the time a band plays barbaric music, great clashes of cymbals and banging of brass. On the floor there are little strips of carpet for people to walk up, quite dowdy. The religious heads, the Sheik al Islam and the Mecca people are the real feature. The *Sultan* gets up for them, and for the Patriarch he advances about a yard towards the edge of a carpet, cloth of gold, in front of the throne. He is like a great egg, and sits half-right or half-left as the case may be, on the edge of the throne, with his hands tightly crossed in his lap. His whole chest and tummy are gold lace. He can walk slowly and get up on to his feet, but is otherwise not very mobile. The people who went up to him backed out of the presence, and then lined the sides of the hall.

The situation here since the ambassador's return is rather easier. Enver has been laid up and the *grand vizier* is recovering power, but the military authorities, under German influence, continue to be most insolent. They actually threatened to take down the wireless on the

Italian and U.S. Embassy Stationnaires while they let German ships keep it up all the time. From the way they talk to the ambassador one would think they were conquerors imposing terms on a conquered enemy. But we are being very patient. Otherwise we should be playing the German game.

★★★★★★

Enver Pasha, as everybody knows, was the dominant military authority in Constantinople and had received his military training in Germany. He became War Minister in Turkey at the time of the Young Turk revolution. To his influence more than any other we owe our rupture with the Turks in 1914.—R.

★★★★★★

To the Hon. Lady Wilson.

British Embassy, Constantinople,
August 24, 1914.

Many thanks for your last letter, which I had not answered yet owing to the wear and tear of these last few days, and the immense deal of work involved by the machinations of the Germans here. They are determined to drag the Turks in on their side, and through their military mission induce them to commit every conceivable breach of neutrality, with a view to forcing us to declare war on Turkey. We are very patient, and do all in our power to allow for the consolidation of the moderate element in the Cabinet which in distinction to Enver, who is the villain of the piece, is desirous, at any rate for the moment, to maintain a genuine neutrality.

The mobilisation, Enver's work, has caused untold misery. The soldiers, called up for the fourth time within three years, cannot be fed, armed, or clothed. They openly state they will desert at the first opportunity—to be fed. They beat recalcitrants in the *gendarmerie* stations, and even flog their female relations if they suspect them of concealing their male relations from the authorities.

Anti-English feeling runs very high. It is sedulously fomented by the Germans, to whom our detention of the Turkish ships has given a great opportunity. Since Sir Louis came back the situation has been easier.

Elsewhere, as far as one can tell, German diplomats have drawn blank after blank, which is very satisfactory to my much abused profession. Events so far, except for the French reverse in Lorraine, have panned out better than we expected.

Our "bloomer" in not catching the *Goeben* is locally almost disastrous, but will not have much general effect on the course of the war. She is of course only Turkish in name. Our fear is that if the Turks become at war with us, the Germans will take her into the Black Sea with other merchant ships they are fitting out here as sort of privateers.

How disgracefully they behaved to the Empress Marie and the Grand Duke Constantine. Serves the latter right, as he was leader of a pro-German party at the Russian Court.

We are all hard up here, but very happy.

To Lord Ribblesdale.

British Embassy, Constantinople,
September 6, 1914.

One line to say that I am well, happy, and very hard-worked whole day, and no time for riding or swimming expeditions. The work is entirely cyphering, and cheered only at intervals by news telegrams. Otherwise we only hear German news, and you know what that is. I much admired the premier's speech at the Guildhall; it was a magnificent piece of real oratory, and most elevated in sentiment. I am glad he has been of the hauteur to see what we are really fighting for, and how we must win. We have, of course, a magnificent position.

I am afraid the war will last a long time, as we shall have to wear the Germans down by degrees. The German Ambassador here says they have food for three years. I don't think this can be true, but no doubt it will take a long time to starve them out.

No time for more.

To the Hon. Irene Lawley.

British Embassy, Constantinople,
September 6, 1914.

Here we live in an atmosphere of lies and violently stirred up anti-English feeling. The prospects of actual war with Turkey seem to be rather diminishing, but the violations of neutrality are just as flagrant as ever. As the prime minister said, we must "take long views," as we can be satisfied with no partial victory. I fancy that the war on two fronts will by degrees force the Germans back within their frontiers. I think It will then be very difficult to make any serious impression on them, as their forts are strong and our artillery not so good as theirs. However, we shall wear them down and starve them out by degrees. I cannot speak of the sack of Louvain.

Even if the population had fired on them they could surely have destroyed the houses where the fire came from and the principal cul-prits; but to sack all the churches, old buildings, etc., is a disgrace, even on their own showing, of the deepest dye. They are the Huns of Europe, and I only hope they will be treated as such and that the Cossacks will not forget. How can one reconcile these vile bucca-neers with the kind of German one knows? What do they think in America? The Americans here are very *bien pensant* and anxious for us to beat the Germans.

The German Ambassador runs about the quay and the hotels wav-ing a newspaper and shouting victory. It will be a curious world after this war—very little money about, I should think, and hardly any to spend on fun; I don't see myself hunting for a long while to come—I don't, in fact, see myself home for some time. I simply can't be spared now; and while our relations with Turkey are uncertain they won't send out anyone else, I don't suppose. The ambassador is splendid; he learns up the names of his ships like a schoolboy, and he is going to take the Belgian Minister into the Embassy when we go back to Pera.

To the Same.
British Embassy, Constantinople,
September 13, 1914.

Six weeks of war, and are the Germans yet in Paris?

Here things go on much as usual. But the Turks are still *convinced* that the Germans will win, and they will stick to this conviction till the signing of the treaty of peace. They were just the same in their own war, and did not think they'd been beat till the Bulgarians were actually at Tchataldja. Of course, it was different in the case of the ministers, but the general public, I mean—and ministers with regard to this war are more or less in the same position as the general public with regard to the other war.

The Turks are not even impressed by the reports of India's re-sponse—which is very remarkable; it must be due to the visit of the crown prince. One should organise tours of German royalty in Eng-land and the colonies, and then people get to know what the Germans really are. Did you see Goschen's dispatch reporting on his last days at Berlin and the emperor's "apology" for the demonstration which took place outside the embassy? It is an extraordinary document. I think our friend Jagow must be genuinely sorry for all this, and especially for the breach with England. The diplomacy of the war on the Ger-man side has been mismanaged—but not, I think, his fault; I fancy the emperor did the whole thing during this big crisis. He is a marvel with his telegrams about God.

All my sisters by degrees will have their husbands fighting, and Percy must have already done a lot; I hope he will get a V.C. or something.

The Turks are less warlike; they have abolished certain commercial and judicial privileges of foreign subjects; and it is thought that this is in reality a peaceful move, as now they can show the public some results for their mobilisation and are therefore not under the necessity of risking a war with someone—a war which only a few swollen heads like Enver really want, and which the civil element in general is *determined* to avert.

The ambassador thinks about nothing but what he can do for the war and doing little kindnesses all round. Heaven knows one can do little enough in what is, after all, a backwater at this moment. It does not really matter if the Turks do go to war. It will only mean their own break up, or at best their becoming a sort of German dependency. However, here we are with our job, to keep them neutral, and we mean to see it through.

How vilely all my old associates, Keir Hardie and Co., are behaving.

Our life here has been extraordinary—in German territory practically, and nothing but German news for a long time. After that awful fighting round Mons, down to St. Quentin we really thought our army had been *vernichtet*, so you can imagine our feelings. Luckily we've had so much work that we haven't had time to think. Now we are a sort of *bureau de presse* and fill the Pera papers with our news. Why is it impossible to have a gentlemanly war with the Germans? The lies they tell in their foul Press, their low behaviour here—the German Ambassador running round to the hotels and shouting victory in the streets—the ungraciousness of their whole way of looking at things makes one feel very bitter.

No one likes the Germans any better after having fought them. The French and Russians did like each other better after the Crimea. Ourselves and the French at least left each other's throats with a feeling of mutual respect. But these cads! I cannot reconcile them with the Germans I have liked. What a dreadful tragedy about Archer Clive. Really what that family has suffered: but it must in a way be a fine thing to have some link with the hosts of great spirits who have witnessed to our national greatness and are in a sense England triumphant while our warfare is still here; and at such moments *I* feel the oneness of the nation with its dead—and those who will die in this war die for righteousness and will be thanked for ever by the little nations for whom they have secured a free existence, un menaced by powerful and interfering neighbours.

So you will be in London; think of me here sometimes: my plans are luckily very much fixed up—till they can spare me

from here. Then—— One feels here that one is doing so very little, and resents the sort of artificial denationalised position the diplomat has to submit to: it *is* merely position; one's character is more nationalised than ever.

The good news, our own and the Russian, has made us very happy—and happy for many things. One can hardly put into words the sort of thankfulness—that after all people are found whose policy is not simply a question of interest, and who value that intangible essence, unseen save at rare moments like the Holy Grail—the Nation's honour.

After all, what would the Belgians have suffered materially if they had let the Germans through? It is quite possible the Germans would have kept their word and retired after peace. It was the idea of the desecration of the streets of their beautiful old towns, where the guilds of the Middle Ages built their cathedrals.

★★★★★★

Charles carried on a faithful correspondence with his aunt, the Hon. Beatrix Lister. She had been trained, as few are, to appreciate the complex problems of European diplomacy. Her constant correspondence with her brother. Sir Reginald Lister, and her frequent visits to him at his various posts, had quickened her interest in the wide issues of world politics. Charles found in her sympathy and perception, and an understanding attention to everything that touched the career he had chosen.—B. W. C.

★★★★★★

To the Hon. Beatrix Lister.

British Embassy, Constantinople,
September 20, 1914.

Many thanks for your capital letter. I remember well what Reggy, and Mallet always said about Germany. We always imagined that the war would begin with an attack on England with the object of destroying the British Fleet: events rather show that England was not the first objective; more than that, the Germans, I think, did calculate on our neutrality. It is a mercy that we have done the right thing: I doubt if we should have, if the Germans had not violated Belgian neutrality. As you say, the whole thing was very badly stage-managed.

I gather from what the German Ambassador has said here, etc., that the Germans meant *as early as July* to declare war on Russia and all other comers. I suppose towards the end of September the German Ambassador used this sort of language after his return from Berlin, when it is probable that the whole thing was discussed: all the other ambassadors had also been summoned home. Then came the Sarajevo murders. I think the Germans thought this would be an excellent chance to catch the Triple Entente more or less disunited—Russia torn between her Slav sympathies and her horror of regicide as a general principle; England sympathizing with Austria on this issue, etc.

She could then declare war on one of the Triple Entente, and find the others not ready to "march." The pace was therefore rather forced and a crisis hurried by the Austrian Note, a document largely drawn up in Berlin. I think Germany was out for war all the time, and not out for a mere diplomatic success. This was surely already secured—seeing the *abject* tone of the Serbian reply to the Austrian Note. And so we have war. I feel rather nervous as to the superior artillery of the Germans and this terrible 42-centimetre gun.

Perhaps we shall not be able to make much impression against the German forts; otherwise, however, I think the situation very satisfactory. It will be a long job, and we may have to finish them by starving them out; but we've got them stiff. I sometimes almost wish we had not got Allies; there will be embarrassment when we come to making peace, and weak Allies may get beaten or give us other anxiety. However, I don t suppose an isolated fight against Germany would be practical politics—too many people dislike them. I think the war will last a long time as far as Germany is concerned.

Constantinople is the one place where she has got sympathizers. Our holding up these Turkish ships and the arrival of the *Goeben* has created a strong feeling in her favour, and the military mission have been consequently able to get the whole thing into their hands. The Turks are *en mauvaise voie*. If the Germans win, Turkey will become a sort of German Egypt. If the Germans lose, Turkey will have to face the victorious Triple Entente Powers in no mood for trifling. The *mot* of a Belgian here now is worth repeating.

One of the ministers said, "*J'ai une nouvelle pour vous: les Allemands sont entrés à Bruxelles.*"

45

He without a moment's hesitation said, "*Excellence, j'ai une nouvelle pour vous: les Allemands sont entrés a Constantinople.*"

It is the literal truth—they arrive train after train, they man the Turkish ships, arm their own merchantmen, sign all the Customs instructions, etc. They are, however, getting unpopular: Faust is beginning to realise that his bondage to Mephistopheles is not an unmixed blessing. I don't think the Germans have any definite plan. It is simply fishing in troubled waters; their idea is to hurry the Turks into war with someone so that they may ultimately get involved against Russia and create a diversion. It is a cynical policy which quite disregards Turkish interests. Of the Turks, Enver is the villain of the piece. He is swollen-headed and crude, and the Germans have promised him Egypt and the Caucasus and Salonica.

P.S.—French strategy is hard to understand. I think that after his first failure to get through the Germans Joffre's idea is a retreat on the Marne, which is very defensible country and suitable to the kind of campaign he desires.

To the Hon. Irene Lawley.

British Embassy, Constantinople,

September 21, 1914.

I don't know that very much has happened since my last. We have been through a phase of apprehension again, and the experts think war is more likely. The German officers are said to be making themselves very much disliked and to be even despised as not knowing their job: they have, of course, told the Turks that our officers taught them all wrong. Yesterday the German cruiser went out into the Black Sea, and returned in the evening. Today the *Goeben* has gone out. It is an astonishing situation; the German captain, by molesting one of our corn ships *en route* from the Black Sea, could any day put the whole fat in the fire. As you know, our naval officers have gone. There have been the usual *potins* and indiscretions in this connection.

It is curious to see how the people who most liked Germans before the war, and who were never out of the German Embassy, detest them now. I think they feel they have been deceived, and look on them as one looks on some cook who has swindled one. I must say it is very hard to reconcile the murderers of women and children and the destroyers of Dierick Bontses *ad lib.* with the Germans one knows—the mild art critics and inefficient tennis players and comfortable bourgeois and governesses. I always rather liked Germans, and was very fond of German food and drink; however, they have shown the cloven hoof with a vengeance.

A few days ago we sent off from here about nineteen volunteers, the English colony paying for their passages. Sir L. gave them lunch at the embassy and made them a pretty little speech; we then went down to the boat and saw them off. It made one feel very much out of it. The honorary *attaché* has also gone. He was an old soldier in the Scots Greys, who have distinguished themselves. However, here we are, in fetters.

Did you see the *Daily Telegraph* account of Francis Grenfell's performances and the part Bendor and Percy took in the affair? Wasn't it splendid—was it true? It sounded almost too good, and more like the list of names at some ducal weekend.

I have taken occasional swims, and you will be pleased to hear I've got over the Bosphorus. This is not as good as Leander's performance; he swam the Dardanelles.

Forgive the dullness of this letter. I think the Italians will come in, but how far they will go beyond occupying the Trentino and Trieste depends on many things. How is recruiting in the north of England? They are very antimilitarist, and none of them would join the Boy Scouts in old days.

To the Same.
British Embassy, Constantinople,
September 28, 1914.

Well, not much this week; things seem shaping for war, and it looks as if the Turks had decided to commit suicide. The excitements here leave me quite cold now, as is natural after what has been a two-months-long crisis at crisis pressure of work. It is not over yet. The Turks have closed the Dardanelles—where Leander swam over to visit Hero. I have been in a very golf and hunting mood lately, and am sure that the life of the "deserving" modern man, with his all-day office work, is a rotten thing—that we should have evolved this as our highest form of activity is not to our credit. Down with these big nations and organisations of business, etc., on the enormous scale, and let's have a lot of village communities, each run by the squire and the parson, with their heads meeting once a year to decide really urgent matters, and let's have no trains.

Well, it's silly all this, I suppose, and the hands of the clock must sweep forward without remorse—unless there are cycles of change like Anatole France says in *L'Ile des Pingouins*. There I think we finish up by internal combustion when the last word has been said in the organisation of industry and the enslavement of the working class.

It has been exciting, that is to say we have been *plus ou moins* on tenterhooks all the time—and are still, though now one feels very stolid—but not interesting in the sense that a period of constructive diplomacy, concession hunting, or reform schemes are interesting, or that a period of things like Armenian massacres, which give you a real insight into the country and make you learn about its various rules, would be interesting. The appeal has been to the game-playing instinct rather than the intellect. But it has been splendid, and the ambassador has shown extraordinary nerve and skill. He has told the Turks some home truths lately. They are, I think, beginning to repent their madness, but are more in the hands of the Germans than ever—and the Germans are getting impatient.

Has anything more been heard of John Manners? I saw he was "missing" in the papers. It must be dreadful not to know, and still worse to know if the worst has happened. We heard at first that Tommy was missing—and this was fighting Somalis—but then the next day I think, we heard he was killed.

What a fine performance our Mons retreat was. England is silent as the grave, and I get no letters—only hairdressers' bills of 1912 for five shillings.

★★★★★★

The hour had struck. Charles's departure at this date from Constantinople was his conscious farewell to diplomacy. "Diplomacy is dead," he wrote to a friend; and to another who urged that he should remain at his post, he said, "The date of my birth determines that I should take active service." A *via media* offered itself repeatedly to Charles, that of the Interpreter Service, for which he would have been eminently fitted, but this, as will be seen, was three times eluded. He returned to England to learn the death in action of his brother-in-law, Lieutenant Percy Wyndham, Coldstream Guards, killed in their famous attack at Soupir on September 14th. No letters had reached Constantinople. And on his return to England Charles wrote none.—B. W. C.

★★★★★★

With the Middlesex Yeomanry

NOTE BY HON. LADY WILSON

Immediately on his arrival in England it was arranged that Charles should join the 1st County of London Yeomanry (Middlesex Hussars) as interpreter. Charles's brother-in-law, Lieutenant-Colonel Sir Mathew Wilson, C.S.I., had just obtained command of the regiment, and it seemed probable that they would shortly be ordered to France.

It took Charles three days in London in which to collect his uniform, kit, and charger, then he joined the regiment at Moulsford, where its headquarters were luxuriously lodged in a brick riverside villa. Two or three weeks later, whilst Charles's dressing-table was loaded with books to enlighten him in the translation of the most obscure military commands, an order came from the War Office to the effect that interpreters would be provided for units on their arrival in France, so Charles secured a commission in the regiment.

The adjutant, Captain Neilson, 4th Hussars, was an old friend. He had been at the Cavalry School in Rome whilst Charles was at the embassy, and they had had many a good ride together across the stiff timber of the Campagna, Charles, according to Captain Neilson, not infrequently showing him the way, mounted on a fatigued hireling called Fernando.

The 1st County of London Yeomanry was moved at a few hours' notice from their comfortable quarters at Moulsford to the chilling asperity of the East Coast. At Moulsford the regiment had a grey shoulder of the downs on which to manoeuvre, and the barns of the low-lying Caldecottlike villages afforded excellent stabling for the horses. The men had first-rate billets, in spite of the Thames valley mud, which motor-cycles and remounts churned up everywhere. The news that the regiment was to move was not received with enthusiasm. It was on a chilly morning in mid-November, after nearly twenty-four hours in a troop train, that the Middlesex Hussars reached Mundesley, a village five miles from Cromer. Here they settled down to their new role of defending the coast against all possible and impossible attack.

Charles embarked with ardour on his new task. Some forlorn-looking trenches were dug on the sand cliffs, a machine-gun meanwhile doing some smart practice among the seagulls. A certain amount of spy-hunting gave spice to the early days at Mundesley, but later, when this flagged, the tedium grew intolerable. The different squadrons were scattered in surrounding villages, a narrow strip of grass which ran along the top of the cliffs was all the unenclosed country which could be used for squadron training. Here Charles could drill his troops, between the dreary back-gardens of seaside lodging-houses; sometimes, for better fun, his colonel would be sergeant-major for him. The ever-retreating prospect of active service made Charles restive, and determined him to seek some way of getting out to the fighting zone.

Yet, characteristically, he was able to make the best of a bad job: he hunted with the local harriers—the ploughed fields and cock fences did not come amiss to him, and he crowned a good day with them by jumping his colonel's best charger over a five-barred gate. Another day he was found gun in hand tramping after an elusive partridge; a wordy altercation followed, in which Charles succeeded by skilful dialectic in persuading the farmer that he was not poaching.—B. W.

> To the Hon. Irene Lawley.
> Grand Hotel, Mundesley-on-Sea, Norfolk,
> November 24, 1914.

There is much to amuse us here.

The local spy-hunter has been always with us, like the poor, and has laid all kinds of information against divers persons; the men are always seeing lights being flashed, and on one occasion they actually saw two men whom they chased down the cliff. Spy-hunting parties go out when these flashes are seen, and generally return empty handed. We put in durance vile the minions of a German who has a house ideally situated for signalling out to sea—he himself had been interned—and shut up their women in the kitchen; myself and Benn searched the house and read masses of correspondence, but with no result.

It was a strange scene—the entrance into the house, the lower rooms of which were actually being *used* by one of our patrols; the men with fixed bayonets bringing to us a large smiling woman of the housekeeper type and a young wild-eyed girl with fair hair and a sallow complexion, a ward befriended in loneliness by this family, and the darkness outside.

Then the search and scrutiny of the correspondence; our suspect was a Salvationist, and we found nothing but notes for sermons, also long family letters from relations in Canada and everywhere you please, very affectionate, with x x x at the end. The only incriminating thing was a picture postcard of the *façade* of Frankfort Station—coloured, too. They are jolly letters: tell you how the children are getting on, etc., when they are coming, and so forth; always say they are very busy. The ladies are now released; the men, I fancy, sent to the general.

To the Same.
Grand Hotel, Mundesley-on-Sea,
December 1, 1914.

You will be perhaps not surprised to hear that I have got the sack, *quâ* interpreter. They have said that all the interpreters will now be supplied by the French General Staff, and would I accept a commission in the new armies. This I am most unwilling to do, as it would mean long waiting before getting out anywhere, and so I am trying to get myself a commission in this regiment. It is a bore after one had thought it all fixed up.

Last week we were rather hopeful as to our prospects of going out, but the latest news from the War Office is not very favourable. So we alternate between hope and despondency, and life goes on much the same, for now we have almost forgotten that there were such things as invasion scares or spies. The riding and jumping has on the whole been great fun, but I've been rather lowered lately by a cold and cough. The English winter, unless one is hunting all day, is a poor show, and I confess to a yearning for the sunny slopes of Rome's seven hills; Isa Chigi's last letter, too, describing the peasants going to and from the *fattoria* laden with grapes, called back pictures of days which I am afraid won't return. However, for us now England is a necessity. What I feel is that nothing will be the same after, and that our generation will live in a constant state of war's alarms and penury, and that fun of any sort or kind has left the world.

Today I tried to learn the machine-gun. I don't feel that I am a very promising pupil, but it is a good thing that as many people as possible should know how to work it, and I dare say I could manage to get an elementary knowledge. My friends are very clever at it. I am not mechanically enough minded to be any use at modern warfare and look upon myself purely as *kanonenfutter*. But the East Coast is a long way from the German guns.

The newspapers have *nothing* in them now; it seems very much as if the winter, on the French side at any rate, would be a quiet affair.

I am going to learn Flemish from one of our troopers. It might be useful.

To the Same.

Grand Hotel, Mundesley-on-Sea, Norfolk,

December 12, 1914.

By the way, I'm practically a camp follower myself. I hope to get my commission soon in this regiment. We are still waiting, and if it was a question of starting afresh I should have been a footslogger, but now I've made my niche and learnt a little about the job it would be a pity to switch off to something else—cavalry is more my stunt—apart from rather doing the dirty on the C.O., who looks to my languages. It's bloody for all that. I suppose we shall go as cavalry to Kitchener's army now. It's better for you, knowing you can do something for somebody, and you like that, I expect, but here one feels one is doing very little for anybody. "*La diplomatie est morte,*" Cambon said, and I feel that will be very much the position of dips, for some time.

We go on in more or less the same rut, enlivened by occasional rides over leaps and days with the hounds, and depressed by inefficiency with the revolver and other weapons. They have competitions among the men—saddling and unsaddling, jumping banks, and going into action, *i.e.* galloping up over a bank *en route*, dismounting, firing, and then returning. They have been a great success, and the brigadier is delighted with us.

Riding back from the day's finish, the setting sun behind, the stars overhead, and the little church-towers at intervals on the skyline, war seemed a distant dream and the world to be peopled with just one man and his tired horse. My khaki tunic and nothing else was there to remind me that the same stars looked down on hell let loose in France. Man is such a brute to man at this moment, that loneliness and isolation seem the only thing; he comes into contact with his fellows solely to inflict and suffer pain. This war knocks out the idea of progress as an inevitable concomitant of time, and I am afraid the world has shown that it has fallen behind the world that fought the Napoleonic wars in its ideals of chivalry, etc. Forgive these rather dull reflections; there may after all be something beyond the mountains.

To the Same.

Grand Hotel, Mundesley, Norfolk,
December 21, 1914.

I'm gazetted now, so my position is regularised. . . . Saturday last I went out and had a day goose-shooting; no geese, but a lovely day out on a vast expanse of sand and salt marshes, and streams of these glorious birds over our heads right out of reach, circling and laughing at our impotence. You'd love the marsh with its brown, and greys, and greens, and creeks of oily mud, which we squelched in and out of in top-boots. We secured a few sea snipe, and ate and drank well of strange food, which I think is the chief charm of getting away.

I have read *Sinister Street*. The Oxford part of it is excellent, very true to life, especially the Magdalen life, which I saw a good deal of. What unsatisfactory people! Alan of the sort *sans peur et sans reproche* settling down to be his wife's land agent, and Stella, after her cult of art and Bohemian swank, tediously happy as a *châtelaine*. Cellars could be filled with stuff similar to all those vignettes of the "Underworld," perhaps written with less art and realism, but it isn't really of much interest. Still, it is "some book," with a good deal of psychology.

To the Same.

Grand Hotel, Mundesley,
December 29, 1914.

I have had quite fun lately, looking after a troop in the absence of its proper leader. They must think me silly, and the sergeant knows everything about drill; he is so versatile, has a tenor voice and a fine notion of playing soccer. I am very fussy about the horses, and worry the men about grooming them. It is the only subject on which I can assert myself It takes a long time to get their names. They are almost as difficult to make out as hounds, and do not wear distinctive dresses or paint themselves distinctive faces like the ladies of Rome. Khaki is a leveller.

I have just acquired a new horse, to my great satisfaction. He seems all he should be, in spite of a certain family likeness to a camel. The colonel ramped twelve horses for us, and, Lord knows how, most of them £200 hunters; it seems a shame they should be under fire. I do feel for the horses, much more than for the men, except those I know.

We had a regimental drill one day before the divisional general, a nerve-wracking affair. I was shepherded by my talented sergeant and got through fairly well, only once attracting the notice of the general.

To the Same.

Mundesley,
January 16, 1915.

We've had a very eventful and busy week here—full of drill and two days' hunting. First day very fair. I was on my good horse and did some good leaping; a harrier day slightly above the average but no more, a lot of "orficers" out. Today, a very good day, I was unhappily on a horse that is a good jumper but has no great knowledge of banks. So I was put down twice; no hurt to myself, but my horse was once in the hell of a fix, his foreleg caught in a hard stub on the bank and his hindleg embedded in a deep, muddy ditch: however, with the help of one of the gilded staff of a neighbouring brigade we extricated him. We were rather often hitched by wire. I cycled to the meet nine miles against a very strong headwind, and before I started I had done two and a half hours' drill and about three-quarters of an hour grooming, etc. So it was a very full day.

In the course of the drill we did a little sham fight. I delivered a finely conceived flank attack on an almost impregnable position and was shot several times myself and had to admit defeat, but the attempt was very glorious. The drill has not been a particular success, but my manners have become more confident, and I lay down the law on a great number of subjects I don't understand in the very least. I don't think the men can be very fond of me, as I am fussy about horses and like to see them groomed every now and then, but they did me the honour of asking me to figure in a group they were having done of the troop.

To A. F. Lascelles.

Mundesley,
January 17, 1915.

Still at Mundesley, and "the front" receding into the dim distance.

I *knew* Julian would do well: only think, last winter or so, he was wanting to be an artist and chuck soldiering. I only hope he will be lucky. I strongly dissuaded him from his artistic leanings, and with some effect, though everyone else was doing the same. He is such an obvious soldier. I only wish I was—when I halt between two opinions as to which is my right, and am detected by irate generals making a muddle of off-saddling.

The Yeoman is a curious creature, but with a good music-hall sense of humour; his faculty for losing his kit makes me feel among friends.

To the Same.

Grand Hotel, Mundesley,
February 7, 1915.

We have had a pretty strenuous week, winding up with a day spent on the muck-heaps of our stables and clearing away masses of manure in pouring rain. So you see what Jacks-of all-trades we are nowadays. The day was a Saturday, so the men were not best pleased.

On Friday I directed a skeleton force—that is, two or three men with flags who represented armed myriads. I walked up and down the line on a prancing charger, not unlike Gustavus Adolphus. (I again appeal to Scottites to remember gratefully Dalgetty's horse in the *Legend of Montrose*).

Another day we did patrol work—a summer pastime in my view— as the officer has to stand stock-still near some object of note, such as a bridge, and wait till his men send in reports. He gets very chilly in the process, so does his horse. We have also had riding school and jumping on to each other's horses. Active little people like you might shine at this game, I confess I don't. However, once the stomach is well on the saddle it is simply a question of sprawling, and the horses stand any amount of this. I can manage the little troop horses, but not my own prancers.

The brigadier's inspection was a success, and he liked our squadron very well, and this in spite of the fact that we were drilling with drawn swords, which lessens the control of the rider over his horse, as you can imagine. I made one egregious blunder—from ignorance, not loss of nerve—which I am rather getting over at drill. Drill is largely a question of swank and flourish—of a ringing voice when you are drilling and a theatrical wave of the sword when you are leading. I am supposed to have a fine word of command which shakes the rafters, and so on.

I am taking an easy day today, as I was inoculated yesterday against—I don't quite know what! But you see how we cling to the belief we are going to the front. Touching, isn't it? I am sorry for the victims of such persistent fallacies, but error may sometimes be the mother of truth.

To Ferdinand Speyer.

Duke of Cambridge's Hussars,
February 8, 1915.

Many thanks for your letter—which interested me very much.

Sir E. Grey's only chance of averting war was to declare "solidarity" with Russia at the outset of the crisis. If he had said England would in no circumstances come in—the other alternative you suggest—he would have simply increased German determination to go to war with Russia.

You say we promised military help to Belgium. Do you refer to the correspondence published in the White Book, Grey Book, etc., which, as far as I can remember, shows that some of the things Grey said might be construed in this sense, or to some undertaking on the part of Grey hitherto unrecorded? I wonder how much anything we said might have influenced Belgium's attitude.

Of course, I don't mean the *general* support, which we were to give, but rather promises of immediate military action. I rather fancy that the Belgians took the line they did, not so much with the idea that they could at once be got out of the wood by their allies, but because they thought a fine defence of the principle of neutrality, cost what it might, was for themselves the most far-seeing policy to pursue; Belgian permission to the Germans to pass through their territory would have been a blow to all the smaller States of Europe. I believe, however, that it is the case that certain members of the Cabinet were only induced to vote for the sending of the expeditionary force to France because they thought it would clear the Germans out of Belgium. Curious how the right thing is done for the wrong reason, for by the time the expeditionary force was out the Germans were quite secured in their possession of the greater part of that country.

I am on the whole inclined to agree with Vandervelde that Belgium did the most politic, as well as the most honourable thing in resisting. She is, after all, herself profoundly affected by this issue of neutrality, as a sanction that States are prepared to enforce by arms, and she would have created a precedent against herself by any other course of action.

I wonder what we should have done if Belgium had not resisted. I am rather afraid we should have missed the big issues—and come down on the wrong side of the fence, at any rate for some time.

I am surprised at the enormous reserve of men Germany appears to have. It is quite uncanny—but I dare say *The Times* has exaggerated.

It is great, your becoming a business manager already: you are a nut. I am glad. I saw F. McLaren a day or two ago; he came with his naval armoured cars and had a field day with us. He was in good form. He is under Wedgwood, the land-taxer, whom I liked very much.

I am having quite fun with the military life, though I feel my khaki is a sort of fancy dress, and that I am very much of a civilian all the time.

★★★★★★

A few days were to bring a momentous change. Several Balliol friends of Charles had just obtained commissions in the Royal Naval Brigade, and a hurried visit to London decided that he was to sail with them. "It was difficult saying goodbye to dear Harry," he wrote of his colonel from the ship *Franconia* about ten days after the date of the last letter, and again he expresses regret for the Middlesex Yeomanry and its colonel, But he was glad to be off.

Now God be thanked who has matched us with His hour,
And caught our youth and wakened us from sleeping,
With hand made sure, clear eye, and sharpened power . . .

These are the words of one of the band of new Argonauts—for so we must think of them—with whom Charles sailed from London port that February day, not in the same ship, but with the Divisional Staff.—B. W. C.

Letters from S.S. "Franconia," with Headquarters Staff

The Divisional and Brigade Staff of the Royal Naval Division were commanded by Brigadier-General Aston, K.C.B., Royal Marine Artillery. (General Paris, who had commanded at Antwerp, was afterwards sent out to relieve him on the Peninsula.) Charles was Interpreter to the Staff as "a Headquartersman." The battalions "Hood" and "Anson" and "Howe "sailed with the *Franconia* from Tilbury, and were not disunited until the whole flotilla reached Port Said.—B. W. C.

To the Hon. Irene Lawley.

Cunard R.M.S. *Franconia,*
March 5, 1915.

. . . . I suppose this is just wisdom, and that those who have lived would always like their lives over again. Well, I shan't regret this stunt, whatever happens. It is the most exhilarating feeling to be again on the sea of the ancient civilizations and dream of the galleys of Carthage and Venice—or farther back still—of the raft of Odysseus, and wonder why Dante put him in the *Inferno* (*Canto* XXVI). He is certainly a soul difficult to judge by moral. But I should have thought that passionate curiosity and yearning for knowledge would have counted for something with the All-knowing. I feel like a pinchbeck Odysseus—longing for the same things, but with the limits and valour of some little City clerk, and no power to return and slay the suitors of my Penelope—*in posse.*

I am reading the *Paradiso* now, *Canto* XXXI; the end having the rather dry bit about the election of children to the heavenly heritage is simply stupendous, with all the Dantesque qualities of nervous description, mystic ecstasy, passionate seeking after the divine and bitter irony combined. He says of the Church triumphant that the Barbarians, as the Roman senators burst into their view as they advanced on Rome, could not have been more amazed than he at the sight of the redeemed.

Io, che al divino dall' umano,
all' eterno dal tempo era venuto,
e di Fiorenza, in popol giusto e sano.

I love that last line, don't you? You ought to read all this when you get back to the hills and cypresses of Florence. It is a mistake to stop at *Siede la terra*, and so on. You might, however, in God's good time send me out a little Dante by post—Temple Classic is the best edition. . . .

These are glorious times. I hope I shall like campaigning as much as Julian does. I *wish* you were here. You'd love it all so—why don't you try?—get out with Lady Paget's show to Serbia when you've had a real rest. Or why not here? but I don't understand our arrangements. I fancy they are pretty complete.

★★★★★★

The following letter is from Malta. Patrick Shaw-Stewart describes elsewhere the meeting with Balliol friends. ". . . . When Charles caught the R.N.D., as one catches the last train, at the end of February, he was an interpreter and sailed on the *Franconia* with the Divisional Staff. The 'Hood' was in a poky little Union Castle boat called the *Grantully Castle*, and we only saw him now and then. At Malta he blew in on us, and we spent a noisy evening ashore."—R.

★★★★★★

To the Same.

Cunard *Franconia*,
March 10, 1915.

Things have proceeded pretty peacefully since I wrote, except for rather stirring times at a certain island. It does not look at all real—Malta—when you come into the harbour: there seems no way in and no way out of the great yellow walls that slope up from the sea, beaten by wave and sun and exhaling a sort of yellow dust into the southern air. Then it is so very seventeenth century—baroque without Bernini lavishness, under the restraint imposed by the original knightly uses to which the island was put as a bulwark against the Turks. The houses have often got flat roofs and bay windows with green shutters. They are nearly all built of the same yellow-whitish stone. No green to be seen till you have got well into the town, and then occasional ribbons of very bright verdure with a dry, stony background of hills. The outside walls of the fortress-city are grown over with bougainvillaea and look on to neat little cemeteries—and the graves already prepared and stone-faced, and cypresses growing in the corners and down the central path.

The people talk no known language. Italian worse than English. And the women wear an extraordinary head-dress. It appears they were over-complaisant to the French troops of occupation at the time of the Napoleonic Wars—so much so that they scandalised their own priests who devised and enforced this head-dress as an emblem of shame. It was to be worn for a hundred years. The hundred years are at an end, but this dress is still enforced. The Naval Division did not have long time enough to prove that humanity remains much the same. The ladies are with few exceptions plain. Patrick's ship was also in port, so we went and dined and to the Opera and generally razzled—"Jack on Shore" to the manner born.

I did some laborious purchases on shore and left them all beyond retrieve on the quay, and for no legitimate excuse as we were as sober as you would have us be. We saw Ivor Windsor in fine dark blue uniform with silver chain epaulettes. He had been seeing the captain of the *Emden* who was in chokey there. This hero is in real life rather glum and dry and not the Bayard of romance our newspapers said. I didn't see him.

As we went out a French battleship *Léon Gambetta* came in, and we all cheered her and her band played "Tipperary"; we got tremendous cheering going out of port. This voyage alone is most heartening; to think of all of us going from end to end of this roguish old sea—unescorted—we only had torpedo-boats up till the end of the mine zone—just as if it was our territory—passing our strongholds on the way and seeing everywhere evidence of the great military and diplomatic conditions we have made—it's too good to be true. Malta was full of French ships and bristled with guns. You never get this sense of *power* at home.

Ship life has gone on its daily round. The rest of the ship count over its blessedness among ships in that it is honoured by a Divisional and Brigade Staff. And the mild radiance still lights our lives. I am neither fish, flesh, nor fowl, being viewed with suspicion as a Headquarters man and yet not sharing in the glories of the red hat and lapel tabs. But I am happy enough, as I've made several friends.

★★★★★★

The Hood was in port at Malta when the *Franconia*, with the Divisional Staff, came into harbour. The first meeting of Charles with the battalion in which he had so great an interest strengthened the wish which he had already formed to be with the regiment, as one of its subalterns, in which were so many of his friends.

The *Grantully Castle* was a small Castle Line ship, and the subaltern officers' mess was afforded little space and few luxuries, but one of them had brought a piano on board, and no record of the Hood Battalion on its way to the Eastern Mediterranean would be complete without mention of the rare pianoforte recitals and choice programmes given on those winter nights in more or less stormy waters. The musicians were Lieutenants F. S. Kelly and Denis Brown.—R.

★★★★★★

To Lord Ribblesdale.

Cunard R.M.S. *Franconia*,
March 10, 1915.

We are still at sea and more or less in the straight, and don't know when or where we are going to land.

We had a jolly time in Malta, That absence of green and the ramparts all round give an impression of artificiality; it is like a stage fortress or the great palace that the Magician drops from somewhere to conceal the princess he is guarding from the hero in a fairy story. And the sea never seems to have settled down since the descent of this Magic rampart into its depths.

I saw Patrick and Oc. Our whole flotilla was concentrated in the port; they have a very jolly battalion, which I should like to join in some capacity as soon as the Staff Intelligence Corps gets properly organised.

In a divisional staff all the men are so senior that one has always to be out with the "Sir." They are as nice as they can be, but a regiment is better fun, and it is more of a unity; a Staff is an amorphous body collected for no particular reason and with no particular traditions or tones, and a divisional staff is so large, and lacks the intimacy of a Brigade Staff, with its brigadier, its brigade major and staff captain. Still, bless the staff for getting me out here, and I'd sooner be a door-keeper, and so on, than dwell in Norfolk all the summer. So, I feel I am as lucky as anyone can be—so much more than I deserve.

Bless you. Did you enjoy your time in France? I suppose the Dunkirk heroine is back to her harness.

★★★★★★

This refers to the bombardment of Dunkirk, May 2, 1915, where his sister was serving in the Duchess of Sutherland's Hospital. Shells exploded close to the building, and the wounded had to be taken out on to the sea beach. Dunkirk, for hospital purposes was evacuated after this.—R.

★★★★★★

To Mr. C. Starkie.

R.M.S. Franconia,
March 10, 1915.

I am afraid I never answered the letter you were kind enough to write to me about Gisburne doings, in which, as you know, I am keenly interested.

You will have heard that I am off—somewhere—and I write to you now from the high seas. I am glad to be out of Norfolk and for it at last, though I have now got a Staff job—interpreter attached to the Naval Division—which I do not like so much as regimental work, especially with my own regiment under Sir Mathew. Still, it is a good thing to get to the front as best one can.

We have had a very smooth voyage and been in no way disturbed by enemy submarines nor by storms. I fancy we go too fast for submarines, which can only take on a slow-going boat.

I am glad that the German blockade has proved such an egregious farce so far, and resulted in such heavy losses for them. Out here, seeing all our sea-power and the way we take troops from one end of the sea to the other—unescorted—has impressed me much. The Mediterranean is like our own territory.

What a run you must have had that Worthy Hill day.

★★★★★★

The next halting-place was Lemnos. Neither the island nor its hero are very distinct amidst the allusion. *Dr. Smith's Classical Dictionary* tells us that Philoctetes, the famous archer in the Trojan War, was left behind by his men in the Island of Lemnos because he was ill from a wound which he had received from the bite of a snake. This is all that the Homeric poems relate of Philoctetes, but the cyclic and tragic poets have added numerous details to the story. Thus they relate that he was the friend and armour-bearer of Heracles, who instructed him in the use of the bow, and who bequeathed to him his bow with the poisoned arrows. According to some accounts the wound was not inflicted by a serpent, but by his own poisoned arrows. He was cured and soon after slew Paris, whereupon Troy fell into the hands of the Greeks.—B. W. C.

★★★★★★

To the Hon. Irene Lawley.

R.M.S. *Franconia*,
March 14, 1915.

This will not be a good letter as I am very hurried to catch our ship's post, which has come upon us as a thief in the night after a long expedition to the big town on this glorious island where we are for the time halted. This was the Island of Philoctetes, the Homeric hero, whom the Greeks found a disagreeable companion, as he had had his foot bitten by a snake, and been marooned on these rocky hills *en route* for Troy. Patrick and Oc. and I went today to the chief town and asked the natives who he was. They told us he was an Argonaut, and that the ladies of the island were so much *éprises* by him and his companions that they killed all their husbands, so that the handsome strangers might take their place.

This is a very interesting mix-up of the story of Jason, who, on his return from the search after the golden fleece arrived here and found the place solely dwelt in by women who had killed all their menfolk—I forget why—and who had a rather serious flirtation with the queen, whom he left, indignant at his treachery. Philoctetes, the natives added, lived two hundred years ago—hastily altered to eight hundred—and was a very good man who liked possession, and who liked all the building very well done.

Oc. met a little Greek shopkeeper who had known him in Omdurman, and pointed him out to the duly impressed crowd of natives as "the son of Mr. Asquith." So you see what fame is. Here they talk every known language. I like getting back to these jabbering people in the costumes of all ages, one man with his bowler on his head and his great red sash and baggy trousers; another in perfect tailor-made clothes but with a dirty cloth wrapped round and round a wrinkled, sunburnt, crab-apple of a face. The various degrees of shaving were also interesting.

It was a dear little town we went to, with its turquoise harbour and frowning fort built high above the house on a great pile of rock, and another great mass rising next it to show God can always go one better than man. There was a little mosque in the centre of the main square, and near it a Moslem cemetery overgrown with purple wild irises and asphodel. We were very well received, and the police all turned out to make omelettes for us and order our wine—you never saw such wine—it tasted partly of liquorice, partly of turpentine. I think one would get to like it, but at the first contact one feels it would add a new terror to crucifixion. Then we had some white wine very like Muscat. Along the road we had glimpses of neighbouring islands. Samothrace, where Poseidon sat to look on at the flighting on the plains of Troy; and once we saw Mount Athos, snow-capped and Deeding up into the sky, and where now sit thirty monasteries.

The fruit blossoms are just beginning to come out, and the village orchards will soon be one mass of pink and white. It is curious to think such an ideal spot should have been the cradle of so many cruel legends, and that Hypsilele's tears have watered the soil where the peasants grow their almond-trees. Jason, I think, was unduly criticized over this incident; the poor man was, after all, on active service—heroes were never off it. But heroes want watching. A nice fireside young man like me is the sort. Domestic—and no fire-eater. My Turkish is getting on very well, and if I light on a theme of which I know the vocabulary, I am almost impressive—but too quick speech rather flummoxes me.

P.S.—Have I given away our halting-place? Don't give *it* away to anyone else—unless of course it is generally known.

★★★★★★

The following is from Lemnos. A letter of Sir Ian Hamilton to Lady Wilson tells how the news of the great battle in the Dardanelles reached the Naval Division. "As to your second question, 'Which G.O.C.-in-C. came on board the *Franconia* at Lemnos and brought news of first landing at Gallipoli?' I was the only G.O.C.-in-C. in Eastern waters. I went on board the *Franconia* on the night of the great naval battle of March 18th when the *Irresistible*, the *Ocean*, and the *Bouvet* went to the bottom; the *Inflexible* and the *Gaulois* being very badly knocked about. I brought news of this historic engagement, and well remember the immense sensation it created in the Naval Division."—R.

★★★★★★

To the Same.

R.M.S. *Franconia*,
March 19, 1915.

I wish you were here. I'll tell you who *are* here—all the staff of the newly appointed *generalissimo*—and the man himself. It is going to be a very big show, and the figures of troops one hears quoted increase by leaps and bounds. There are constant arrivals moreover; and you can see Australians and French jostling one another on the little quay outside the chief town. The opinions of our gallant fellows of the French are very funny—the sort of old Frenchman who appears with a goaty beard and spectacles whom one often sees excites much interest.

I am still in a condition of rather "unmasterly "inactivity, as I have nothing whatever to do on the ship, and am not turned on to any odd jobs; I've rather mixed feelings about this. I am sick of Turkish vocabularies, with which I never seem to make any progress, and get on shore as much as I can to talk to the natives, a lot of whom know Turkish and so give me good practice; and I think I am improving—I wish I was doing more; I am still full of fears that this may be a second Norfolk. I am afraid chafers like myself fret themselves too much.

You will have our news before you get this in all probability. It is for the present not too good, and will probably lead to rather prompt action on our part.

To the Same.

s.s. *Franconia*,
March 22, 1915.

We are still here, marooned like the hero of the festering foot and expectant. When with the assistance of my housekeeper, who is to solace my declining years, I write up all this time, it will be interesting to see how Britain manages her affairs. First hustled out post haste. Stores all over the place, in the wildest confusion. Then held up in this spot for days—about to leave every afternoon, yet never leaving. Then a case of *reculez pour mieux sauter*. Then I suppose the final spring. I don't feel the Germans would have quite done it in this way. Priceless people aren't we? The horses have arrived only to be yoicked off *senz' altro*. No letters come here.

The Balliol men collected one evening and dined, and afterwards we sang the songs of our native heath with great gusto. The new staff is brilliant but affable like the archangels, and applauded our singing efforts without stint. They are nicer than the Naval Division Staff; less conscious of dignity and the weight of office, and they've got some people who really do know what we're about, and have been in the Near East.

I went on shore yesterday and had a jolly walk among barren stony hills, windswept from end to end. Little peasants, their heads well wrapped round with nondescript cloths and brightly coloured petticoats, winding up and down the hill paths on their donkeys. I like to see sunburnt faces. I then came down into the town and talked Turkish with my friends at the little wine-shop. In the evening I talked with an old Constantinople friend of mine now on board. He is our great hope, and knows everything: talks Turkish like a marvel, and is sound, not a crank like most Balkan experts.

To the Same.

s.s. Franconia, Port Said,
March 28, 1915.

We have left our island and have been whisked off ostensibly for Alexandria, then suddenly diverted here. I have seen a certain amount of this place, and it certainly has a character of its own. The naked and unashamed petty roguery and its unredeemed ugliness and ramshackleness are quite by themselves. It is all a huge joke at which everyone is smiling, bearing with flippant calm all minor worries such as dust and flies. The latter are almost the "friend of man"; a man is quite unconcerned if they sit on the end of his nose or wriggle into his eyes, and there are flies even now. What will there be in August?

The natives wear a jolly blue overall and a *fez* sometimes wrapped round with a *hoja's* white duster. The ladies are often seen in the streets in black dresses like a man's habit veiled up to the nose and with a funny little brass ornament connecting the veil with the hood above. They don't look beauties: beauty is indeed rather absent among the people of this side, and the type is generally low. Everyone talks Italian. It was rather a disappointment not going to Alexandria, but there may very possibly be some fighting here. There was a little fight a few days ago.

Our real object, however, in coming here is not to defend the Canal but to collect our *armada* and to straighten out our stores, etc., which in the case of the Naval Division are in a condition of some disorder. The *Armada* is still destined for the greater game. But many roads lead to Rome.

I can't help smiling at the boastful attitude of the papers of about a week ago as to Allied exploits in the Dardanelles. I am afraid we are rather quiet about our performances in that part of the world just now. I see the Admiralty have admitted in rather cryptic language that the attack on the 18th was not altogether a success. It dramatically synchronized with the arrival of a certain distinguished general officer, (see earlier note) who naturally witnessed the discomfiture of our ships.

Isn't the general note of optimism that prevails rather singular? I think we shall be through with the job by the end of the year, but July does seem rather early closing. Things seem going well for us in Italy. I am still more or less without occupation and have nothing to do besides working up my Turkish. For the time that we are here I shall try and get attached to Patrick's battalion. I am painfully getting this intrigue through now, lobbying and waiting for the great, who are today having an access of the work malady and not, as usual, comatose in the smoking-room armchairs. I think it will be successful, as my people have really nothing for me to do here. (*Later.* My intrigue is through.—see Mr. Shaw-Stewart's letter, following chapter.—R.)

The chances of seeing a shot fired here are very slight but not absolutely nil, and we shall be safely behind our forts.

With the Hood Battalion at Port Said

The story of the doings of the Naval Division is no longer told from the Franconia with the Headquarters Staff. The letters that follow are written from a Donald Currie steamer lying in harbour at Port Said. Charles was now gazetted to the Hood Battalion of the R.N.D.—and was meeting many Eton, Oxford, and Cambridge friends, all, like himself, full of eager anticipation of the vicissitudes and possibilities of war.—R.

★★★★★★

To Lord Ribblesdale,

April 2, 1915.

I am now a fixture in my battalion. I would have sooner been a supernumerary in view of my inexperience of infantry work, but they wanted me to take a platoon and I could not refuse. My company commander, one of the best, can say *"Ejectum littore egentem accepi"* (I hope he won't have cause to finish the quotation).

This is my first taste of camp life. The sand is the chief hardship—one day we had a horrid sandstorm, and it was impossible to go out without all the chinks of one's face being filled up with black sand: all our tents were finely dusted all over.

There is jolly bathing quite near and rude plenty; everything you get in the town is excellent, and we eat and drink like fighting-cocks. I am very fit. Today we were inspected by the G.O.C.-in-C, and complimented on our appearance.

I marched past with all the swagger of the rawest recruit; very self-conscious. My company has fine material, nearly all Naval Reserve men: hard nuts. I feel a sort of baby among them. There are many over thirty-five. The sun was brilliant, and the bayonets flashed like magnesium when it is burnt.

To the Same.
Mediterranean Expeditionary Force,
April 3, 1915.

This letter is written in *medias res* and the lavish disorder and glorious romance of the tented field with the transports in view that are to take us to ———.

It has been very jolly getting into the battalion, there are so many likeable people. I have got a platoon and bellow out orders which I understand through a glass darkly, but which are carried out punctiliously by my men, who are old hands, having been mostly stokers.

I have taken to camp life with zest, and I bathe early every morning in the rather soiled sea of this place, and sleep out in a Wolseley valise, a Jaeger bag, and my fur coat. It is coldish in the mornings, but the angry dawn over the ships' funnels is a grand spectacle as is the moon that whitens great stretches of sand in the evening, and throws her light on the rigging of the fishing-boats, shaped like the ships of Odysseus on the Greek vases and black against their star-lit backgrounds.

We live in plenty—rude plenty—not too many clean plates, but heaps to eat and delicious prawns for nothing practically. My company commander is a topper and a champion swimmer, as hard as nails and a real fighting leader; not so knowledgeable as Wilson—bless him—but a grand man. I do not fancy this is going to be a second Norfolk: even if we stop here we have the enemy nearer to us than at Mundesley.

Patrick and Rupert Brooke are down with sun, but not seriously. I am marvellously well and in fine condition, thanks to these few days on shore.

To the Hon. Beatrix Lister.
Mediterranean Expeditionary Force,
April 3, 1915.

. . . . I am afraid there is very little to say. We have been joy-riding about the Mediterranean under conditions which, up till now, made the idea of active service seem very remote. A Cunarder with its American bar, six-course dinner, and other accessories does not connect itself in my mind with anything but a transatlantic trip to Newport.

We were inspected by the G.O.C.-in-C. the other day, and really made a very good show. It is an exhilarating sense, marching in front of a line of strong men in step, their bayonets bright in the sun and the great adventure in their eyes. They all wear shorts now and step along very gaily. The G.O.C. was pleased with us and said so. The division, as you know, is fearfully and wonderfully made, and combines all the elements in its officers—the guardsman, the marine, the Balliol man, and the retired merchant service officer. It is remarkable how they have welded together. The war news looks very good, and I believe the end will soon be in sight. We shall now be able to reap the fruits of the Battle of the Marne.

To the Hon. Irene Lawley.

R.N.D., M.E.F., c/o G.P.O.,

April 5, 1915.

One little line before the mail, after two days of purgatory on these sands—duststorm blowing all the time and not a chink of an honest, open countenance clean within half a mile of it. Tempers all rather ruffled, and food highly flavoured with sand. Were we birds our gizzards would by now be in the very best form and mastication a pleasure. I was Battalion Orderly Officer yesterday, so I had no relief from the attentions of the sand, having to stay in camp all day. I distinguished myself by ordering a sergeant-major of the battalion next us to turn out his light. I was not only *ultra vires*, but trespassing on a most cherished privilege. So my confusion was dire: otherwise the day was uneventful.

All our mails we hear have gone to India—a very good place for them to go to, though some little distance from where we are now. Plans are still vague, and we are kept sitting on our haunches waiting for the *mot d'ordre*. It is, of course, impossible to give the men any work in this plague of Egypt. We had hoped yesterday that the sand might have been accompanied by locusts. One or two fine specimens, yellow and fat, flitted in to call on us. The men are in a state of cheerful grouse, and long for the quiet and peace of the Gallipoli Peninsula. We've had to chuck sleeping out as one would have been buried and dug out perhaps thousands of years hence. I censor some of the men's letters. They all talk about their knees getting burnt by the sun—we have put them all into shorts—and that they can't say anymore because of the Censor.

★★★★★★

The following more or less retrospective letter is written to a great friend of his Eton and Balliol days. It is dated from the Ægean, but properly finds its place here in view of the constant

70

references to school and university comrades.—R.

******

To Rev. Ronald Knox.

Hood Battalion, R.N.D., M.E.F.,

April 26, 1915.

No, I am not lonely at present, nor particularly uncomfortable. I am in a very jolly battalion—the "Hood." It is great fun having some small executive command as I have in the "Hood."

I fancy the original idea of the Admiralty was to force the Straits with ships alone. The R.N.D. were to come into the show as the force that was to do the dirty work of the ships, land occasional demolition parties, garrison forts the ships had cleared, and so on. Then came the gradual conviction that this was an impossible programme. Some marines were landed about the middle of March. My platoon got badly potted on ground which had been thoroughly searched by the ship's guns, and it was shown that ship's guns could not permanently rid ground of snipers or concealed trenches.

Result: the gradual aggrandisement of our force with Australians, Frenchmen, and so on, and the addition of a general officer commanding-in-chief He arrived about March 18th, and witnessed the sinking of the *Irresistible* and the *Ocean*. After that all naval operations on the grand scale were deferred, and it was plain that so long as the Turks held the peninsula and the mainland of the Asiatic side they were in a position to drift floating mines down the current and prevent the passage of ships. So we were taken to Egypt and encamped at Port Said on a sandy stretch of the station. . . .

Port Said is a merry sink of the minor iniquities—sunny and unashamed. Nothing there of interest except the people, a very low type of Arab, who accepts his degradation in a cheerful enough spirit, and has on the whole a very good time.

******

From Port Said Charles sailed, to quote him, "to an island of marble, to brilliant blue landlocked bays, sage and balsam, and bees." The rest of this letter to Rev. R. Knox, which bears evidence of having been written at different times, finds its place with some letters written on the eve of actual operations in the Dardanelles.—R.

******

About this time Mr. Patrick Shaw-Stewart, of the R.N.D., thus describes Charles joining the Hood Battalion.—R.

71

At Port Said Charles introduced himself by most subterranean methods into the Hood. He pulled as many strings to get off the Staff as others to get on to it—and in about three days he had a platoon. The four subalterns of the company were then Charles, Rupert Brooke, Johnny Dodge, and me. I had dysentery all the time at Port Said, so I missed the spectacle of Charles drilling stokers on Yeomanry lines—an entrancing one, I have been told.

There is one particularly circumstantial story of how he marched a body of men on to the parade-ground before the eyes of the Brigade, and in his resonant parade tone ordered them to halt in words more suited to the evolutions of quadrupeds. When I staggered on board about April 10th he was firmly ensconced in the battalion, and evidently had no intention of leaving it. It became a very jolly family party on board ship. At the same table Charles, and Rupert Brooke, and Oc, and Denis Browne, and Johnny Dodge, and Kelly, and me. Rupert and Charles, who were great friends, were its pivots.

In the same way Lieutenant Denis Browne writes to Mr. E. Marsh of the unforeseen meetings in the new conditions of war:—

Our party goes on happily. Charles Lister is a great gain even to those who don't understand him. He has the kindest heart imaginable, hasn't he? We laughed a good deal over the Divisional Notes on the character of the Turks, particularly at one which said they did not like night attacks because they hated the dark and invariably slept with a night light. Charles parodied them inimitably.

★★★★★★

These extracts from other folks' letters spoil, perhaps, the run of the actual correspondence, but still they give a sort of local colour—to use a horrible term.—R.

★★★★★★

Letters from the Ægean

The following letter was written off Patmos. The ancient city lay on the eastern side of the island, with the harbour on the sea, rather lower than the modern town. The natives still show the cave where St. John wrote his Gospel in banishment. About April 12th the Hood Battalion had sailed from Port Said on the *Franconia*.—B. W. C.

To the Hon. Irene Lawley.

April 15, 1915.

We are still yachting in the Mediterranean, more remote from the feeling of war than when we were on the dust-heaps of Egypt, and living the daily round of ship life, with its strangely made menus. You don't know what "*cardoons*" are—they sound like one of the degrees of black blood—yet we have them; not to mention *hominies*, and Yosemite girdle cakes, and Schoongesicht wine from Table Bay.

I am trying to learn signalling, which is a useless accomplishment, I fancy, but I must above all give the impression of zeal, as I always feel my position is rocky and my accomplishments far behind those of my brother officers. They are so versed in machine-guns, physical drill, and all the other accomplishments of the foot-slogging soldier. I feel that anything I know is worth very little. Our best officer is an ex-cavalry man, but he has seen service in the Matabele and Boer Wars—and I have seen service at Mundesley.

I smile at these wishes for a rapid passage through the Golden Gate. The nearest we have been to the G.G. is some fifty miles, and I feel the gilt of potential heroism wearing off amid the sands of Egypt as quickly as it was tarnished by the mud of Norfolk. I cannot write you any more about seas and sunsets, and shall not take up my pen till we have some tale of blood to our credit (at least, I suppose I shall, from what I know of the speed of our movements). But you would like the island of the Apocalyse. A city of dazzling white crowns it, and stands out brilliant long after the hills have been merged into the gloaming. I wonder if it existed in the time of St. John, and gave him the idea of the heavenly city.

★★★★★★

The "Golden Gate" was one of the gates of the city of Constantinople. In the Middle Ages Constantinople was besieged by the Arabs soon after the Hejira, and we read that "from dawn of light till evening the line of assault was extended from the Golden Gate to the eastern promontory. And when the Greeks wrested Constantinople from the Latins in 1261, they broke an entrance into the city through the Golden Gate."— B. W. C.

★★★★★★

To Lord Ribblesdale.

April 16, 1915.

This is again on board ship, bound for an "unknown destination." This, I suppose, is the *saut* after the *reculement*. But I fancy we shall wait about a bit more at our islands. I am very much happier in the Battalion than on the Staff, and there have so far been no contretemps with the platoon, which is tame and has good petty officers. The stokers look after themselves. You just tell a petty officer to get something or other done and it is done with unobtrusive regularity. It is impossible to do any drill on board ship except rather uncomfortable Swedish exercises, which, I suppose, are beneficial. They are certainly disagreeable, and done with little enough grace by most of us. Then there is practice in machine-gun work which I have continued since the *Franconia*, and semaphore signalling which I am trying to learn. This is difficult; a pretty thing if well done, but of doubtful advantage. I do not think that signalling is possible in face of an enemy—you would show yourself too much, certainly with flags.

We are sailing between wonderful islands of an opal colouring with cobalt blue shadows between the rocks and ravines. We passed the island of the Revelation, and saw a gorgeous white city on the top of one of the hills, which must have inspired the idea of the heavenly city. It remained in sight long after hills round had sank into the twilight. The sea under the setting sun is really wine dark.

We have got some horses on board, which have done pretty well and look very jolly in their boxes with their heads out. The men are having a fancy dress ball tonight, and we have to think of dresses, etc., for them, which is a business. As towels are about the only material

74

available the problem is not easy.

I go on talking Turkish to our little interpreter. I acquire quite quickly, but do not make real progress, as he is very bad at English and never knows what I am talking about. What impression did the mishap to those ships about a month ago make on the English public? I see we made a clean breast of it. All love.

★★★★★★

This following letter is from the Island of Scyros, known as the Island of Achilles. It lies with Lemnos and Imbros off the coast of Ancient Thessaly. A cycle of legends relate the conquest of Scyros by Achilles. There was a sanctuary of Achilles known to tradition, and the actual worship of the island is of a hero or god. Can this be St. George? The ancient city of Scyros is now the town of St. George.—B. W. C.

★★★★★★

To the Hon. Irene Lawley.

Hood Battalion, B.M.E.F., c/o G.P.O.,
April 20, 1915.'
(Union Castle Line.)

We are still waiting, in a neat bay formed by the Island of Achilles. Here he was hidden among a bevy of maidens, and dressed in female attire by his mother Thetis so that he should not be taken for the Trojan War. Thetis knew that he must die if he went to Troy. Odysseus, however, suspected this, and came to the island dressed as a merchant with draperies and female *gewgaws*, but amongst them was a sword, and Achilles at once gave himself away by showing interest in the cold steel. So he went to Troy and there died.

The island is made of pink marble, out of which sage and balsam and every kind of wild flower grows. It is humming with bees, and there are groves of olive- and thorn-trees in the ravines that run down to the sea from the mountain tops. In the middle of the island there is a little *nek* of brilliantly green cultivated land. The water in the island's bays is an extraordinary blue, and cold to swim in. Oc. and I and my company commander, who is a very fine swimmer, tried to swim back from the shore one day. Oc. and I had to chuck it, as we got chattering cold; my C.C. did the distance as easy as pot. It is about two miles, and we must have swum about a mile and a quarter. Today we three all did a shorter swim from shore of about one mile.

Patrick and I went a walk on the island, and we met the only inhabitant, a charming man in blue baggy trousers, who gave us lunch consisting of a sort of milk-cheese and some good damp brown peasant bread. We went home in a native boat, rowed by an old fisherman and his wife, who sleep in the boat and light fires in it. We have had two field days—one brigade, one divisional. The brigade day was pleasant. We lay in the sun on a hillside and built ourselves little stone *sangars*. The divisional day consisted in aimless walking about over very rough country, which fed the men up thoroughly and spoilt their boots.

What have people at home made of the *Manitu* incident? Curious that the Turks—— Well I won't say any more.

★★★★★★

The attempted sinking of the *Manitu* referred to was by a German destroyer which *missed fire* after magnanimously giving the crew five minutes to leave the ship. It carried guns for the 29th Division. The *Franconia* and several destroyers were at the time anchored off Scyros.—R.

★★★★★★

I doze over "Infantry Training," practise signalling, and read Anatole France. *Les Sept Femmes de Barbe bleu* is a fascinating example. *La Chemise*, the last story, of the search for the shirt of a happy man is charming. Then I have started on *Monsieur Bergeret à Paris*. I rather like the quiet, rather Christmas-numbery manner, with mild touches of the *scabreux*. It makes for better writing than the broader improprieties and far more subtle atmospheres.

The General Staff, in an access of gaiety, have thrown six mail-bags into the harbour of an island which shall be nameless. So perhaps your last letter "shall suffer a sea change." I haven't had it anyway.

Life is so very quiet, and there seems no end to its peace. Our distance from active service seems to increase rather than decrease. But I suppose this cannot go on for ever.

I am every day happier at having left the Staff, and the sight of one's own men lying down in line among the stones and scrub of these jolly hills warms the blood. I hope I shall be brave; I am sure they will.

To Lord Ribblesdale.

Hood Battalion, B.M.E.F.,
April 20, 1915.

One line to say I am still guiltless of blood and that the yachtsmen in the Mediterranean pursue their ordinary avocations and cruise

76

from island to island. We had some excitement the day the *Manitu* was attacked and got a number of signals advising us in one sense and the other; we stuck, however, to our course and met with no mishap, hearing later in the day that the raider had been scuppered. There are one or two men-of-war about here, and occasionally we see dummies which would take me in but which deceive no one who is an expert at all, so I don't suppose the Germans get much hoodwinked.

I have been swimming a certain amount twice since we have been here, an island smaller than our previous anchorage, stony, uninhabited, but with wonderful wild flowers and humming with bees. Its fragrance meets one as one comes into harbour. I like that smell of land. Platoon commanding is most amusing, and it is a very good thing that I have left the *Franconia* and the General Staff. Life is serene and war seems remote. No more now, as I must catch mail.

★★★★★★

The following extracts from letters written by Denis Browne and Patrick Shaw-Stewart to Miss Lawley from the Ægean Sea, give some idea of their life during this time.—R.

★★★★★★

There's a fancy dress ball tonight for the men, and they're making wonderful confections out of nothing at all; the vain spark in my platoon is going as Queen Elizabeth. His skirt is my burberry, his stomacher my cabin curtains; his wimple (not historic, but one must wear something on one's head) is a boot-bag, and his veil a blue antiseptic bandage. Perhaps he's Queen Eleanor, but as he hasn't heard of her, we call him Queen Elizabeth. The rest are rather shy; they are too bashful to go as Greek athletes in a towel, which would be charming—and all the most magnificent want to go as old dames or niggers.

We went to Scyros and lay in harbour there for a week—these were the weeks in which the Mediterranean Force lost its chance of doing something in the Peninsula—and there were days where we performed evolutions up those beautiful but stony hillsides, and there was one day when no-one left the ship except by great ingenuity, and Charles and I exercised it and explored the whole barren southern half of the island all through the most perfect spring day, and ate bread and milk-cheese given us by a solitary shepherd. He was very delicious that day and very ardent—a frame of mind "which always made me marvel (modern war has never had any attraction for me). Before we left Scyros, Rupert Brooke died and we were all very sad.

77

★★★★★★

Rupert Brooke died in a French Hospital off the Island of Scyros April 29, 1915. He was 27 years old. His letters, recently published with a preface by the late Mr. Henry James, speak eloquently for his reputation and character.

Mr. Edward Marsh writes me: "Denis told me that Charles was one of those who turned the sods of Rupert's grave, and stayed behind after the burial and covered the grave with great pieces of white marble."—R.

★★★★★★

To Lord Ribblesdale.

Hood Battalion, R.N.D., B.M.E.F., c/o G.P.O.,

May 9, 1915.

At Scyros, we had a blow in the loss of Rupert Brooke. He died of blood poisoning and we buried him in a grove of olives tucked deep in a rocky ravine under Mount Paphlee.

αἱ δὲ τεαὶ ζώουσιν ἀήδονες.

To the Rev. Ronald Knox.

April 1915.

We are now at the last lap, waiting our turn. Our ship is anchored in a glassy, sunlit sea—enemy coast on every side—not a breath of air, not a sign of movement. It is still a sheer impossibility to believe that we are at war.

To the Same.

Hood Battalion, B.M.E.F.

Rupert Brooke died of blood-poisoning caused by a germ called *the pneumo coccus*. He had been rather pulled down at Port Said and suffered from the sea, so the *p.c.*, had a favourable field to work in. There was no doubt as to his fate; he died within twenty-four hours of the ill making itself manifest. He was buried in an olive-grove hidden in a ravine thick with scrub that runs from a stony mountain down to the sea. The grave is under an olive-tree that bends over it like a weeping angel. A sad end to such dazzling purity of mind and work, clean cut, classical, and unaffected all the time like his face, unfurrowed or lined by cares. And the eaglet had begun to beat his wings and soar. Perhaps the Island of Achilles is in some respects a suitable resting-place for those bound for the plains of Troy.

★★★★★★

Rupert's was certainly a perfect death, and a very fitting close to a fine life; but it is rather a bitter thought that he should have seen none of the soldiering he had devoted himself to with such ardour, and that the gift made so gladly should have been accepted before Experience gave him any return. For anyone with a mind alive, this war is primarily a search after the new, and appeals keenly to one's sense of curiosity.

Landing of the Hood Battalion on the Gallipoli Peninsula

On June 27th Sir Ian Hamilton wrote to Lady Wilson—

The Hood Battalion made a feint of landing up at the head of the Gulf of Saros towards evening on April 24th, and continued threatening a landing until after dark on the night of April 25th. As I wrote you yesterday, the only individual of the force who really landed up there was Freyberg.

This is what happens later as described by Mr. Shaw-Stewart—

After several days hanging about we landed on April 29th. Then Charles began to scent the battle and to be really happy. The third night the battalion went up to the firing-line, and took part in the *manqué* advance of May 2nd. That day everyone who saw him says Charles was superb: he was hit by a shrapnel bullet in the retirement and tried to conceal it, till he was given away by his breeches being filled with blood—so his sergeant told me. That meant a long dreary blank for me, especially as Oc. was wounded on May 6th and Denis on May 8th. (He came back only to be killed on June 4th.)

To Lord Ribblesdale.

May 9, 1915,

The next evening (April 30th) the colonel gave us a little address to the effect that now we were in for it, and on the morning of Sunday we found ourselves lying off the shore. For a day, we sat and watched a rather leisurely bombardment of the little scrub-covered cliff sides and rounded green hills of an apparently tranquil coast-line. Not an enemy within miles: a sea like glass, and the whole notion of real war still remote and illusory, and all this time the landing was being made and our foothold on enemy soil dearly bought some fifty miles farther down the coast. The next day routine unrelieved was the order, and we did Swedish exercises in the sight of the enemy—rather sick at heart at these delays.

We were then moved down to nearer the scene of action, and for three days watched our ships pound the hills and woods that crowned them. It was a wonderful spectacle, the shrapnel going up like little white clouds and then bursting high up and sending down a spray of smoke like a firework, and the lyddite green and yellow which could only be seen when the shell had actually burst on the ground, and looked like some angry protest of the gods of the soil, in the form of deadly vaporous exhalation from the earth's inner chambers. The row of one's own guns is very deafening. The enemy shrapnel make a shrill ghostlike scream as it goes through the air overhead, but no more. Occasionally little ant-like men could be seen making their way up the cliff faces or creeping over the scrub-covered hillsides. And once or twice we saw Turks in retreat catching it from the ships' guns.

The night of Thursday we were landed and passed a chilly time on a wind-swept plateau-like field with the flare of smoking towns on the skyline, as red as a red dawn. The next day we passed quickly in digging and landing stores, and occasional shells fell in the water near where I was working. That night we drank rum and dug ourselves little nests in the heather, so we were warm and woke up fresh. We then dug trenches, occasional shells passing over our heads. I don't think we were ranged: one or two, however, fell just short of us. That night at about midnight we were woken by a tremendous volume of rifle and machine-gun fire which seemed at our very doors, and we passed about an hour in a state of more or less alarm.

We were then marched out through a marshy ravine overgrown with lovely water weeds and olives, grey in the moonlight, to a line of trenches immediately behind the firing-line and sat tight, spent bullets from the firing-line and from rather remote snipers whistling over our heads. One of my men got hit. Dawn showed our men advancing and many Turkish dead. One of our officers who advanced up a certain gully which was the critical point of the Turks' attack counted hundreds of dead. They must have lost *enormously*.

We then advanced, my company in second line. When the leading company had got about 2,000 yards or so in front of the front line of fire trenches they got heavily shrapnelled by the Turks. With no adequate trench cover and no time to dig themselves in and no support on either flank. Result: orders to retire. The same thing happened to other troops sent through and round us. My company being in the second line retired last, and by the time we were moving the whole of our front was being searched with terrible effect.

One of the shrapnel burst on the ground about thirty yards behind me and a pellet ricocheted the ground and struck me in the off-buttock. I thought it was a piece of stone at first. I had already been hit by several spent pellets without any effect. One went through coat and shirt and hardly marked my skin; another knocked in my water-bottle. However, this third one found its billet, and I was soon bleeding like a pig and walking indifferent well—I never fell down. It was an irritating moment, as I should have been there to rally our boys after the retirement. They did well, considering the trying circs, and their relative rawness. I never saw a Turk within shooting distance: the other companies did, and did some execution; not much, I fancy.

I was under fair shell fire for about one hour or so and light attentions from snipers. One bullet went between me and my petty officer as we sat together. The battalion has since been in the firing-line all the time and done very well, getting a bayonet charge on one occasion. I should like to get back quick, because I have seen just enough to tantalise. It is rather like love-making in this. The *mise en scène* was magnificent, and there is no sound like the scream of enemy shrapnel through the sky.

My return to the beach was easily accomplished for me on a stretcher, not so easily perhaps for the poor orderlies who had to carry me, and I had a feeling of great peace as I lay on my back and looked at the blue overhead. I was then put on to a lighter and then on to a trawler, which was full of wounded, slight cases for the most part, and there we were, rather toasted by the close proximity of the boilers. Here I saw several of our people; we dropped about eight officers or so, slightly wounded in every case; as to men I don't really know, so I will give no figure—certainly not more than eighty and very few killed, but it happened all within an hour or so.

From the trawler we went on to an Anchor Line ship, a dowdy old boat but comfortable enough. Rather a shortage of doctors to cope with the numbers on board—and to bed in our battle shirts. I found our adjutant here and one of our company commanders, so I wasn't lonely. I saw no very distressing case except a poor man who had been hit in the back of the head and had a compound fracture in the thigh and was quite off his chump—and my next-door neighbour. We did what we could for him.

I write from Alexandria, where we went, after a short wait, round the scene of action's vicinity for more wounded. I saw Letty and Mary Charteris here and Harry. (Sir Mathew Wilson, in command of the 2nd Mounted Division.—R.) All the 2nd Mounted Division are here now; and it was a great pleasure seeing the boys once more, Mary was in great looks. Letty rather pale. It is a Capua this place, and full of rank and fashion. So the wounded, no matter how slightly, have much sympathy. My injury was rather doubted, and I fear I was not in a position to give optical proof. But *"Blessed are they who have not seen, yet have believed."* Off we go to Malta now. I shall be back again soon—a week or so.

Constantinople During July and August 1914

In the leisure and comfort of the Blue Sisters Convent Hospital at Malta, whilst recovering from his first wound, Charles wrote, in the form of a letter to me, a full and graphic account of the run of events and the varying phases of feeling at Constantinople during the months of July, August, and September 1914.

This MSS. letter—much of it in pencil—worked out to over 15000 words when I had it typed and suggested to me the possibility of getting together his letters, for he had several more or less regular correspondents besides his sisters and myself. The Vice-Provost of Eton, to whom I had shown the MSS., encouraged me to do so, and the Blue Sisters letter thus became responsible for this volume.

I should have liked to use the MSS., just as he wrote it, but this was not his own wish. Writing to me on June 3, 1915, he begged me to get it typed quickly, but added that he did not think it "could be used for a time," so I reluctantly defer and confine myself here to a few selected passages. On the news of the death of the Archduke Charles tells us "long faces were pulled by those who wished to appear knowing," but entertainments and dinners went on much as usual.—R.

We gazed on distant war-clouds through the light glow of Japanese lanterns. . . . The change came with the publication of the Austrian Note. The feeling that predominated at Constantinople at the outset was more or less a reflection of that which, as far as we could see, obtained in London; sympathy with Austria was considerable amongst diplomats. Austrians are generally liked as personalities, and from Constantinople the Serb can be observed rather too closely to pass for a *chevalier sans reproche*. I had just been a trip to New Serbia, and returned with unfavourable impressions. The Italians were upset about the turn of events. They had wanted that year to take their course and hatch out the Austria-Serb conflict in due time when Italy would be ready to play her hand.

The premature announcement was not to their liking. The French had, from the outset, a rather clearer vision than ourselves of the German behind the scenes. The Germans in conversation were quite unequivocal in their approval of Austria's action, and were decidedly "out" to make us think that after all there would be no trouble. They sometimes said that the Austrians would climb down as they had done before. At other times they were full of stories of mutinies on the Black Sea front, Russian unpreparedness, and so on. The first and last time I dined at the German Embassy, Von Wangenheim was on this tack. As the crisis took its course we saw less of our German colleagues.

At this time, even amongst "the intimates" of the Young Turk Party, there seems to have been complete ignorance of Enver's intentions. Charles goes on to say—

The Turks, I fancy, in so far as they understood it all, were in the first phase not sorry that Serbia was to get a trouncing. Later, they rejoiced in the thought that thieves would fall out and honest men come by their own, and they calculated on a Turkish re-conquest of Salonica, for Greece was at that time their *bête-noir*.

On a long railway journey, from Smyrna to Constantinople—we had by this time come "in" as belligerents—Charles says—

My train was packed with soldiers answering the call. They seemed already rather German in their sympathies and not unwilling to be again called to the colours, but friendly to me as an individual.

Previously—that is before we came in—he says—

At Constantinople, there had reigned the leaden calm which precedes a storm. The days of suspense when it was a question whether we would participate were very grim, and all that time we carefully avoided our French and Russian colleagues. We felt a sort of shame about meeting them. During the time that server and a gentleman, which was the reason for the dislike of the Irish members. His comments on the statesmen of the day are most illuminating. He sized up Lord Salisbury very well as "a really weak man." His friendship with Chamberlain seems to have been one of genuine comradeship.

Parnell turns into the strange, mist-enveloped silhouette of the mediaeval alchemist. His interest in astronomy, his efforts to get gold out of quartz, and his childish beliefs and superstitions make one even more conscious of his utter remoteness and intangibility. He thought much on death and its terrors, and yet was a man of marvellous courage—a mediaeval trait, I think, I can't make him out at all. I suppose his intense refinement and high-strung nervous system found just what was wanted in Mrs. O'S.'s liberalness. Parnell's mind seems to have been clear and comprehensive but not subtle, and his power of expression and turning a phrase limited except when dealing with broad issues.

I have also read the *Koran*—or rather most of it—and will let you know what I think of it. The Prophet is as insistent on the genuineness of his mission and the virtues of his book as the populariser of a patent medicine, but has considerable lyrical gift. But more of him later. Bless you.

To the Hon. Mrs. Percy Wyndham.

Blue Sisters, Malta,
May 27, 1915.

What I meant by the Naval Division being a "washout" was that it is not being used as a division. The battalions are attached to other brigades of the 29th Division, and have individually done *very well* and suffered very severe losses. I think the chances of its being worked as a division were always slight, as it had no divisional artillery or cavalry. So long as this campaign lasts *I can't think* of going back. Now that more of our men are coming out it is possible that the Naval Division may again become a unit. The news of the *Majestic* is rather disquieting. I think the submarines have appeared on the scene just too late. Had they come earlier in the day—— Even now it will be awkward if the ships have to discontinue their work in any way till the submarines are bagged. Operations on land seem to have settled down into normal trench warfare. Reinforcements constantly pass through here—including crowds of doctors and nurses.

My pellet was extracted more than a week ago now, and the gash is followed, after my journey from Smyrna, we at least knew we were men. Work grew brisk enough; reports from the provinces poured in. The Turks had viewed our entrance into the field with mixed feelings; they had hoped we should look on and, in company with themselves, play the part of the fox that sucked the bone for which the lions were fighting. They were rather impressed by our intervention; but I doubt if they thought we could really do much to benefit our allies, who in their view were certain to be beaten crushingly. The Turk has very little idea of sea power as a factor in war. He imagined that England could not come to very much harm, but he could not conceive sea power as an aggressive force in world warfare.

In Government circles pro-German feeling was on the increase, and reached its climax with the arrival of the *Goeben*, following closely on the embargo we had placed on the ships Armstrongs were building for Turkey.

All these days the ambassador was on leave; he returned soon after the *Goeben* arrived, to find the situation compromised beyond hope. The initial error had been in our impartial recognition of the transfer of the German ships to Turkey. Once that had been conceded; once we had failed to demand internment in a certain time, and, failing such internment, sent our ships up the Narrows—then but little mined—we could only work for the postponement of the final rupture between Turkey and the Triple Entente Powers.

★★★★★★

Note: Sir Louis du Pan Mallet, K.C.M.G., became Ambassador to Turkey in the early part of 1913. He had previously been Private Secretary to Sir Edward Grey (1905-7) and Assistant Under-Secretary of State for Foreign Affairs (1907-13).—R.

★★★★★★

All sorts of rumours were rife as to the condition in which the *Goeben* had arrived; and for a long time, she failed to make an appearance. We all thought Germany was waiting to see the *Goeben* restored to health before she finally pushed Turkey over the brink. The fateful date was to be September nth; this was the date fixed for a great naval review in which the whole Turkish fleet was to take part. The review made less impression than was expected.

The *Goeben* appears to have done nothing to disturb the peace—

> She used to sail up with her band playing, packed with German sailors—not a Turk in sight—and made a point of passing very close to the Russian Embassy at Therapia. The chief impression she gave was one of great breadth amidships.
> . . . The *Goeben*, however, was not the sole symbol of German domination. One day, on the polo ground, we met some apparently Turkish soldiers who had obviously lost their way. They were spoken to in Turkish by the Zaptieh hard by, but without success. Then one of our Russian colleagues brought himself to speak the enemy tongue, and it transpired that these men had been deliberately brought in from Germany to garrison Turkish forts. Trainloads, in fact, arrived daily. After the taking of Brussels, Djavid said to a Belgian friend of mine: "*J'ai une nouvelle pour vous—les Allemands sont entrés à Bruxelles.*" He answered: "*Et moi, excellence, j'ai une nouvelle pour vous—les Allemands sont entrés à Constantinople.*"

This is what he has to say of the German Ambassador at this time—

> The figure which stands out amid the multitudinous detail and petty incident of these days is that of Von Wangenheim. He was a tall, well-made man with a dark, lowering face, somewhat marked by duelling scars, and a close-cut moustache. His features were well cut and their pose solid. There was a grimness about the clean-shaven chin and a cold stare about the sunken blue-green eyes. I liked the man. He was very fond of horses, and actually took the trouble to get hunters all the way out from Ireland for the Constantinople drag hunt In his Junker way he liked the English, and was very hospitable to us in better times.
> He talked very freely to everyone, and as early as June, after a brief visit to Berlin—where it was supposed he would take up Von Jagow's position—used to inform his barber every morning that "the war" would take place in the autumn or late summer. To the young he was full of chatter, and flattered them by his anxiety to hear their views. While German influence was stronger and more uncontested than in Marschall's time, I do not think Wangenheim ever bulked so large in the eyes of the Turks as his massive predecessor. He lacked the quiet strength, the awful silences of Marschall, and could never control his

natural excitability. Morning after morning he used to sweep round the neutral embassies like a tornado with reports of German successes, which in due time kind friends repeated to us. . . . The *Goeben* and *Breslau* used often to set forth under his orders, and his control of the Turkish military and naval organisations was complete, except in so far as he had differences with Liman von Sanders, a hot-head who managed to quarrel with every one sooner or later. Liman's temper was reported to be even less under control than Wangenheim's nerves. . . .

Liman was certainly of the view, shortly before the war, that the Turkish Army was quite incapable of taking the field, and he told Enver as much. When the fat was in the fire he had to box the compass, and has since been engaged in a task he has known from the outset to be hopeless. All the time I was in Turkey, members of the German military mission took the line that the task was impossible; they said they disliked the Turks, thought them stupid and unteachable, and despaired of any results. I have often wondered if the Germans at Constantinople were unanimous on the question of the advisability of bringing Turkey into the war. . . .

It is difficult for us to make out the Turks' attitude towards Germany. I don't think the Turk has any liking for the German; he looks on him as useful, and has boundless confidence in his efficiency. It was this conviction, that Germany was sure to win, which had to be met. . . .

There is, after all, something to be said for those who were throughout convinced that it was in Turkey's interest to go to war on Germany's side, such as Enver and others of the soldiers. Turkey could alone hope from the Central European Powers for any reversal of the Balkan settlement arrived at in 1913; France was herself at war and therefore unable to lend Turkey money. This fact precluded any possibility of peaceful regeneration and raised the spectre of internal disruption and the fall of the Enver regime. Add to this the dazzling nature of the German promises.

Charles thus describes his impression of the *grand vizier's* attitude towards European intervention and advice in Turkish affairs—

He (the *grand vizier*) was a good French scholar and pugnacious in conversation, but a very oriental Oriental. He was never happy in the Stamboul frock-coat, and in the morning wore Arab costume. Before the Central Powers days he used to beg his Western friends to keep their enterprise and finance away from Turkey; Europe was trying to get the Turk to do things that were beyond his power; the Turk was too stupid to organise himself in any way: his only chance was to stagnate and remain in the East—speeding up he declared to be hopeless.

The role played by such a man in the present drama is enigmatic. He was, I think, sincere enough in his wish to keep the peace, for he saw the risks attending a rupture. He failed to realise the impossibility of playing with German influence, backed as it was by the *Goeben's* guns, and thought to the last that he could avert the inevitable. He remained in office, telling himself, perhaps, that *he* will be the influence for moderation, and that *he* will enable Turkey to cut her losses by his diplomatic skill. Then he liked prominence.

He realised that he could only appear equal to certain of his colleagues by retaining his tinsel trappings of high office, and that, German influence apart, he had never been really master in his own house. His devotion to Enver was almost doglike. My chief, in happier days, dined with the latter at a huge banquet and the *grand vizier* was also present. Throughout the repast he drew Enver out and made him tell stories of his marvellous escapes, asking him for his views as to Destiny, and other high subjects; listening to the oracle in speechless amazement.

In all these grave contingencies and complications, it appears that—

The dogs of the enemy embassies refused to recognise the state of war; the Wangenheims had to pass our demesne to go for their evening ride, and their greyhound bitch Fly never missed the opportunity thus afforded of paying a friendly visit to an Irish terrier, Mike, of Nicolson's, and a bull-terrier pup then under my care. Fly was at times accompanied by a pointer, spotted, grim, and underhung, who was sometimes on the verge of blows with Mike.

Mike was equally without political conscience, and we sometimes had to enter enemy territory to lure him from the Calypso-like charms of Fly.

This is also a passage of not unpleasing interest—

During the early days of the war Wangenheim rode for more than an hour with the huntsman of the Constantinople drag-hounds—Maiden by name—who had been huntsman to Sir Watkin Wynn and had fallen from this high estate to a measly £90 a year, plus a residence on an upland farm buried in the woods above the polo ground. His Excellency was full of commiseration for the poor English who had been bungled into the war against their will and interests; who had lost one army at Mons, and who were bound to go under. There seemed to be nothing of the "Hymn of Hate" spirit in him; nothing but pity "for his good friends," On more than one occasion, too, he talked to others of an early peace wrung from France, of a *guerre* Platonique with England, ending in the union of Western Powers against Russia as *Kultur's* arch-foe. As events developed his tone changed.

Charles's application to the Foreign Office for a year's leave of absence from his post was at last successful, he writes:

I left about a month before the final rupture. Events took their course, and the Turk, as the successor to the Emperors of the East, took his place at the side of the man he believed to be the Emperor of the West, to divide with him the world's spoils. In the same spirit, moving along the same groove of historic fatality, the Turk of a former era *coquetted* with Napoleon, to be hauled back from the abyss by the strong hand of Sir Stratford Canning, but Sir Stratford had not to contend with the guns of the *Goeben*.

With the Dardanelles Expedition

To the Hon. Irene Lawley.
Blue Sisters Convent, Malta,
May 16, 1915.

It is lucky this place has been built under Spanish influence and escaped the floridities of the Italian baroque, which was oozing into its most luxurious form about the time the knights came here and started to build, in about the sixteenth or seventeenth century. The part I like best is the little *Vittoriosa* harbour, where the admiral lives. It is a narrow inlet of brilliantly blue water, like a canal of Venice, with great *palazzos* with pilastered *façades* here and there, and jolly little jutting-out flat-roofed houses with ship's images over the door. All the roofs are flat, and geraniums grow in the windows.

My convent is not actually in Valetta, but on a hill called St. Julians, and I am most comfortable with the nuns. They are Irish and charmers, and wear little blue head-dresses—Eton blue—which hang down their backs like veils. My wound is practically healed up, but I was unfortunate enough to find the bullet, and the doctor is determined to have it out, and I have not sufficient strength of will to withstand him. It is, after all, hard luck. He has had scarcely a single case on which he could operate among our lot, and I should feel under a grievance at that if I was a surgeon—wouldn't you? My operation will not be a severe one, and I shall be back again in a short time—say a week. So write to the old address, if the fancy takes you.

I can tell you nothing of what is happening at the scene of action from here, and feel in a complete fog about it and dying to pierce the gloom and hear something. This sort of enforced absence feeds me up, and I'd give anything to know what the battalion was doing. Oc. was hit about three days after me, I gather, and not very badly, though the Italian papers said *gravamente ferito*. I hear Princess Teano has been over

91

in England looking over Red Cross things, etc. I suppose the Italians will be in by the time you get this. This new factor is in our interests on the whole, as the Adriatic question will not be solved in a sense so wholly favourable to the Slav if Italy figures in the conference after the war as a participant, and therefore more entitled to a hearing than if she were simply there as a neutral. It also cuts off another food supply from Germany. But we can win without her.

I saw Ivor Windsor, (A.D.C. to Lord Methuen), at tea at St. Antonio yesterday. He is in great form and very busy. They have done a lot for the wounded, on their own, organised accommodation for six thousand. It is badly wanted, as the actual accommodation on the spot has been lamentably deficient, and has entailed casting the wounded about on transports from port to port with a very inadequate number of doctors and orderlies on board.

Alexandria was Capua, *le tout Londres*. But here too there seem quite a number of people—though such tired warriors. The beauties here are for the most part floral; though the flapper *del popolo* is occasionally of dazzling beauty, she wears off as soon as the southern Italian, and becomes hunchbacked, wrinkled, and frog-like.

The Maltese come up between six and seven to our hospital, and crowd round the doors and are most effusive; funny black dresses, with black cotton gloves and toques. We are the sort of "lions" that don't bite. You would have laughed at our reception on the quay. *Le tout Malte* turned out covered with brassards and badges of the Red Cross, and the ladies lavished on us slabs of Fry's chocolate and glasses of rather tepid lemonade, and cigarettes. I never smoke cigarettes, but could not say "nay" to such a charmer as the young lady who made me the offer. She is almost as good-looking as you are. The Maltese are very pious—one hears bells going all the day long. I like it, it is soothing. You would like the governor's, (Lord Methuen), country palace. The garden is a paradise—orange groves and pergolas of geraniums and little loggias covered with creepers.

To the Hon. Beatrix Lister.

Blue Sisters Convent, Malta,
May 25, 1916.

Ever so many thanks for your letters, which gave me so much pleasure.

You will have heard from father of the details of my wounding.

I have had the pellet actually removed now—being subject to an operation about a week ago, and am now stitched up and a little gash near the groin. The pellet worked right round. I expect I shall be fit for duty shortly.

I am splendidly looked after at the convent by some delightful nuns, who are excellent nurses and angels of kindness. They put themselves to every sort of trouble, and are most anxious about our welfare. They make a marvellous open jam tart, and their pastry generally is worthy of the highest encomiums. So with all this there is little to complain of.

I always thought that the Italians would come in, but I am rather surprised they have entered on war so soon, and at this moment the Russians are doing indifferently. Evidently the Salandra Government must have been determined on war for some time, and under the impression that longer delay would give the enemy more time to put his defence in order and recast his arrangement of forces.

War is the only way the Italians will obtain the Trentino and Trieste, and the crushing of the Central Empires the only guarantee that they will retain any acquisitions they make. Were they to accept the Austrian offer, and remain neutral, they would find that after a few years of peace Austria would take back what she had given, if she were able to do so. She must therefore be really knocked out, and the best way for Italy to ensure this is for her to take a hand in the game. It is in British interests that Italy should voice her views at the conference which will end this war as a participant, not as a neutral. As a participant she has more claim to be heard, and if Italy is at the conference simply as a neutral, Adriatic questions will be settled in a sense wholly favourable to Slav aspiration.

Lord Methuen has been most kind to me, and as soon as my stitches are a little more healed than they are at present I shall go and stay at St. Antonio, (Palace of the Knights of Rhodes.— B. W. C.), which is his country villa, a lovely spot, with marvellous geraniums in great masses all over pergolas. You would admire them. It is a great flower country, all over the fortifications there are lovely dollops of bougainvillaea.

✶✶✶✶✶✶

Writing to me May 1915 from the Palace, Malta, Lord Methuen says: "Having done my best to break your leg, the least I can do is to look after your son. Finding hospital accommodation for 7,000 men and all its attendant complications, makes me appropriate your son in a few days as extra A.D.C. He can remain until a wounded Scots Guardsman comes here for rest, and if your son is not well and is happy he can stay on. He has an old Eton friend in Windsor."

Lord Methuen's horse kicked me with very considerable violence on my patched-up left leg in a gateway, out hunting with the Duke of Beaufort's hounds in March 1914.—R.

★★★★★★

To Edward Horner.

Blue Sisters Convent, Malta,
May 25, 1915.

I am so sorry to hear that you have been wounded, and I must write one line. P. got your letter *en route* for Scyros about your having got a load of earth on the torso, so I suppose this is a new injury.

My military history has been a record of futility. Two months' cruise in the Mediterranean, then three days watching the battle from afar off; then three days on shore, ending in an hour or two under shell fire and my wound in the backside. I shall be back again in about a fortnight, and I think I want to be, as I've had so very little show. If I'd been longer there I might feel differently. I hate being nursed.

I am at a convent . . . the atmosphere of piety—smiling and un-ruffled—is very congenial to me. They also make a very good tipsy-cake and an open jam-tart beyond praise. I have a jolly Maltese doctor who quotes Dante to me.

Leonie Leslie is here with Shane. She is, I fear, very sad, but wonderfully brave. He is very interesting about Parnell. I have just read Mrs. O'Shea's *Life* of him. It doesn't appear from the letters that P.'s intervention on behalf of O'S. in 1886 was a concession to blackmailing on the latter's part, as the Irish M.P.'s say, or that there was a real *ménage-à-trois*. Had there been the slightest suspicion of a *ménage-à-trois* at that time, it would have come out in the divorce and O'S. would not have got his verdict.

Gladstone's trustees, it is supposed, suppressed what conversation passed between him and Mrs. O'S. This is a pity. She makes many statements to the effect that she was a go-between for Parnell with Mr. G., but cannot substantiate them. If Mr. G. knew of their relationship all along, his sudden horror in 1890, at the time of the divorce case, is rather a poser, though I do not of course see why he should have shown himself a moralist while O'Shea continued to be accommodating.

O'Shea is pot at all the sort of loathsome, *souteneur*, bookmaker type the ordinary "lives" represent him as, but a very intelligent ob-

not yet healed up. The operation was painless enough, as they froze the spot, and well done by my charming Maltese doctor. Even the stitch he put in a day or two later did not hurt. But I am immobilised and take no strong drink, so it is rather dull, and makes me so dependent on cabs. I have got through a lot of reading, including Mrs. O'Shea's *Life of Parnell* and the *Koran*, besides numerous novels of the lighter order. I have also nearly finished my retrospect, which I shall send you if you are still in England, or father or Laura, if you are not.

I am sorry to say that my naval capacity has received acknowledgment from the naval hospital authorities, and that on Monday I am to leave my dear Blue Sisters and be put into the naval hospital, which is a sort of prison life. No leave to go out before two o'clock, and you have to be back before six o'clock. With the Blue Sisters we have perfect freedom, and are so well fed and looked after. They are all saints, but in some cases really wasted as spouses of Christ—pretty, fresh-complexioned, bright girls, nearly all. It is also a nuisance leaving my doctor, who knows my case, etc. But my bondage will not be of long duration, as I am fit now but for the silly slice in my thigh.

The Italian paper now publishes, day by day, snippets from the Italian *Libra Verde*, and it is of interest to see what efforts the Germans especially made to keep the Italians neutral—as it shows Italian intervention to be rather a serious blow. The Austrians seem to have been, as usual, *une pensée en arrière* and sceptical as to the extent to which Italy was prepared to make herself unpleasant. The Italians have up till now—I have read the *L.V.* up till the middle of February—conducted the argument with great skill and show of legality. Mrs. Leslie has been a great standby, and introduced me to some nice Maltese.

A Roman archaeologist—English—has been digging here lately, and I have seen something of him, which was a nice link with Roman days. Otherwise, except for its bookish side, life has been uneventful and dull. If I'd known I was going to be here so long you might have come out; but, alas, we never know, and I didn't want to suggest it in case I should be bundled off. Miss Maxine Elliott and Angela Forbes have done finely in this war. I suppose they have a prompt understanding of human needs. Father cabled me that Julian was still in danger, but better than might have been expected. I am very upset about him. I have written to him.

★★★★★★

Amongst others whom Charles refers to especially as having been most kind and welcome friends at Malta are Mrs. Lawson and her two daughters, all of whom he admired.—R.

★★★★★★

To Lord Ribblesdale.

No date.

Lord Methuen was most kind to me. I went about with him round hospitals in being or in preparation. He has worked like a Trojan, and his charm of manner to the men and nurses and doctors must hearten them up in their work. He is a marvellous walker, and if you lose sight of him for ten minutes, he is round the corner and three hundred yards down the street, and you have to be after him at the double.

I stayed about four days at the palace, and was much pleased with the Marsala there; but I am better without, I think, as it heats the blood and raises bumps, which I've lost since I got on board and put myself on to whisky and soda. As a senator I am sure you would have applauded Lord Methuen's eloquent harangue to the "Doblins" and "Munsterrs," many of whom are now convalescent, on the drink question. There is no holding these brave fellows; the Australians are like a young ladies' school in comparison.

To the Same.

Blue Sisters Convent,
May 29, 1915.

God! how sad it is about Julian. It's the bitterest blow I have had since this war and am likely to have. You must not make reservation about the "ultimately satisfactory issue." I'd sooner spend my life in trenches than have any other issue.

You will see that I did not have very long of war's alarms, and that our performances that morning, through no fault of our own, were hardly brilliant. If the C.O. had not retired us we should have been annihilated—perhaps cut off, as the Turks were gathering on our flanks. Since then the battalion has done very well and seen a lot of fighting. That day they showed great steadiness for raw troops, but their situation was impossible.

To Lady Desborough.

Blue Sisters Convent, Malta,
June 3, 1915.

I can't write what I feel about dear Julian. The void is so terrible for me and the thought of it quite unmans me. I'd so few ties with the life I left when I went abroad—so few, that is to say, that I wanted to keep, and I always felt as sure of Julian's love as he did of mine, and so certain of seeing his dear old smile just the same. We did not often write or anything of that sort just for that reason, and now the whole thing has gone. How much worse it must be for you and yours. All of us loved him so, and I'm sure if I were back with father and Diana we should be in the depths and feel almost worse than I do now that one of our nearest and dearest has gone.

I suppose that if death meant wholly loss, all recollections would be wholly bitter; but the consciousness that we are recalling memories of one who may still be near us makes recollection precious, an abiding realisation of what is, and not a mere regret for what has ceased to be.

I suppose everybody noticed dear Julian's vitality, but I don't think they were so conscious of that great tenderness of heart that underlay it. He always showed it most with you, and with women generally it was his special charm. I think now of the way he used to take my hand if he had felt disappointed with anything I'd done and then found out why I'd done it. I remember a time when he was under the impression I'd chucked Socialism for the "*loaves and fishes,*" etc., and of course that sort of thing he couldn't abide, and he thought this for a longish while, then found out that it wasn't that after all, and took my hand in his in the most loving way.

I don't suppose many people knew of the ardent love he had for honesty of purpose and intellectual honesty, and what sacrifices he made for them, and sacrifices of peace of mind abhorrent to most Englishmen. The Englishman is a base seeker after happiness, and he will make most sacrifices of principle and admit any number of lies into his soul to secure this dear object of his. It is want of courage on its negative side, this quality—and swinish greed on its positive side. Julian in his search for truth and in his search for what he believed to be his true self caused himself no end of worry and unhappiness, and was a martyr who lit his own fires with unflinching nerve. Out stalking he always wanted to do his own work, and he was just the same in his inner life. Surely the Lady he sought with tireless faith, the Lady for whom he did and dared so much on lonely paths, will now reward him? God, it is glorious to think of a soul so wholly devoid of the pettiness and humbug, the cynicism and dishonesty, of so much that we see.

There is a story in one of Miss Kingsley's books of a West African medicine-man who found himself at death's door. He applied all his herbs and spells and conducted all his well-worn rites before his idols, and with his friend's intercessions, without any effect. At last he wearied of his *hocus-pocus*, and took his idols and charms down to the seashore and flung them into the surf, and he said, "Now I will be a man and meet my God alone." Julian from the time I knew him had flung away his idols and had met God. His intense moral courage distinguished him even more than his physical bravery from the run of common men—and his physical bravery was remarkable enough, whether he was hunting, boxing, or whatever he was at.

I think he found his true self on what we all knew would be the scene of his glory, and it is some melancholy satisfaction that his services received recognition. What must make you still happier must be the glorious glowing tone of those letters of his, and the knowledge that his last few months were crowded hours of glorious life, stronger than death in that they abide. I shall never forget how much they heartened me when I came to see you to get your kind offices for this show. The recollection of them will be a constant strength. No one wrote of the war like that or talked of it that way, and so many went from leave or after healing wounds as a duty, but without joy.

Julian, apart from the physical delight he had in combat, felt keenly, I am sure, that he was doing something worthwhile, the thing most worthwhile in the world, and looked on death and the passing beyond as a final burst into glory. He was rather Franciscan in his love of all things that are, and in his absence of fear of all God's creatures—death included.

He stood for something very precious to me—for an England of my dreams made of honest, brave, and tender men, and his life and death have surely done something towards the realisation of that England. Julian had so many friends who felt for him as they felt for no one else, and a fierce light still beats on the scene of his passing, and others are left to whom he may leave his sword and a portion of his skill.

You must have known all this splendour of Julian's life far better than I did, so I don't know why I should write all this. But I am so sad myself that I must say something to you, and because you knew how very fond I was of Julian.

One can seek comfort at this time in the consciousness of the greatness of our dead, and the work they have left behind them, and the love we have borne them: and such comfort is surely yours, apart from any larger hope.

To Lord Ribblesdale.

Blue Sisters,
June 3, 1915.

My own injuries are fast healing, and at the end of the week I shall see my naval people and ask for a berth back to Gallipoli. By dint of intriguing I have saved B. and myself from durance vile in Bight Hospital, where the naval authorities wanted to move me, and where I should have to have kept fixed hours and lived up almost two hundred steps in a sort of eagle's nest.

Ashmead Bartlett has been here, home bound. He was blown up on the *Majestic* and escaped, but without his notebooks, etc., which I believe contain scathing denunciations of all those in authority, and which are just as well at the bottom of the sea. He will talk when he gets home. I hope he will get us more men sent out; but his tone is pessimistic and his statements exaggerations, which he qualifies by about 75 *per cent*, in his next sentence.

So perhaps they will take no notice of him. The Turks are exhausting themselves by these attacks on our trenches and losing great numbers, and with a few more men we could do the trick soon enough. It would be hopeless loss of face if we chucked up now. I don't think we can.

My only fear is Ashmead may paint in such gloomy colours that the Harmsworth Press may plump for a complete bunk. This would be *appalling* and, I think, impossible. Our hold is really *very* firm now, and it's simply a question of more men to effect our advance. I shouldn't write like this, only people at home have become such funksticks and seem only good for anti-German riots in Shoreditch. I should have thought there were other places where the readers of the Harmsworth Press could take part in anti-German demonstrations.

I always supposed the government contemplated some unpopular measure like conscription when they called in the Unionist leaders for this Coalition, and am glad to see you think that may be the reason. I quite understand their wishing the responsibility to be shared. The same considerations would apply were it necessary for the Allies to conclude a peace falling short of popular anticipations, though I cannot conceive such a peace being so much as discussed at this moment.

Madame —— I am told, said the Italians contemplated three months' war, and they have subscribed to the London Agreement of some time ago, relative to the Allies not negotiating separately, etc.

To Mrs. Cornish.

Hood Battalion, R.N.D., M.E.F.,

June 11, 1915.

I have at last read Thackeray and must write to you, because you used to show me his drawings at Eton and tell me what a world was in store for me.

I read *Pendennis* and am now at *Vanity Fair*. I don't know which I like best. *Pendennis* is on a more *tenuis avena*, and I think the satire, the little vignettes of literary London, of the London of servants, is better put in, with more subtlety and good humour, than in *Vanity Fair*, I think Thackeray loves old Major Pendennis, but really dislikes Becky, who I consider a much more likeable and admirable fraud. I spare much needless pity on Becky, and I'm sure I should have married her if she would have married me. But *Pendennis* is spoilt by the Fanny Bolton episodes, and the book is so largely made up of the telling of estrangements between son and mother, which one feels are of a kind that could not possibly have come into being on such slight occasions.

I suppose we have all passed through the school of the larger charity taught by the Russians, and cannot understand Helen's readiness to believe the worst and treat her son's flirt so cruelly. I like the touch in *Pendennis* where Arthur, after having been most affectionate the whole evening to poor little Fanny, tells her that she must always call him "Sir" or "Mr. Pendennis," as their "stations in life were so different." In our greatest intimacies, we still reach out over deep gulfs of class differences. Perhaps the dead of the war, side by side, may fill these up.

Pendennis gave me such sheer pleasure from its remoteness from present days. The word "*Przemysl*" never occurred once in its pages. *Vanity Fair* in those Waterloo chapters is a poignant gripping emotion and gives one pain—the kind of pain one would not miss for anything—and one thinks of dear Diana, in Amelia Sedley's place, waiting for the news of the heroic stand of the Coldstreams at Landrecies. These chapters are self-contained, a piece of magnificent life drama, with all life's rapid passages from laughter to tears, and smallnesses to epic valour. I wish Becky had liked her little boy. I feel Thackeray had made her so charming that he felt he must put something in to make her unpleasant and justify his own dislike of her.

I think Sir Pitt is a masterpiece—both Sir Pitt senior and junior. I'm sure Sir Pitt junior only took to religion from want of occupation, or perhaps a desire to please Lady Southdown. How he rises in the canvas, like an El Greco saint in glory, when he turns Lady Southdown out of her predominant position in the *ménage*. There is no one in *Vanity Fair* so antipathetic to me as Arthur Pendennis. I suppose we are all very like him—by "we" I mean young men in general, but he is a very cleverly written warning—*Fabula de te narratur.*

I've been wounded lightly, and am now going back *via* Alexandria, which is our base. I was only three days on shore and about two hours or so under real fire. My love to the vice-provost and other Eton friends (especially Miss Margaret and Cecilia). What a period of sadness but glory it must be for all you who have watched Eton's life year in, year out.

To the Hon. Irene Lawley.

On Board Ship.
(Extract, undated.)

I have been reading some George Meredith. *Beauchamp's Career* I have always admired from a distance rather. But I must say his touch when he talks of love is so deep and subtle so elusive and yet so true, that one lingers over the chapters and puzzles out each word. Not that it is so difficult, but the greatness of it all makes me always think I am missing something. I don't think the book is very readable apart from the love interest. Beauchamp as a politician is sympathetic but not interesting. However, the whole portrayal is that of a hero, and that end is most moving when he dies to save a little mudlark of a child, *chétif* and half idiotic. "This is all we have in exchange for Beauchamp." Read Lord Cromer's account of the ex-*Khedive*. It is massive, terse, and manly, and puts Lord Rosebery in quite a new light as Foreign Secretary. I always thought he was a bad one. But Lord Cromer says he practically settled our position in Egypt between 1892 and 1894— periods of constant friction with the *Khedive*.

★★★★★★

We take up the history of the Naval Brigade in the following letters after the battle of June 4th, in conjunction with the operations of our forces by sea, in which the Hood and Anson Battalions suffered severely. The Hood Battalion took a Turkish trench and bayoneted the Turks, but came immediately under fire from another trench, and they lost heavily. Colonel Quilter was succeeded by Colonel Stewart. Commander Freyberg as second-in-command. Charles was company-commander, with three subordinate officers.

The unit of the Naval Brigade and its battalions, the Hood and the Anson, had to be brought up to strength with new officers, new N.C.O.'s, and new men. After the battle of June 4th, the Hood Battalion was out of the firing-line. They were detailed for beach work, and, still under-officered, were employed in digging saps, beach fatigue work, sniping, and even unloading lighters and guarding G.O.C.'s. Commander Freyberg, who was seriously wounded in July, was now in command. Charles was in his company from the start and in all the advances under him.—R.

★★★★★★

To Lord Ribblesdale.

Cunard s.s. *Andania*,
June 12, 1915.

I am now recovered and *en route* for Alexandria, with details of the R.N.D. to rejoin. We have about forty-two Naval folk and twenty-nine marines, nearly all wounded and now better. I am very happy at the prospect, and quite (as if I was going out for the first time.

I am still in the thrall of Thackeray, delighting in *Vanity Fair*, the Waterloo chapters read so living nowadays. But the pageantry and brightness of Brussels a week before the fighting must contrast rather with the businesslike look of Boulogne and its pathos. Mrs. Crawley did not don the nurse's .uniform, which so well becomes M. and Lady ——. Alexandria is probably more like the Thackeray Brussels.

I shall never forget the change from our dowdy old steamer to the Alexandria racecourse. *Le tout Londres* and Lord —— at dinner. This nobleman, from a safe seat in the club at Alexandria, said that he heard the —— Naval Division always ran away; I hope he will revise this opinion. Certainly quite a number have not run away with sufficient expeditiousness to avoid the Turkish bullets. Our battalion now numbers about sixty men with four officers or so. Pat, I think, still well, though rumours are rather conflicting. However, most of us are in my case. Did you see our brigade (2nd Naval) got specially thanked by General d'Amade, under whom we worked for several days?

I hope we shall have silenced at any rate some of the criticisms and sniggers which have been our lot since Antwerp. I heard a bad account of Denis Browne. I saw quite a number of our boys hit in the June 4th fight. Their spirit was fine. My platoon has suffered very much, but has done very well. We were invited to "celebrate" June 4th at Malta, but I didn't, as I was not for organised guzzles at a time when better fellows were celebrating it in a very different way.

Several Italians have been through from Constantinople, and they say that there are eighty thousand Turkish wounded there, that the Turks can only continue the war for a month. I think we have got them, shall wear them down, even if we make no advance. I wish I hadn't missed all this fighting, and that I had seen more of the battalion after it had really got into its stride. That first morning was futile, and we had such a foolish role to play. We did it as well as could have been done, but it wasn't the real thing. The division is now being worked as a division, and is no longer scattered. We have now one fine staff-officer who will pull us through. This ship has a Territorial battalion on board, and various other odds and ends, such as A.S.C. and doctors. I am the only officer who has been anywhere near the foe, and am asked for tips by staid old colonels (formerly family solicitors like F—— R—— I expect) and blushing staff captains. I have made many inaccurate and conflicting statements.

My attitude to the Territorials is *très digne*. I call my details to "attention" once a morning as the Territorial colonel passes, but not a second time. I give my boys no work. We have lectures, and were informed last night by one of the medical officers that the female fly takes only ten days to attain to sexual maturity—a creditable performance.

To the Hon. Beatrix Lister.

Hood Battalion, R.N.D., M.E.F., s.s. *Andania*,

June 12, 1915.

Many thanks for your last, which was very welcome. I am waiting at Alexandria to get a ship back to the front. Our orders are so slow coming through, and we have to wait so much for other people. . . . I have seen several other of our officers and heard the gup. The day I was hit the brigadier of the brigade on the left of us came up to our colonel and told him he thought our advance one of the bravest things. Then when we were with d'Amade we got a *most* handsome letter from him on our services, which appeared in all the French papers.

On the June 4th fight our brigade was put up against a very stiff job and got heavily punished, but at one time was holding a whole brigade-front with three hundred and twenty men. We have about one hundred and fifty men left out of the battalion and five officers, including those returned after being wounded. My company-commander has got the D.S.O. We have lost two colonels—Quilter killed and his successor, Stewart, hit in the jaw. We have altogether not done badly. I saw a number of my platoon at Malta wounded after June 4th, and they looked so jolly and bronzed in spite of their wounds. I am happy to get back. If we simply sit tight in our present position the *crac* is bound to come.

Will you send me Julian's poem published in *The Times*. I can't give you the date. The Egyptian papers quote it. Julian is an appalling loss to me. He was the most perfect of friends and heartening of examples, but I am relieved that E. Horner will be all right. I wish I knew more about Rex. Benson. News is so fitful here.

To the Hon. Lady Wilson.

Alexandria, June 18, 1915.

I have been here now for about a week, and am sorry to say have been unable to see Scats, (Sir Mathew Wilson, late 10th Hussars, then commanding the Second Division at Ismailia.—R.), who has been in hospital at Port Said. . . . Our base commandant is apt to send one off at a moment's notice, and Port Said is too long a journey to risk. Alexandria has been pleasant enough, with lots of old friends about and lots of our officers.

Did you know a charming man called Major Bell, who was in Somaliland, and knew Tommy well? He is now a Sharpshooter. The Sharps and ourselves are still at Ismailia. The H.A.C. battery of Major —— got off one of his guns at the Turks—or rather at about one Turk—but the rest of Taylor's brigade have done nothing.

The Hood Battalion was finished on June 4th; we took a Turkish trench filled with Turks, whom we bayoneted. It was, however, under fire from another Turkish trench about fifty yards higher up, from which the Turks could throw hand grenades, etc., and we lost heavily, and did not get supports enough to go on.

Out of nine officers who went with the charge, six were killed and three wounded. We now number about one hundred and fifty men all told, I think. I think the battalion has done well. It has certainly earned a lot of official praise.

Our new Colonel, Stewart, who was hit on the 4th, came back on the same ship as Scats, when he came back from India to marry you. Our commodore and all the officers commanding battalions of our brigade are going to get *Légions d'Honneur.*

I like the poem of Julian's which they put into *The Times*—a real swan-song. And how very sad about Bill Tennant.

To Lord Ribblesdale.

Hood Battalion, R.N.D., M.E.F.,

June 23 or 28, 1915.

Just one line to say I am returning to duty now. They kept me waiting about a week in Alexandria, then put me on to the wrong boat, then kept me waiting ten days for the right boat; so you see they are not in a frantic hurry for the wounded to return. I shan't find my battalion much in the swing of it yet awhile; we are, I fancy, too reduced, and now getting ourselves together again under our ex-second-in-command. (Colonel Freyberg).

Stewart, by the way, who took Quilter's place, may be coming to see you. He is a charming fellow and a fine officer, and, while he will have little to tell you about me, he will be able to yarn to you about *les faits et gestes* of the 2nd Brigade and the battalion in general. The battalion, I fear, is a mixed lot now, filled up with odds and ends from new formations, etc. I saw Harry at Port Said, which was nice; he was there for a sore throat which they feared at one time was diphtheria. He was not looking famous, and rather fed up with canal guarding, Ismailia, however, is a very fine place from all accounts, bathing and good club. Am now back with battalion in rest camp. Big battle in progress, but we're out of it.

To the Hon. Lady Wilson.

June 28th.

. . . On this ship we are in a state of acute discomfort. Some forty-five officers in fifteen cabins—and a coal black ship. . . . But I have been very lucky so far, and one mustn't expect Cunarders all the time. . . . We have a subaltern on board who is in a corps of Palestine Muleteers, nearly all Russian Jews, who ran away from Jerusalem at the beginning of the war to Egypt, and enlisted, and have been made into a transport unit. They have to be spoken to in Arabic and Yiddish-German. They are now going to the Dardanelles. We are having a jolly journey through islands, which we expect to complete tomorrow.

★★★★★★

Charles, after a tedious journey, now had about a fortnight in a rest camp. Two new battalions had been broken up to bring the Hood and the Anson up to strength, and the vexed subjects of brigade organisation, always accompanied by some friction, are described.—R.

★★★★★★

To Lord Ribblesdale.

I find everything very peaceful on my return—a new battalion brought again up to near its proper strength by accessions from other battalions, a line of trenches very solidly made reaching well up towards our goal, and well provided with drinking-water brought by pipes right into the firing-line, and an intermittent appearance of ships. It was tragic, the first arrival at dawn, to see nothing of the great fleet of men-of-war and transports that once was there, but the keel of the *Majestic* sticking out about four feet and lit by a solitary light, similar to the oil lamps put on the graves of the San Lorenzo cemetery on All Souls' night at Rome; but the beaches are busy with life and but little troubled with shell fire. The mischief is done by an elusive old lady on the Asiatic side nicknamed Annie. We can't discover her, as she moves on trollies. She sometimes drops a shell into our camp.

We haven't been in the trenches since June 4th, but will go soon. They are very safe and never shelled. The plan we follow now is to pound away at one little bit of the line and attack that. It answers better than general attacks all along the line, and the general tone is very optimistic and the Turkish shortage of shells very manifest. I am now a second-in-command of a company under a real type, Chalmers by name, whom I'm very fond of, but this will not last for long, when more of our wounded return.

I am the baby of the "Hood." We have been subjected to pie-jaws on the subject of brigade reorganisation, which has been necessary in our case and accompanied by some friction, as it involved the break up of two young battalions to make us up to strength. . . . Soldiers, of course, have much practice in stump oratory, as the most junior platoon officer is supposed to lecture his men. I have studiously avoided doing so. I love our rest-camp life except for the dust storms. Soldiering is a grand life, and I never thought I'd like it so much.

I must now censor men's letters.

To the Hon. Mrs. Percy Wyndham.

I have got two delightful letters from you, darling, one describing your being shelled at Dunkerque and the other from Lilfeild telling me about the charge of the Essex. What a magnificent performance.

I have found the battalion in a rest camp—some miles from the firing-line—living comfortably enough and sleeping in pyjamas, except when we are standing by, which is rather our usual condition, especially if an attack is in contemplation. I have been in fine health since landing, except for slight *mal-de-mer* caused by an excess of rum last night. I look forward to the rum nights with all the zeal of an old sea-dog. It is a glorious liquor.

We have really got on well since I left, and while there may have been unnecessary losses, there is no ground for pessimism. The French are fighting splendidly, especially when they are on their own, and their bombardment of trenches is a masterpiece—marvellous rapidity of fire and accuracy. We are well round the Turkish flank on the Krithia side, thanks to a fine attack by the 29th Division, who have done marvels. It was well prepared for by artillery, and there were practically no Turks in the trenches, bar wounded and dead, when the men came up. If only the same had been done when we attacked on June 4th.

I went up into the fire trenches yesterday, and they gave me a great feeling of confidence. The Engineers are getting water right up to the firing-line by means of pipes. The trenches are for the most part bone dry, but they haven't always been so. Patrick is in great form. I, of course, did not see any of his activities in the field, but all say he is an excellent officer, very cool-headed and active. I am glad he gives me a *bonne presse*.

To the Hon. Lady Wilson.

Hood Battalion.

(No date.)

We each of us have our dugouts, which are about two feet or so down from the surface. They would be a protection against shrapnel, but of little use against high explosive, which is what we are visited with from time to time. Luckily the Turks are very short of shells and so do very little "hating."

There is a gun called Annie on the Asiatic side which gives us now and then five or six about tea-time. I am told it was much worse last week. One unfortunate hero, who had been hit in the hand, came back and was hit in the ankle his first day *de retour* while lying in his dugout. So his time in the Peninsula has been short.

It is a great difference from when I was last here, considering we are fighting a trench-war, like in France. We have pushed our line up very well, and made our position very solid. The co-ordination of the various units' activities is far more efficient, and in my view we have the situation well in hand.

Our friends are all flourishing. Oc., (A. Asquith), very fit after his bullet, and Patrick looking a holy man in his bright red beard, which might have been dyed with henna. He has done so well, and is *gai comme un pinson*.

To the Hon. Beatrix Lister.

Hood Battalion, M.E.F.,
July 1, 1915.

......Gallipoli has lost much of its charm of scenery since I got back. The place where we are camped has been changed from a smiling olive grove to a dust-heap. But everything is much better organised—splendid trenches, heaps of delicious water, and easy walking. The whole force is in great heart, and progress, if slow, has been considerable. The French artillery has quite found its length, has any amount of shells, and is doing magnificently. The new French general (Gouraud) is a great success and *some* thruster. Duststorms are our only grievance. We get very fond of our rum ration.

My brigade has not been in the trenches for some time, but is now fit for work again. We wanted a good deal of re-organisation, but at this moment we are pretty strong. The only real discomfort I have had so far in this war was my passage from Alexandria to this place on a vile ship, where we were packed three officers per cabin, and which took about a week to do a forty-eight hours' run—what with dawdles and muddles.

To the Hon. Mrs. Wyndham,

Hood Battalion,
July 5, 1915.

Many thanks for three letters which I got all at once, I fear Julian was destined for a higher fate than hanging about Hazebruck.

Rest-camp life I really find pleasant enough, and my dugout is now fairly well organised, though I had two wet nights, owing to holes in my waterproof sheets which treacherously let the water-pool there find its way to the apertures and pour down on my devoted head. Shells come down from time to time. Yesterday three burst on our lines without doing any damage, bar riddling poor Patrick's best khaki tunic (luckily he was not in it, but it was hanging on a tree) and covering his sleeping-bag with soot. One fell in the lines next to us, killing two and wounding ten men. So it is purely a matter of chance.

I have had one or two amusing working parties. One of digging saps right up about sixty yards behind our firing-line and a hundred and sixty from the Turks' firing-line. It was at night, so I saw nothing but the usual fireworks and flares and rifle flashes, but very much doing. I went up yesterday to see where we had been working, and had a most interesting new and close, but perfectly safe position. I did some sniping at a Turkish loophole and had two shots hitting the iron round the loophole quite neatly. The men love sniping, but I think it is a safe enough pastime both for ourselves and the enemy, as the trenches are very solid.

I fear I shall not do many more joy-rides for a little time, as we are on beach fatigue for about ten days or more. I am rather annoyed at it, but the general view seems that we ought to wait a bit longer. I have for the moment got a company. But this won't last long, as other wounded will be returning. I sleep in pyjamas now, as we are no longer standing by—so life is practically picnicking with little interludes of shell fire. I am getting a good judge of where a shell is likely to burst, as I expect you were also after your Dunkerque trials.

To the Hon. Lady Wilson.
Hood Battalion, R.N.D., M.E.F.,
July 5, 1915.

Many thanks for your letter reporting on the last phases of Middlesex history at Mundesley.

My life since my return has been very peaceful, and I don't think there is any chance of our doing anything for some time, as we are detailed for beach work till further orders. We are still rather uncoalesced and we haven't a great number of officers. This is illustrated by the fact that I am *pro tem*, commanding a company, and for troops like us one really wants rather a full complement of officers.

Our camp is really very pleasant, and the shade of the olive-trees and the breeze neutralize the fly and dust nuisance. At night our camp looks lovely with the little lights in the dugout shining through the sacking and waterproof sheets and the olive-trees in relief against the night sky and silvery in the moonlight. The darkness, moreover, hides the grassless state of our lines. We had shells in yesterday—four into our lines which did no damage, ,But shelling is so much a matter of chance. The beaches are the most extraordinary places, full of dugouts, etc., and just like London, for no one knows who his next-door neighbour is, and to find anyone is practically an impossibility.

The Beach take themselves very seriously, and one would think that no one else on the Peninsula is in any danger whatever.

The Turks have pushed up a fresh army corps from the other side of Constantinople, who arrived here very exhausted after fifteen days' forced marches. They were at once pushed up into an attack, at which they made a very poor show, losing about three hundred men yesterday, and not pressing home an attack which might have rather shaken us. The brigadier commanding in the trenches was suffering from the prevailing Peninsular complaint when he heard this attack was going forward, but acted with great decision. Picnicking and shell fire is not half a bad fire life, and I am very well and happy, though disappointed we are doing so little. K.'s fears about the ineptitude of shelling weeks before we have the troops for landing ready, and the fallacy that the R.N.D. and the French would suffice have been more than justified.

To Lord Ribblesdale.

Hood Battalion,
July 6, 1915.

Life continues to be peaceful and picknicky, and I have for the first time, fired a rifle in anger. This was in the course of a joyride to some advance trenches of ours, where we are within a hundred yards or so of the Turks. I fired two shots at a Turkish loop-hole and hit the iron immediately round the aperture. Sniping must be very good fun. The men in the trenches seemed most cheerful and pretty comfortable, though they don't get too much sleep, as heat and flies stop their getting it by day and rifle-fire and watches stop them at night.

I am rather annoyed at this continual state of inactivity, as we can't really get to know our men or train them if we are always doing fatigues and living under the eye of the Turkish gunners. Our new men want a lot of shaking down. We have not enough officers, moreover, and this is a bad thing in the case of 2nd home troops, which is what we are now.

F. Robinson is on the Peninsula now—at least, I suppose he is, but I have not had time to get at the Lancashire lines, and only been able to visit our lines rather occasionally.

Some offence has been caused by our new Eye-witness—— a writer without an equal in describing Pimlico—likening the famous West Beach to Blackpool. Its inhabitants take the shells rather seriously and would resent this flippancy. The dugouts on the beach are masterpieces of the sand-bag style, and very cool and safe. The very latrines are like the houses of the great.

To Mrs. Graham Smith.

Hood Battalion, R.N.D., B.M.E.F.,

July 6, 1915.

I have just got two charming letters from you which gave me great pleasure. I am delighted to hear you are walking again. I expect you could do all the walking that is wanted on this Peninsula. Trench warfare has debased and made dull a noble science, and anyone with a leg to stand on and a fairly sound stomach is fit for it. I went from Malta to Alexandria, where I was about a week before they found me a ship to take me on here, and from Alexandria it was about a nine days' journey. First we were taken down to a ship, about a thousand of us, which could accommodate three hundred. Then we were made to wait about three days till our new ship was ready to start. Then at Lemnos no one knew anything about us, so they had to improvise arrangements for us, which led to another three days' wait. No easy matter getting back to the front.

Our return to the Peninsula from Lemnos was a strange experience. When we first anchored off Cape Helles in May there was a huge collection of ships of all kinds, all lit up making an effect like Brighton Pier illuminated. At present all there is to be seen are a couple of hospital ships, a few destroyers, and a green shape protruding from the water, the keel of the *Majestic*.

On land, however, the difference is tremendous. Considering how early operations developed into trench warfare, we have gained a lot of ground, and places which we thought reasonably near the firing-line earlier on are now rest camps. Our brigade has done nothing since June 4th, when it was very badly cut up, and we are likely to be on working parties for some time. The Turks occasionally shell us in this camp, and they are very assiduous in their attentions to the beach; but they do not do much damage, and the absence of the ships' guns to keep down their fire has not made so much difference as I expected. I suppose this is due to the fact that the Turks are short of shells.

Our dinner was spoilt, as the dexy with the soup in it was riddled. So were two khaki tunics of Patrick's, luckily hanging on a tree and not on his manly form. These sort of things make us feel we are at war. The bathing here is very pleasant, though care has to be exercised in avoiding dead horses. Once out of their reach the water is deliciously cool and clear.

The Turks behave well to the wounded, give them first aid and sometimes return them to our own people after dressing them. Oc. has been made lieutenant-commander (same as a major) and has got his company, a meteoric rise.

To the Hon. Irene Lawley.

Hood Battalion,
July 7, 1915.

It is delightful, having the *Inferno* by one again, as the most hard-hitting, poignant *cantos* are to be found there: they are in a sense more universal than the mystic ecstasy and transcendentalism of the Paradiso, to which one must be to some extent attuned and have steeped oneself in the spirit and spiritual theory of the Middle Ages. I think the finest thing in the whole Divine Comedy is the twenty-sixth *canto* of the *Inferno*, where Odysseus tells Dante of his last voyage, and the wreck of his ship on the Mount of Purgatory.

We expect to go up to trenches very shortly, but I fancy we shall at first only be in support. The change since I was last here is enormous. We really have got on—have consolidated our portion in a remarkable manner. The trenches are splendid, and for the most part bone dry. The rest camp where we have our dugouts is pretty quiet, though occasionally shelled. It would be untenable if the Turks had enough ammunition on the Asiatic side. I write under the shade of an olive-tree, reasonably cool, as there is generally a south wind blowing, but rather fed up with the dust. There are also lots of flies. But there is no real discomfort, and deliciously cool water.

Patrick, who is practically the oldest inhabitant, never having been wounded, has grown a glorious red beard of the colour of henna. He is a thundering good officer and has quite a reputation. Since our last "push," on June 28th or so, we have marked time and the Turks have obligingly attacked us. They are supposed to have lost practically a whole division since that date. Gourand (O.C. French troops) will be a great loss. He was blown by a shell over a wall and broke both his legs in falling. He had got the French well together—and was a real *Coeur de Lion*.

To Lord Ribblesdale.

Hood Battalion, R.N.D., M.E.F.,
July 8, 1915.

Many thanks for two letters which I have just got, and for the cutting from *The Times* giving Julian's poem. It is a beautiful poem, and I like to think how fond he was of all his days of war, I saw it in Alexandria, but should like one to keep. I so liked the verse about the horses. It is very true of them here. They hardly turn their heads when the shells come, even if they burst quite near. They have not had such a bad time or lost any great numbers since I've been back. I've not seen one actually hit and maimed, though shells burst everywhere round them.

They have made dugouts for them behind walls, with mud partitions between—no overhead covers; and the battery horses all look fit, though on the fat side, as might be expected in this trench warfare, where they have relatively little distance to move. They seem a good stamp of horse. I have heard of one or two chargers having been killed, and am on the whole not sorry that Reynolds is in Egypt, where he has a good master and is looking very well. (A very good bay horse of mine which went to Egypt with Sir M. Wilson. He won the jumping prize, beating a class of 87, at the Cairo Horse Show, 1916).

Lygrove sounds a charming place, if we any of us ever have money to hunt or own horses again. The return to settled life is very difficult to conceive at present.

There are many rumours as to the future of the R.N.D,, occasioned, I suppose, by the temporary removal from our section. This has never happened before, as there have never before been enough troops to admit of it. But in France I understand there are frequent choppings and changings.

To the Hon. Beatrix Lister.

Hood Battalion, M.E.F,
July 12, 1915.

I have several charming letters to thank you for, which have in due time dribbled in. I am looking forward enormously to reading your collection of Granny's letters. All the time I have been back the battalion has been inactive, either in camp or digging trenches, unloading lighters, guarding G.O.C.'s, and other humble occupations, and I fancy we should all like a change. The working parties tire the men and interrupt their night's rest, and the long time in camp gives them time to think of the food they are getting, etc., and leads them into grousing. If men have plenty of real work they haven't time to grouse.

However, things are settling down pretty well. . . . It is distressing to look on the havoc modern warfare, with its trenches and dugouts, makes with the kindly earth. I doubt when the soil here will recover its old look and these gaping wounds be healed. Also all the grass is trodden in and there is very little green. In the lines a little vineyard has been spared from the ravages of the spade and looks like a bright little emerald in the midst of the dirt and dilapidation.

Oc. Asquith and I went up into the French trenches one day. The trenches are built all round a great Turkish fort which they destroyed with shell fire and then stormed. They call it the *Haricot*. The Senegalais were in much evidence; they are marvellous sleepers, and do not mind the flies crawling all over their faces. Our men can't get sleep in the daytime in the trenches because of the sun and the flies.

The French officers were extraordinarily nice and welcoming. They looked perfectly spick and span and were beautifully shaved. Our people don't keep nearly so tidy. They adore the 75 like a sort of goddess, and the French 75 may indeed become the new centre of French worship, now that they have got rid of God. They have had most difficult ground to get over.

We have had one night in the trenches since I've been back, well behind. We were shelled on the way home. My stick was hit by a spent piece of high explosive which had burst about two hundred yards away. It was of course absolutely done. They drop a few shells into our camp now and then, but they have not a sufficiency of ammunition to make themselves really disagreeable. We, I am told, will soon have plenty of shell both here and in France. This morning there was the very devil of a bombardment from about 4 a.m. onwards, and I think a considerable advance has been made both near Krithia and on the right of our line.

The situation is well in hand. Whenever we concentrate gun fire on a little bit of the Turkish line and then push men up, we advance. We have a lot of troops; coming out, and we have now contrivances by which our ships can anchor and shell the shore without fear of submarines. One of these last has been lately caught by nets. I think we shall be through with this job here by the end of September, if not before.

To Lord Ribblesdale.
Hood Battalion, R.N.D., M.E.F.,
July 18, 1915.

We are now in the trenches. We went in about three days ago. They are old Turkish trenches, with one or two admirably protected dugouts, which we suspect the Turks have been made to hollow out for the German officers. It is fairly whiffy, and there are quite a number of dead in the neighbourhood, and the tell-tale stocking or end of boot is now and then seen protruding from the trench wall. We get our share of sniping, even in the support trench, which I have seen most of. One has to drop nimbly past certain critical corners. But there is no need for anyone to get hit if they keep down. The Turks are sniping from a long way off and fire on the chance. The communication trenches are rather ticklish by day, though safe enough by night. There are occasional dead bodies where people have been killed, and it is an awful job getting our men past them: they have a sort of supernatural fear of trampling on their own dead; this kind of feeling of awe is felt also by the men in the case of the Turkish dead.

We get all we want to eat. The Eastern tea and biscuits and jam are excellent, but for a jam variety known as the Sir X, Y. brand, with a picture of the inventor on the label. He is a characteristic Millbank type, with the urbane glance of the sweating mill-owner of the 'forties. He gives us away, because the French used to give us wine in exchange for jam, but are now tired of doing so, as they always get this sample foisted upon them. What a good example of Gresham's Law.

Trench life means a good deal of repose but very little sleep. This is not so much due to the enemy as to the torrents of raw levies coming up to do working parties or to relieve pals or to look for their proper *places* in the line, and so on. I have had my toes trodden on by every officer and man of a Scotch Territorial Division. They come up in driblets, carrying the most weird cooking utensils, and with every sort of impedimentum. They never know how many of them are coming, and if you ask them each man says he is the last.

Then after about ten seconds' interval fresh men come up, carrying what appear to be portions of bagpipes. They are always getting lost and held up. Last night I *had* to get them out by dint of jumping on the top of the communication trench parapet and kicking dust on to their heads, and at the time using the most violent language. The humours of trench warfare are really delicious. Our men are in fine fettle and have worked awfully well, taking things up to the firing-line with hardly any rest.

Patrick keeps a most lucid grasp of affairs, even with the Scots standing on our toes, when the trench is a seething mass of humanity. I had no idea the difficulty of getting men in or out of the trenches would be so great. The trenches are bone dry just now, rather hot and dusty, but there is always a breeze. I am very well and happy. The trench soil is limestone and chalk, rather white and trying to the eyes.

To the Same.

Hood Battalion, R.N.D., M.E.F.

July 22, 1915.

We have now done with our time in the trenches and emerged from four days' very hard work with great credit. This is due to our acting C.O. Freyberg, who will come and see you when we get home.

Our digging operations, carried out at night within about two hundred yards of the enemy's trenches and under a certain amount of rifle fire, have not only made our own position quite secure but rendered untenable for the Turks a small portion of our sector which they still held in between our extreme right and our right centre. They have also given us a point of vantage from which we can enfilade Turks retiring before the French on our extreme right.

Oc. has been extraordinarily dogged, and is practically responsible for all this corner, which will be known as Asquith triangle. He hadn't a wink of sleep all the four days, and Patrick and Kelly also distinguished themselves, and in one night dug a long trench connecting Asquith triangle with our main support. Six men of this company were killed and wounded, and I think the company of another battalion working with them lost about as many. Patrick and Kelly remained above ground the whole time, and it is a wonder they were not hit. Their petty officer who was doing the same got killed. This trench will be called Shaw-Stewart Street.

Our last two days my company joined Oc. in the fire trench. The fire trench is heavily sniped, and before I had been in two minutes I got a bullet through my helmet, which was a salutary warning and made me keep my head well down. My company was chiefly occupied in operations against a little advanced post the Turks had pushed up against our lines like this. There was a sandbag barrier separating us from the Turks. One night we took this barrier down and pushed it about ten yards up the Turkish communication trench. As things were before, the Turks could have come up quietly and dropped bombs into us.

The next day we were more ambitious. The artillery—an Australian battery and the French—shelled the advanced Turkish post for about twenty minutes while we massed, with a covering party of men with bombs and bayonets and a main body of men with sandbags, in the trench, ready to rush out up the old communication trench and push our sandbag barrier still farther forward. It was not feasible to take the Turkish advance post, as it could not be held in face of Turkish guns on the hill slope opposite.

Our shelling was magnificent. We realised the importance of rushing in *immediately* our shelling ceased. But as it turned out we were rather too close, for a shell fell among our people and buried six of them, who were however, dug out unhurt or only slightly wounded. The shell luckily did not burst. This was followed by a Turkish shell which fell right in the middle of us as we were all crouching for the rush, hit Freyberg in the stomach, killed another man, and covered me with small scratches, which bled profusely at the moment. We had by now got our original barrier, so I got our covering party out and rushed them up the trench over quite a number of dead Turks, while my company commander, a grand fellow called Egerton, most valuable organiser, did the same with sandbags.

We stopped our men just short of the Turkish advanced post: threw bombs in which did not light and would not burst, and at once started the new barrier; not a Turk in sight The snipers, however, soon came back and made work at this point difficult, so we moved back and contented ourselves with a gain of about forty to fifty yards on our old position. The men, once they had recovered from the shaking they had got from these two shells, behaved very gallantly. We had only one man killed, and the East Lancs (Kitchener's Army), our neighbours, who helped us very cordially, lost their company commander; sniped because he put his head up.

Our Commodore, General Paris, and General Hunter-Weston are all delighted with us. The latter now feels quite easy about his line.

The serious thing is Freyberg. He was sure to get the battalion and is such a splendid soldier. He got a D.S.O., you know, for swimming ashore at the Gulf of Xeros and lighting flares. I told him to look you up when he comes home. A stomach wound is always dangerous, but I think his chances of getting over it are good. He has been *awfully* good to me.

I have been hit in about six places, but all *tiny* little scratches, so they will send me to Imbros for a fortnight or so. It is a delicious place. Buy me a wedding present for Violet—I should suggest *Storia di Mogor*, a translation from the Italian of the *Memoirs of Minucci*, a Venetian who was a doctor at the Court of Aurungzeeb.

I have had no pain, only slight discomfort, in this clearing station on West Beach, where one can get nothing—not even a second cup of tea.

To the Hon. Beatrix Lister.

My injuries are very slight and do not even want dressing now, and the operation was a great success, as we got our barrier at least forty to fifty yards farther on and have quite secured our trenches from the danger of being bombed by the Turks. The position was like this, and we advanced our barriers from point X to Y. When I went out there were no Turks about: the artillery had scattered them to the four winds; but they soon came back, and we had only just time to get our sandbags up.

Our days in the trenches were very hard work, what with garrison duty, getting water and ammunition up to the firing-line and improving our fire trenches themselves, and we hardly closed our eyes all the time. It is hard to sleep in the daytime owing to the flies. But it was never very hot, and we always had heaps to eat and drink. I have never, however, been so conscious of the uses of a water-bottle.

The battalion worked awfully hard and emerged with great credit in the highest quarters—all our friends, Oc., Patrick, and so on, are the most excellent officers.

I am in the hospital at Imbros, a most delightful island, full of lichen-covered grey rocks, trees, and orchards—every sort of delicious fruit—and a glorious blue sea. It is much cooler even down here near the beach than the Peninsula, and a real land of plenty. The hospital people are most kind and put themselves out in every way. I get Guinness's stout for dinner.

I am reading d'Annunzio's *Trionfo della Morte*—apart from his luscious and eloquent treatment of the passion he is supreme at describing the drear life of the provincial *noblesse* of Italy and its underlying dramas of squalor and pathos. He is tedious when he goes too deeply into the morbid psychology of his heroes.

To Lord Ribblesdale.

I am afraid you will have thought it very odd my not wiring about being wounded, etc., but it was quite impossible, as the authorities would allow no private wires to go through. The wires are retained for official messages only.

My wounds were very slight—mere scratches. So now I am back

to duty again. We are still in our old rest camp, acting as Army Corps Reserve, and likely to be used in the coming fighting, but not as first line of attack, which will be undertaken by new troops. The division was told they would be taken off the Peninsula at the end of the month, but it has now been decided that not a man can leave, so I suppose there will be something doing.

We get fish for our breakfast, as we have an enterprising officer who goes and bombs them, then dives and picks them off the bottom.

As to my convalescence, I was first of all in hospital at the clearing station on the beach, where I wrote to you. It is a vile place. The men only get bread and cheese, and officers can't get a second cup of tea or sugar with their bread and milk. I then went over to Imbros with a sort of "world's fair" boat, with Sikhs and Turkish prisoners. The Turks told me all the Germans had left the Peninsula, and that they were fighting alone now—this is true of the higher command, but not of the machine-gun section. They praise the heir apparent, who when he went round the wounded said to them, "*Inshallah*, you will go home when you are well." Enver said to them, "*Inshallah*, you will go back to the war when you are well."

George Brodrick took me to lunch while I was at Imbros, and Sir Ian was most kind and affectionate in his inquiries after you and the rest of the family. He lives very simply, though well. We had excellent fish and potatoes and stewed plums. I should be rather more luxurious if I were G.O.C. in-C. Sir Ian chatted pleasantly on the demoralized state of the Turks and on Egyptian antiquities, notably a cat-goddess with a lovely young woman's body he saw at Luxor—his recollections in our present conditions of monkery filled all with anguish.

The hospital at Imbros was rather congested with pale-faced officers whose tummies had been upset by the suns of the Levant. So I got into the interior as soon as possible, and went up to a charming village called Panaghia, where I stayed with the resident British. I gorged on fresh vegetables excellently cooked by a handy Greek. I used to go jolly rides all over the island on pack-ponies, brushing through masses of Persian lilac and oleander on either side of my stony path.

I went to one or two little monastery churches, kept tidy by one or two old monks who do damn all, and once a year give the countryside a "jolly" out of the endowments of these little churches, and I did one famous climb to a shrine of the rather controversial St. Athanasius. The highest hill in the island is crowned by a little shrine of St. Elias, built of shell and red tiles. St. Elias for some reason is the great saint of thunderstorms, and I suppose connected with the old Aryan sky-god, whose holy places were always on hill-tops.

I am now returned to duty, flourishing and very happy to get back to the battalion. We are still Army Corps Reserve, but likely to be employed—*Parturiunt montes.*

We have lately been common objects at Divisional Headquarters, and sat round Staff officers discoursing to us, like the disciples of St. Francis and Savonarola round their masters, and we had one very amusing morning making and firing off bombs. They are most undependable, and the fuses either ignite practically before they are lit or never at all. The bombs I saw were so remiss in going off that I feel they are almost suitable toys for children. I lit one and threw it with a catapult. I disclosed my lack of deftness in striking matches, a characteristic of very early days.

General Paris talked to us today. He looked most young and cheery—brighter than I have ever seen him. He has a little poultry-yard at Headquarters and two roosters, a white one called Hindenburg and a buff Orpington called the Grand Duke—Hindenburg never allows the Grand Duke any play with the hens, but drives him away.

To the Same.

Hood Battalion,
August 10, 1915.

Many thanks for your letter and the Gisburne news . . . I should think Jock's fondness for hunting will make Mrs. Y. friendly, but I dare say a visit would help matters. Hunting seems so very remote now.

I approved your comments on Lord ———'s scheme. He must be off his rocker. The soldiers, I hear, say the war will last at least another two years—particularly the French. I think if we are to go on for this time we shall have to run things in a different way to what we are doing now, as it seems agreed we are, at this rate, financially good for only one year. How we are to take our horns in I don't exactly see, so it is a pretty dilemma. Here we hear every day that Warsaw has fallen, which must mean a further prolongation.

Apart from financial considerations, a long war is not altogether against our interests. It gives us time to pull up a number of unconsidered trifles in different parts of the world, which we should otherwise not have time to look at. Of all the Allies we have so far been the only gainers. The smashing up of German influence in the Far East, in the Persian Gulf, in the Pacific, in South-West Africa and in West Africa is an enormous gain.

I have written Diana at length about recent fighting here. Results are so far shrouded in mystery. I don't think no news is always good news. The Hood Battalion, acting as Army Corps Reserve, have done no fighting. We are not even sleeping in our clothes. The men get instruction in the "use and care" of the rifle and receive rather halting lectures on how to dig latrines in trenches, and other topics of martial interest. So all is pretty peaceful. We are so very callow just at present and our drafts so raw that it is not a bad plan some initial ignorance should be dispelled. The men's health is not quite as bad as it was, but is distressing us all a good deal. They cannot get rid of this mild dysentery. . . . It affects their spirits and makes proper feeding an impossibility. However, we've been here since May 6th, and should be thankful nothing worse has made its appearance.

To the Hon. Irene Lawley.

Hood Battalion,
August 11, 1915.

Many, many thanks for your letter, which I loved getting. The Prophet is much given to self-repetition, but he has a glorious power of making his clouds into angels with sweeping wings, and giving nature a soul, and great lyrical fire. He is also an old fox, and the skilful use he makes of Gabriel and *Allah* to get him out of domestic difficulties commands respect. It is a pity Gabriel is not at the disposal of the modern husband—or wife. He is an "affable archangel" as far as the Prophet is concerned, and makes special exemptions for him not accorded to other believers.

The Prophet was not too humanitarian, and was at times inclined to compromise with idolatry; but there is a fine statesmanship of the patriarchal type about the man. And he generally must be admitted to point out the evil consequences of unbelief as coming from God, not from his own armies. I can't find any positive order to kill the non-Moslem, and to the "People of the Book" he was, administratively, most lenient. Mary in the *Koran* conceives under a date-tree near a stream of running water—a graceful image.

I have been wounded again since I wrote, but it has been a very light affair and only kept me away for about a week, giving me the chance of going to Imbros, a dream island, where the mountain paths are choked with masses of Persian lilac and the mulberry-trees are almost dark blue. I did little rides on pack-ponies all over the island the

122

two days I was there and soaked myself in mulberries. I wonder there is not some Islamic legend making of the mulberry a transformed nymph; the juice of the fruit is the nearest thing to blood in trees and flowers. You can't think how delighted one is to guzzle in fresh vegetables cooked by Greeks. Except for onions and potatoes they are the great dearth here. We get plenty of fresh meat, and I haven't eaten bully beef—which I don't like—since I have been on the Peninsula. I like all the other ration things, especially the men's stews and desiccated vegetables, etc. The form of bully beef is repellent.

Annie has been very quiet lately, and altogether we get precious little shelling now. I feel we are not going to do any fighting for some time—we are such a long way short of strength, both in units *quâ* Division and in officers—so you can be sure we are pretty safe. I believe we are being sat on by a commission which is to decide our fate. It is about this struggle against dissolution, which can only end one way, and to feel one is more or less out of it.

Patrick, alas! is not with us *pro tem*, as he is Army Corps liaison officer, but we see him quite often and the job gives more scope for his abilities than the little hack-work we do here in the way of instruction. I am, *vice* him, a company commander, which is rather comic. I leave all to my second-in-command, who is a sort of Dugald Dalgetty and was himself a C.P.O. and can jaw on any subject under the sun. Asquith is battalion second-in-command and a most distinguished and respected figure. The men even take his advice about investing in War Loan.

To the Same.

Hood Battalion, R.N.D.,
August 13, 1915.

You will have got my letter telling how it all happened. "It" is really the two vaccination marks on shoulder and one on arm. It is now practically well, though I still have it dressed, and it has done just as well in camp as it would have done in hospital, where I should have been much more bored. Sick men are the last kind of company one wants if one is sick oneself, and yellow faces give me the pip.

We have done nothing since I got back to the battalion. But time has gone pretty fast, as we have an agreeable mess. The fighting on this side has been in itself costly and unproductive, but I fancy our attacks of the 6th and 7th (I forget dates) did have the effect of keeping Turks on this front who would have otherwise gone to the other front and opposed the new landing. We may have even done more.

The new landing, intended to lead up to a "threat" at Maidos, is so far a partial success. It appears we got to all the critical points, but were not in sufficient force to hold them. A landing operation is like getting men over a bridge—you can't pass more than a certain number over within a certain time, so at the outset you have always strictly limited forces confronting unlimited forces on the enemy side. The last information to hand is to the effect that both sides are digging like badgers. We have, however, more troops to land, so it is possible that we may be able to break the Turkish line yet.

But once we settle down into trench fighting it becomes a slow business, and additional divisions dropped in don't make very much difference. I don't know what troops we've got to play with. At present it looks rather like a game of noughts and crosses, little landings here and there and Turks in between them. I trust the Germans haven't a large force to detach down to this part of the world to coerce the Balkan States into giving them a passage and so effect a junction with the Turk.

Life is rather inactive, but we are comfortable enough, and the only distressing thing is the shaky health of the men. I have kept very well, and have initiated ovens for my people, so that they get roast as well as boiled.

P.S.—I feel that we shall never fight or move, and I shall not know what has happened if I wake up one morning and don't see Achi Baba on the skyline.

★★★★★★

Let me here insert a letter to a friend from Mr. F. S. Kelly, of the Hood Battalion, which bears upon the position and the prospect of affairs in Gallipoli at this time. As it also refers to Charles it is not irrelevant.—R.

★★★★★★

Charles returned to the Peninsula somewhere about the end of June, when the original battalion was very much reduced in numbers by the heavy losses incurred on May 6th to June 4th. It was just about this time that everyone began to realise that a continuance of the campaign on the lines hitherto laid down was very unlikely to achieve any success, and there was a consequent depression among all the ranks, which, if it had been unchecked, would have undoubtedly had a serious effect on their moral. It was precisely in checking this that Charles's influence was, by universal consent, invaluable.

The heat, the swarm of flies, the horrible stench in the trenches, seemed to have no effect at all on his cheerfulness, and above all he didn't know what fear was. I can well remember the sensation created early one morning in the battalion on our right when they saw someone walking along out in front of their trench apparently quite unconcerned.

It was Charles, to whom much the simplest method of solving a dispute that had been vexing the Staff and other authorities— as to whether there was or wasn't a trench at some particular point in "No Man's Land"—was to go and see. This was just about the time that he was wounded the second time—on the occasion of the rushing of a Turkish sap with some bombers. The last time he was wounded was pure ill-luck.

To Charles's friends no praise would be excessive. I knew him before the war, but have never had an opportunity of cultivating his friendship before we were thrown together in the same battalion. I have certainly never known a more original character, nor one of more sterling worth, nor one either with a more exquisite sense of humour. On his second return from hospital from Imbros, he came laden with fresh fruit, vegetables, wine, and other luxuries, which, in the absence of transport, had to be left on the beach while he came up to camp to arrange for a limber party to be sent down for them.

We all waited its arrival with impatience, and when eventually the party came back to say that there was no gear there, and it became obvious that a stupid servant who had been left in charge had taken his eyes off it, there was a savage outburst of anger from all of us, and imagination ran riot in devising punishment to fit the offence. Charles's suggestion, however, as to what one *could* do with such a man was: "I think we must make him an officer."

To Mrs. Graham Smith.

Hood Battalion, R.N.D., M.E.F.,

August 14, 1914 (1915)

Ever so many thanks for two charming letters I have had from you. Clare's young man sounds very attractive, and I should think a great riding man, which is what she wants.

The last few days here have been exciting, though we have rather played the role of Sister Ann, and waited for the cloud of dust to rise in the distance. The results to date of the new landing have not been brilliant, and the "thrust" at Maidos has not materialised. Our operations have been quite of secondary importance, simply meant to keep the Turks busy here and stop them sending troops away in any great quantities, and the sanguine estimates of a capture of Achi Baba, etc., have been rather beside the mark.

The 29th lost a good many men in the latter fighting; the actual results in capturing trenches, etc., are nil. I think the Turks have also lost prettily heavily, as they did some counterattacking. We are again supposed to be short of shells. Such is life. It is disappointing, but, of course, no one knows how many troops we have got to play with.

Our mess have snaffled a Frenchman to cook for us, of whom we have great hopes. Our only fear is that he may be coveted by some of our generals, etc.

Rumours say that the 2nd Mounted Division (Scats and the rest of them) are fighting on their flat feet on the Anzac front. It is certainly the interesting front just now. I am gloriously well, and have a pleasant mess and plenty of books, so the tedium of always being in the same place is obviated. We always get breezes, so don't suffer much from heat.

To Mrs. Lewis.

Hood Battalion, R.N.D., M.E.F.

Many thanks for your very kind letter. Cigarettes would be most welcome; but send me a nice, damp plum-cake. If made damp and packed in tins they keep splendidly. There will be just time for you to get one cake out to me. We shall be through in six weeks' time I hope.

No home-coming for me till then. We sailors (!) have been here from the first, and will see it out.

It will be a bit sad coming back. . . . Think of Taplow nowadays. At least out here there is enough to do to stop me dwelling on these things.

I got well from my wound in a week's time. Hospitals give me the pip, and I was very happy to get back to camp among my pals. Great fun we all have at our camp table. We do ourselves very well here, you'll be glad to hear; but there is no Scott to bring me my boots in the morning. Give him my love, and Freddy. (Scott, the hall-porter at the Cavendish Hotel. "Freddy" is Scott's fox-terrier.—R.)

Be good and look after the family well. Get *The Times* of July

23rd and cut out the Gallipoli news. It is about the Hood Battalion, although they don't give names.

To Lord Ribblesdale.

Hood Battalion, R.N.D., M.E.F.,
August 19, 1915.

We are again in for a spell of work, and have just had Monday to Thursday in the reserve trenches—comfortable lines a good long way back. We shall shortly go up again into the firing-line, which is very nearly as safe, as I don't think we contemplate doing any more attacking on this side till some real progress has been made on the other side. We seem quite jambed on this side, and all efforts to advance which have been recently made have been costly and unsuccessful. Every division tells the same story about its drafts. They come out insufficiently trained, so there is a feeling of staleness about the whole show on this side. We justify our existence by pinning a certain number of Turkish troops here. The Turks, I imagine, hold this line lightly with a few good troops and an enormous number of machine-guns, which are German manned.

It is exciting H. being at last in a show and the Middlesex having their fling, which they so longed for. I am sure they will do well; they are much better troops than Kitchener's Army, I feel. The 9th Corps have been a disappointment. They neutralised the effects of the expansion of the Anzac position by complete inaction after a virtually unopposed landing at Suvla. As troops they were not thought much of here. One I talked to did not know which hill was Achi Baba, and this after five days in the trenches, for they came here first before going to Suvla.

Is it true, by the way, that Billy Grenfell has been killed?—this would be too cruel news. It is a good thing Ivo is still too young. We have had rumours of it out here.

I went for a visit to the firing-line yesterday, but saw nothing of any particular interest. At one point an old Turkish communication trench runs right into a sap of ours. We have a huge sandbag barricade with a loophole whence there is always protruding the point of a rifle. I fear the monotonies of trench warfare are still with us, but the discomfort is not serious and shelling is very intermittent. The Turkish shells are bursting very indifferently.

Freyberg, after an absence of twenty-five days, has returned. This must be a record for anyone hit in the stomach. He was brilliantly operated on, and the gash is perfectly healed. He saw H. in Egypt, and was probably the source of H.'s information as to me.

I am glad you liked the MS. It is the sort thing to put by, I think, and might be of interest when the events of the last few months have faded into the distance of time.

Look up *The Times* of July 23rd. The last paragraph of the official news from Gallipoli describes the achievements of the Hood in the trenches that led up to my being wounded. I see Sir I. H. says we took the redoubt. Our orders were really *on no account* to take it. How news is made up. Do get that number. Mrs. Lewis can put the cutting in her scrapbook. Give her my love.

To the Hon. Mrs. Percy Wyndham.

Hood Battalion,
August 23, 1915.

Since last I wrote I fear my worst anticipations as to the Anzac move have been realised, and it was so very nearly a brilliant success. The Turks were surprised, as they thought we were going to land in Asia and in the Gulf of Xeros, and it was only the dilatoriness of the O.C. 9th Corps which prevented us getting right across to Maidos and cutting off the Achi Baba army.

If they reinforce heavily at once we shall be through by the autumn. If they don't ——. My fear is that the Germans may do a push through Serbia, get there before we've done our job, and play old Harry with everything in this part of the world. I only hope Sir Ian will be honest and state his requirements in the most explicit and insistent manner.

We have been in the trenches lately—in reserve to the other brigade—and are now going up to hold the sector ourselves, which is fun. We have a jolly little cornfield in front of our old trenches, where was a tree on which a lot of pigeons and doves settled. If only I had had a shot-gun. There were also a lot of jays and little doves.

We have just had a new draft—eight officers and two hundred men. The men impress every one very favourably. . . .

How tragic about Billy. I almost dread my home-coming. So many of our old joy-places will be full of ghosts. And here one does not have that feeling of the void and the ghosts which have taken the place of dear living forms. Julian and Billy were very close brothers, so one hopes they will somewhere be united again. Shall write again shortly.

To Mrs. Hamlyn.

Hood Battalion, R.N.D.,

August 23, 1915.

I must write and thank you very warmly for the Clovelly cake, which was eaten with enthusiasm, and was in pleasing contrast with our normal fare—not that that is so bad, but *toujours perdrix*——.

Since my second wound we have been very quiet till the last few days. The Naval Division are once more in the trenches. We had three pleasant days in a reserve trench—well behind—with any amount to eat and drink, and not too oppressive heat. When one gets away from our dust-heap of a camp the country is very smiling.

The men were pretty happy in the trenches, and pleased me.

We have now got a large new draft of men and some new officers. I am for the moment in the giddy position of company commander, with three subordinate officers. I've had a company before, but never so many underlings, and I feel rather embarrassed. The latest thing in officers in the R.N.D. is no worse than the latest thing in Kitchener's Army, judging from the specimens I saw in the hospitals and rest camps at Imbros—young men of tender age with queasy stomachs, to whom you and I with our Levantine experiences would feel very superior.

I met Jones, (Sir Louis Mallet's former butler), at Alexandria, where he is with Sir H. McMahon. He is longing to fight, and regrets his age. I hear Francis is Raymond Asquith's senior officer in the Guards.

To Mrs. Graham-Smith.

Hood Battalion, R.N.D.,

August 23, 1915.

We have been pretty quiet lately, and I have had a certain amount of time for reading.

What do you think of Lewes's *Life of Goethe*? He is rather inclined to moralize and obtrude his own personality, but it is a good biography, I think. Lewes, of course, devoted rather unnecessary space to defending Goethe for actions which need no defence. Why, for example, should Goethe have made an honest woman of Friederike? I should like to have seen Goethe more than almost any other great man, with his ideal beauty and piercing eyes. He is a much greater man than writer, really.

What an odd lapse his writing a treatise on the Gift of Tongues in the Acts and on the real nature of the Ten Commandments. It is curious great men have been seduced into serious discussion of futilities by the spirit of their age.

★★★★★★

This is his last letter to me from the hospital ship *Gascon*. I refer to it in my memoir. At the same time he began a letter to his sister Diana. His nurse advised him not to go on writing it, as he was very restless and ill at ease. He assented, saying there was no hurry, and put the few lines he had written to Diana in one of the books he had been reading.—R.

★★★★★★

To Lord Ribblesdale.

Hospital Ship,
August 26, 1915.

Just think, I have been wounded once more, the third time. We were in a trench, observing the Turkish trenches, when suddenly they fired some shells into our trenches. I went along to see what had happened, got my people back into a bit of a trench they had had to leave, then went down the trench, thinking the show was over, and then got it, being struck in the pelvis and my bladder being deranged, and slight injuries in the legs and calves.

I have been operated on, but am sketchy as to what has been done. I am on a hospital ship, comfy enough, but feeling the motion of it a good deal, and I have to be in bed and cannot change my position. The hours go slowly, as one does not feel very much up to reading. However, I got to sleep all right.

I feel this will be a longish job, and I don't know where I shall do my cure—perhaps Alexandria.

My doctor is quite happy at the way things are going. The shell that hit me killed one man and wounded the others.

Forgive this scrawl, but it's not easy to write.

★★★★★★

In my memoir, I spoke of Sir Ian Hamilton's Honours dispatch. A few days ago I wrote and asked whether I might quote its actual words. He has approved of my doing so, and, indeed, seemed to wish it. Here it is.—R.

(Copy of Original.)

For brilliant deeds of gallantry throughout our operations. On July 16th he was specially brought to notice for heading an assault against an enemy's stronghold. Again, on July 21st, he personally reconnoitred a Turkish communication trench, and, although wounded (for the second time), he returned and led forward a party to the attack. Subsequently he was a third time wounded and has since died, to the sorrow of all ranks who knew him.

One more letter and I have done. Colonel Bernard Freyberg, D.S.O., now commanding the Hood Battalion in France, sent me this letter only the other day. It is dated July 30, 1916, and is written by Lieutenant Ivan Heald, of the Hood Battalion, to Colonel Freyberg.—R.

There is, I learn, some hope that a little memoir will be published by a friend of Charles Lister's. Would it be possible for you to let the author know something of the splendid lead which Lister gave to the junior officers who served with him in the Hood Battalion? Charles Lister was a tower of strength to us, and you. Sir, I am sure, will agree that his wonderful personality was a great aid to you in your task of rebuilding a battalion of fighting men out of the salvage left from the disaster of June 4th.

We had seen our hopes of speedy victory smashed before our eyes; our few men were broken with the endless drudgery of trench digging, and everyone was yearning for relief.

Then follows a passage which I've quoted in my memoir, in which Mr. Heald speaks of Charles returning to the battalion—his wounds healed—and assuring them "joyously" that they were having the time of their lives. He goes on:

Henceforward, who were so cheerful as the Hoods? There was no mess in the Peninsula, I'll swear, so merry as ours, with Lister leading such rare wits as Asquith, Kelly, and Patrick Shaw-Stewart—Lister always on the most uncomfortable packing-case, declaiming and denouncing with that dear old stiff gesture of his, which we came to know so well.

But the strongest impression I have of Lister was his eager sense of duty. Throughout the war I have never met a man in whose heart there burned so steadily that first fine flame that sent us all cut soldiering. He was ever on the look-out for something useful to be doing. His willingness to sacrifice himself seemed part of some high secret religion of his own; and those who mourn for him must realise that this, coupled with his serene disdain of danger, inevitably meant his fall sooner or later in the campaign. We were six months in the trenches after he died, but I, for one, know how much his example helped me to carry on through that dreary stretch. The legacy he left us was rich indeed.

The Gallipoli Campaign
By Douglas Jerrold

The second departure of the Naval Division overseas was as un-expected as the first. We have seen how the whole division, less one Field Company of Engineers and the Hawke, Collingwood and Ben-bow Battalions, had finally been concentrated for Divisional training by January 28th. The next day came the first orders for overseas. They affected only two battalions, the Plymouth and Chatham R.M.L.I. battalions, and the Staff of the Marine Brigade, but the event is note-worthy, not only because through the issue of these orders the last chance of concentrating the whole division for serious divisional training passed away, but still more, perhaps, because it gave rise for the first time to those rumours that the division would never again be employed as a separate formation in the field, which, from that date, hardly ever ceased to be current, and were hardly ever wholly with-out foundation. (Captain M. C. Festing, R.M.L.I. (Brigade-Major), and Captain C. F. Jerram, R.M.L.I. (Staff Captain). Brigadier-General Trotman was in command of the force).

That the Naval Division should never have been concentrated except under fire, is merely an incident in its history. It was in the most literal sense a fighting division. The rumours which made up the mess-room gossip through the whole course of the war, rumours of dispersal, transfer to the army or to sea service, or condemnation to garrison duties, were, however, more than an episode in the history of the division: they were part of its daily life, the very atmosphere it breathed.

The two Marine Battalions which left Blandford for Plymouth on February 1st, under Brigadier-General Trotman, sailed for an un-known Eastern destination on February 6th. The general belief was that the balance of the division would be dispersed on different independent operations, and rumour gave East Africa as the destination of a number of battalions. Not till the 17th February, when Mr. Winston Churchill inspected it, did the hopes of the division revive. The inspection was held in pouring rain, under the most unfavourable conditions, but the verdict of the First Lord must have been a favourable one, for the next day the orders came for the rest of the troops at Blandford to prepare to follow the Marine Battalions. Exactly a week later, the division was again inspected by the First Lord, and two hours later by H.M. the King.

On this occasion the inspection was unusually detailed, Mr. Winston Churchill inspecting every battalion, except the Nelson battalion, which he had seen on his visit the week before. At 11.30 the Royal Standard was hoisted and the king's inspection began; after which, the division marched past the saluting point in column of companies, and later marched again past His Majesty on their way back to camp in double column of fours.

This was the end of the division's training. The 26th and 27th, the last two days spent by these units at Blandford, were occupied with the distribution of ammunition and iron rations, and the overhauling of equipment and kit, and on the evening of the 28th the whole of the division, with the exception of the partially trained Collingwood Battalion, the Third Field Company of the Engineers (by now at Blandford, but also untrained) and the Hawke and Benbow Battalions (still at the Crystal Palace), marched out of camp by Black Lane to the town station. The next day the troops embarked at Avonmouth, and sailed the same day; General Paris and the Headquarters Staff, General Mercer and the 1st Brigade Staff, the Drake, Nelson and Deal Battalions, the 1st Field Ambulance, and the Motor Machine Gun detachment of the R.N.A.S., on board the *Franconia,* and other units in the *Braemar Castle,* the *Gloucester Castle,* the *Grantully Castle,* the *Minnetonka* and the *Astrian.*

The decision to send the division overseas was, as we have said, unexpected. It is doubtful, however, if it was premature. Officers and men had everything to learn of the things which active service alone can teach, but it is a reasonable view that they were otherwise adequately trained. Those who consider no training adequate which is not comparable in its duration to that considered necessary for the corresponding ranks of the regular army overlook, perhaps, one very vital difference between a professional and a volunteer formation. The average civilian soldier must usually learn the business of soldiering in less time than that required by regular officers who join their regiments virtually straight from school.

After all, the converse holds: no one expects a regular officer, who retires and goes into the City, to begin as an office boy, and it would be strange if a really competent professional or business man were to find serious difficulty in mastering the work of a company commander. The same, *mutatis mutandis,* holds good of lower ranks. There were cases where this was hardly appreciated, with the result that units, brigades, even whole divisions, became routine-bound, over-trained, stale. This danger was avoided in the case of the Naval Division, and, in this sense, it was right to regard all, save the three recruit battalions, as already in February, 1915, fit for service overseas. If, however, it is reasonable to assume that, in marked contrast to the division which went to Antwerp in 1914, the division which left Blandford on this occasion was fit to take the offensive, it would be idle to pretend that the decision to send it to the East was equally uncontroversial. Nothing in the war (not even excepting the Antwerp expedition) has been the subject of weightier criticism than the decision reached in February, 1915, to embark on extensive military operations in the Near East.

To understand the operations in which the Naval Division was so soon to begin to play its part, the circumstances leading up to them must be briefly outlined.

At the end of 1914, the dominant facts in the general situation were the staying of the German offensive on the West, and the ominous threat of a decisive German victory in the East. Turkey, known to our military advisers to be still one of the most formidable military powers in Europe, had declared war on the Allies on October 31st, and must be expected at any time to make her presence felt on the Russian flank unless her armies could be engaged elsewhere. This in itself was serious enough, for the Russians were already sufficiently hard pressed by the Germans and Austrians; but it was only part of the story. Serbia was threatened with an Austro-German invasion, and such a threat, if it materialised, might be expected to bring to the aid of the Central Powers the armies of Bulgaria and Rumania.

In such an eventuality, would Italy feel herself able to intervene on the side of the Allies, a step which she was at the time actively contemplating? These dangers were so grave that they could not be ignored. They had to be faced, on the contrary, with energy and resolution. Whatever may have been the faults of the Allied strategy, the errors of generals or politicians, the need for some action to prevent the threatened disasters in the East is, if not unchallenged, at least unchallengeable. Those who attempt to review the 1915 situation in the light of our success in 1918, and still suggest that, because the war had to be won on the Western front, it had to be fought on that front, forget that the drain imposed on the German, Austrian and Turkish resources in 1915 and 1916 by the vigorous prosecution of the war in the East, was as decisive in the battle of armies as the battles of attrition in France and Flanders in 1916 and 1917.

Is it seriously arguable that disaster could have been averted if Italy had remained neutral, if Serbia had been crushed, and if Russia had been faced by a German-Austrian-Turkish offensive, before the British armies were sufficiently powerful (which was not till 1916) to initiate a vigorous and continuing offensive in France? These considerations in themselves afford no argument for, and are not mentioned here in defence of the Gallipoli expedition, its strategy, its tactics, or the adequacy of the preparations made for it; but they are unanswerable as arguments in support of the Cabinet decision (arrived at on February 16th, 1915) to send substantial forces to the Near East. (See, for a fuller discussion of this point, Corbett: *Naval Operations*, Vol. II.) It was in pursuance of this decision that the main body of the Royal Naval Division were ordered overseas later in the month.

The decision to employ the new "Mediterranean Expeditionary Force" (as it came to be known) in the historic attempt to force a passage for the fleet through the Dardanelles, by seizing the Gallipoli peninsula, was more controversial. This operation had been considered directly Turkey came into the war, but had been put aside, in view of the then success of the Russian armies and of the critical situation in the West. No more had been heard of the Dardanelles till January 2nd, when the now menacing situation in the East was brought urgently to the notice of the government by a request from the Russian commander-in-chief for an early demonstration against Turkey, with a view to relieving his armies from pressure on their flank. Lord Kitchener, through the Foreign Office, at once agreed; and the Admiralty immediately sought the views of the Admiral Commanding in the Eastern Mediterranean (Vice-Admiral Carden), on the possibility of rushing the Dardanelles, an attack on the Straits being clearly the most direct threat which a naval power could bring to bear on Turkey. Admiral Carden replied by telegram that, in his view, the Straits could not be rushed, but could be forced by extended operations directed to the systematic reduction of the forts.

It would be outside the scope of this history to examine the tangled story of the manner in which the government finally, on January 28th, committed themselves to endorsing this project. It is sufficient for our purpose to record their decision, which was arrived at independently and prior to the decision to assemble in the Near East a substantial military force. The only military movement to which this decision, by itself, gave rise was the dispatch of the two Marine Battalions to the East on February 6th in advance of the rest of the division. These battalions were not to form part, as has been often assumed, of any military force, but were to act under the fleet in what were definitely assumed to be purely naval operations, involving the landing only of reconnaissance patrols or demolition parties, operations normally within the province of a naval commander.

Towards the end of February, the position was that the preparations for the naval attack (assisted only by the Marine Battalions) were well advanced, and that the concentration of troops to exploit any naval success, or to operate in the Balkans, if that theatre should appear later more profitable, was proceeding. If the naval attack had succeeded, there would, of course, have been no Gallipoli campaign; but when the naval attack, begun at last on February 18th, proved inconclusive, and then had to be broken off because of the weather, Admiral Carden suggested speeding matters up by a military landing on the peninsula. The proposal was rejected by the War Office as involving an irrelevant diversion; the assumption still was that the main work of reducing the forts could be achieved by the navy alone.

The Admiralty appear to have indorsed this view, and Admiral Carden was so informed, but he was asked, at the same time, to confer with General Birdwood, and told that "if he was of opinion that the army could help him, he was at liberty to submit suggestions." (Corbett: _Naval Operations_, Vol. II.) The same evening (February 24th) the War Office sent out similar instructions to General Birdwood.

This development marked the first definite step towards the ion to attempt to force the Straits by conjoint naval and military operations, and, for this reason, February 24th is one of the critical days in the history of the war; and not for this reason only, but also because, on this day, the government appeared first to be moving towards the conclusion that the Dardanelles operations must somehow or other be carried to a successful conclusion,

There was, however, still a firm belief in the chances of a purely naval success. It was not till the beginning of March that events at the front, in which the Plymouth Marine Battalion took a gallant if unsuccessful share, brought about a decisive change in the prospects of the purely naval campaign. Admiral Carden's plan had been to force a passage through the Straits, by a series of progressive bombardments against the forts which guarded the whole length of the Straits on either side. The long range guns would keep down the fire of the forts, while the ships with lighter armament closed in to effective range and destroyed them. The long range bombardment would then lift and come down on the next group of forts, and in due course these also would be closed and put out of action. The same procedure would be applied, and of course at the same time, to any mobile batteries which the enemy might bring, in support of his permanent defences.

The first naval attack, on February 19th, had had, as we have seen, to be broken off before the merits of the plan could be tested, but, when the attack was renewed on February 25th, the fleet, standing in close, compelled all the outer forts to cease fire. Next day, demolition parties from the fleet, covered by Marine detachments, were put ashore to complete the work of destruction. These parties, which displayed the utmost gallantry and energy, did no small amount of damage, and further landings on February 27th and March 1st and 2nd added to the tale of destruction. As far as the outer forts were concerned, everything indeed seemed to be proceeding according to plan. It was quite otherwise with the more important attack on the inner forts, which had been begun on the 26th, and had proceeded as weather permitted, but without any sort of success. The main objectives of the fleet were, of course, the groups of forts at Chanak and Maidos, guarding the entrance to the Narrows. Before, however, these could be effectively bombarded, the smaller "Dardanos" group had to be subdued, and the minefields at the entrance to the Narrows (by Kephez Point) had to be swept.

Despite all efforts, neither task had been accomplished, nor had any material progress been made by the evening of March 3rd. The fire of the forts, indeed, whose position was accurately known, could be kept down, but all attempts to deal with the mobile batteries had failed. It was becoming increasingly clear that without the occupation of some commanding position on shore, which would enable the fire of the ships' guns to be effectively controlled, or the forts to be taken in reverse, no further progress could be confidently expected. General Birdwood, who had by this time conferred with Admiral Carden, appears to have advised Lord Kitchener in this sense, and the next day's operations made the situation even more clear. These operations consisted of landings by the Plymouth Battalion at Kum Kale and Sedd-el-bahr.

Both landings were unsuccessful, and their failure was significant. The plan in each case was much the same. The parties landed in open boats without much opposition, but, once landed, they were unable to make any headway. The idea was to advance inland and hold a line in each case some two miles in length, on the Asiatic side from Kum Kale pier to Yeni Shehr, and on the peninsula from Morto Bay to Cape Tekke. These lines were to be held for three hours, while an exhaustive search was made for guns, gun positions and ammunition dumps, and while the work of destruction and survey, hitherto undertaken piecemeal, was carried to completion. Instead, the landing parties, though consisting of two companies each, found themselves held up almost on the beaches, while the Turks were occupying strongly entrenched positions in the neighbourhood of the different objectives.

Against these it was found impossible to advance, even with the assistance of the ships' guns.

In the circumstances, there was nothing for it but to withdraw, and even this proved to be difficult, though, in the end, it was successfully accomplished.

This failure was important because of the light it shed on the prospects of the purely naval attack. The destruction of the outer forts, at least, had been considered, until now, to have been relatively satisfactorily achieved. It was now seen that the Turks were not only undismayed at our success but still in a position to maintain by force of arms their hold on the coast-line even at the entrance to the Straits, and even there to bring mobile batteries to bear at their pleasure on our fleet and transports.

In spite of this it was decided to persist, and the attacks on the inner forts were renewed on March 5th and the following days. These, like the former attacks, were, at the very best, negative in their results, and the situation was thus dubious when the War Council met on March 10th, to take a final decision regarding the question of the military force to be sent to the Near East.

The crux of this question was the 29th Division, which it had been agreed to send out in February, but which Lord Kitchener had since felt unable to release. Though it is clear that no definite proposal to abandon the naval attack in favour of joint naval and military operations was under consideration at this date, there can be little doubt but that the decision, now finally reached, to send the 29th Division, marked the definite acceptance by the government of the Near East as an important military theatre. It meant, in particular, that, if the naval attack failed, the government were by this date determined to push the attack home by military measures, if such were recommended by the authorities on the spot. The necessary corollary to these decisions was the appointment of a commander-in-chief, and Sir Ian Hamilton was selected almost immediately after the meeting of March 10th. Sir Ian's written instructions make the government's position unmistakable. (Second Report of the Dardanelles Commission, paragraph 18.)

> Having entered on the project of forcing the Straits there can be no idea of abandoning the scheme.

It is, of course, equally clear from the instructions that the government still hoped that military intervention would not be necessary to subdue the forts, and that, as Sir Ian Hamilton puts it in his *Diary*, (*Gallipoli Diary*, Vol. 1.), "the Cabinet did not want to hear anything of the army till it had sailed through the Straits." But these were pious wishes. The written instructions above quoted (reinforced by a subsequent telegram from Lord Kitchener) decided the issue. The only essential precaution enjoined by Lord Kitchener was that extensive operations should wait on the arrival of the 29th Division.

The fact that the government had by this date definitely faced the possibility of combined operations did not mean, however, that in their view the naval attack need not be pressed. On the contrary, high hopes were now entertained of extensive Russian co-operation against the Turkish forts on the Bosphorus and the Turkish armies if we could force the Dardanelles; and Admiral Carden was urged on March 11th to further efforts. Only in preference to an attempt to rush the Straits across unswept mine-fields were combined operations on an extensive scale to be undertaken this side of Constantinople. Admiral Carden agreed to the Admiralty proposals, and the plans for a final attempt on the Narrows were put in hand and were ready by March 15th. The next day Admiral Carden was forced under medical orders to resign his command, and the date of the attack was postponed while the Admiralty exchanged telegrams with the new naval commander, Vice-Admiral de Robeck, who was able to assure them that he was satisfied that the proposed attack was sound, and that he was anxious to carry it out.

In these circumstances, the historic action of March 18th was decided on, and with that decision the active participation of the Naval Division in the Gallipoli operations begins.

It must not be imagined, though it is indeed hard in the light of events to imagine otherwise, that the situation seemed, to those on the spot, anything but reasonably promising at this time. It is indeed poignant to recall the high hopes with which the Naval Division had started out to the scene of war. Rupert Brooke has left on record his own peculiar enthusiasm:

> I had not imagined that fate could be so benign. . . . I am filled with confident and glorious hopes. (*Rupert Brooke: A Memoir*, by Edward Marsh.)

He was not alone in his excitement. The Englishman's protective irony could not indeed be expected to survive the splendour of that voyage through the Mediterranean, When the first breath of spring was in the air, the sea was brilliant like a jewel, and "*sunset and dawn divine blazes of colour.*"

Not even Malta, that suburb of the East, could break the spell. Africa lay behind them, the Greek islands and Constantinople lay before them. The spirit of adventure was in the air of spring, and no jarring note intruded on the Eastern Mine as the transports worked up the Mediterranean from Malta in the second week in February and weighed anchor in Mudros harbour. Later, with the too facile genius of our nice, even primitive islands of the Aegean Archipelago became Anglicised, but as yet those tranquil shores were the embodiment of a classic, if somewhat arid, simplicity. Thucydides' description of primitive Attica comes inevitably to mind as we wander in memory among these barren but fragrant hills, and see the scattered peasants eking out a peaceful existence from the small patches of cornland and vineyard which they had won in the course of a struggle with nature extending through many sunny, if penurious, centuries.

And in the harbour itself the scene was not only unfamiliar, but without parallel in the modern annals. Indeed, as John Masefield says, you might have thought that all the ships of the world were gathered there. From the *Queen Elizabeth,* then the pride of the fleet, to the smallest variety of tramp steamer that ever carried yeast from Edinburgh to Grimsby, every type of craft was represented. Coming to rest in such an anchorage, the battalions of the Naval Division suffered no sense of anticlimax.

At 6 p.m. on March 18th, the division, still in the original transports, sailed out of the harbour eastwards. Steering W. and N. of Imbros, the transports arrived off the western shore of the peninsula at 5.30 a.m. on the morning of the 19th. Down the coast, the flotilla moved on to Cape Tekke, and came up with H.M.S. *Dublin* at 6 a.m. There, at the entrance of the Straits, destroyers went cruising round, and *Queen Elizabeth, Dublin, Glory, Albion* and *Inflexible* were keeping up a desultory bombardment on the Turkish forts. The first sight of these historic waters, famous beyond all other channels of the world, held out, to the untrained and enthusiastic eyes of the young officers and men on board the transports, the promise of early developments. The great ships, gathered off the entrance, appeared in truth to dominate the scene. Every moment the men expected orders to disembark. From the decks of the troopships the Turkish infantry could be seen lining the cliffs. The hour of battle seemed at hand.

But in fact the movement of the transports, a demonstration planned to divert the attention of the enemy from what should have been the closing and critical stage of a great naval attack, was no longer required. The great naval attack had failed, and within two hours of their first sight of the enemy, the Naval Division received orders to return to Lemnos.

There was in one sense no reason why the failure of this naval attempt on the Straits should have been regarded as decisive. The disaster which had led to the breaking off of the engagement, though believed at the time to be due to floating mines, was caused, so it has since been established, almost accidentally, by a minefield laid by the Turks on the night of the 17th and 18th in waters which we could have cleared. Unaccountably, this minefield had been missed by our sweepers, and the result was a heavy loss in capital ships, but the loss need not have been regarded as likely to recur if the operations were renewed: in other words the original plan was not necessarily shown to be incapable of fulfilment.

The admiral, however, was not long in deciding not to make any further unsupported attacks on the Straits, and, on March 21st, he formally notified Sir Ian Hamilton of his decision. The effect was to commit the army to an attack on the Gallipoli peninsula. Sir Ian Hamilton's instructions from Lord Kitchener were such as to compel him to undertake such military operations as were necessary to enable the fleet to reach Constantinople, unless he was convinced that no operations of the kind were possible; and, after a personal reconnaissance, he was already reasonably satisfied that this object could be achieved by military operations against the Gallipoli peninsula.

When, therefore, the admiral notified him, on the 21st, that he would require military assistance if he was to get the fleet to Constantinople, the only question left open was the time and the place of the military attack. The time was the immediate question. The chance of a surprise had been jeopardised by the naval operations. A further delay would render a surprise impossible. Despite the grave difficulties, General Birdwood was in favour of an immediate landing. Admiral Wemyss held similar views. In addition to the Naval Division, there was on the spot approximately the strength of an Australian Division. An immediate landing, it was urged, might be comparatively unopposed, and might mean the capture of Achibaba almost without a struggle. Meanwhile other troops could be brought on the scene.

But Sir Ian Hamilton had no hesitation in rejecting the plan. The 29th Division could not be expected for a fortnight or longer; the Naval Division transports were not suitably loaded for landing operations; troops from Egypt could not arrive for some days. The force might indeed reach Achibaba, but what chance had they of remaining there, unsupported by artillery (save a few Australian guns), without Engineers' stores, periscopes and tools? In the absence of detailed preparation for the landing, the supply and the transport arrangements for even twenty thousand men must inevitably be inadequate; if bad weather arose they must break down completely, and weather conditions could not be expected to become settled till mid-April at earliest. Above all, there was Lord Kitchener's precise instruction that no extensive military operations should be undertaken till the arrival of the 29th Division.

In these circumstances it was decided to postpone the attack, and to make, in the interval, the most careful and detailed preparations; and on the 22nd March the Naval Division transports sailed from Mudros to Port Said, where they were to re-ship their stores, and await the concentration of the remainder of the force.

The disembarkation of the division was completed by Monday, March 29th, and on that and the following days the R.N.D. S.A.A. column (Major Carter), the R.N.D. Supply Column (Major J. D. Buller, A.S.C.), the R.N.D. Sanitary Section and the 19th Mobile Veterinary Section joined the division. On the 1st April, orders were received by General Paris to send a detachment to take over a section of the trenches at Kantara on the Suez Canal defences, and a composite force consisting of two half-battalions from each of the 1st and 2nd

Naval Brigades (Drake, Nelson, Howe and Anson Battalions), under General Mercer, left for Kantara by rail at 7 a.m.

On April 3rd, the division was inspected at Port Said by the commander-in-chief, Admiral Pierce and his flag captain (Captain Burmester, R.N.) being present. The inspection passed off successfully, at least according to Sir Ian Hamilton, who notes in his *Diary* the next day that the division "marched past very well indeed." For a division, not by any means at its best on a parade ground, this was satisfactory. The day has, however, a painful significance, as it marked the beginning of Rupert Brooke's illness, an illness not then, or for some days, diagnosed as serious, but which was to lead to the untimely death of one of the most brilliantly gifted Englishmen of his day.

It is easy to find defects in the writings of men of genius—because they set in their own works a standard which inevitably they cannot always maintain—but only poets of the younger generation have ever doubted that by the death of Brooke England lost not only the greatest of her younger poets, but a voice which would have championed the cause of humane justice without discrimination in a world where, later, such voices were to be few.

Two days later the arrangements for the transport of the Naval Division had taken shape, and the re-embarkation of stores began. On this day, also, the Anson Battalion were ordered to Alexandria to act as beach parties for the 29th Division, who had just arrived, but whose transports, like those of the Naval Division, had been loaded as for a peace-time change of station. The Anson left Alexandria at 4 p.m. It is interesting to recall that this battalion, which, as it happened, had the most honourable part of any in the Naval Division at the landing on April 25th, was detached and sent to Alexandria, in the belief that it would be required solely for routine fatigue duties. Nothing but disappointment was felt by the Anson officers, at this time, with the task believed to be before them.

The remainder of the division proceeded at top speed with the work of re-embarkation. Time was indeed pressing. It was now a fortnight since the last naval attack; and the admiral had consented to break off further active operations, only on the understanding that they would be renewed again by April 14th at earliest. A slight interruption to the embarkation was caused by a reported attack on the Canal defences at Kantara, on the 7th, with the result that at 11 a.m. all troops in Alexandria were ordered to "stand by." The attack proved, however, to be nothing more than a reconnaissance by a mounted patrol, some sixty strong, which was beaten off without loss, the enemy not venturing within effective range; and, at 2 p.m., the division was able to "carry on."

The next day, 8th April, the first Naval Division transport (the *Braemar Castle*) sailed for Mudros. On board, were General Trotman and his staff, and Colonel Matthews and the Plymouth Battalion of Marines. The *Braemar Castle* was followed by the *Cawdor Castle* (Chatham Battalion), the *Gloucester Castle* (Portsmouth Battalion), the *Inkonka* (Motor Machine Gun Squadron), the *Royal George* (Commodore Backhouse, R.N., and staff, and the Howe Battalion), the *Grantully Castle* (Hood Battalion), and the *Somali* (1st and 3rd Field Ambulances and details R.M.A.). All the transports had their tow of lighters, not for the disembarkation of the division (even at this eleventh hour, when every element of surprise had been sacrificed to completing the preparation and equipment of the force, there were not enough lighters to enable the whole force to be landed simultaneously), but for the use of the 29th Division.

The departure of these transports left in Egypt only the headquarters of the division, and General Mercer's 1st Naval Brigade, who were required for the re-embarkation of horses and mules. As soon as this had been completed, the brigade and the divisional troops embarked on the *Alnwick Castle* (Deal Battalion R.M.L.I.), the *Ayrshire* (R.N.D. Engineers), the *Franconia* (D.H.Q. and H.Q. 1st Brigade, Drake Battalion, Div. Cyclist Company and Signal Sections), the *Minnetonka* (Nelson Battalion, S.A.A. Column and No. 2 Field Ambulance) and the *Astrian* (Divisional Train). As the transports arrived at Mudros, they were ordered to proceed to Trebuki Bay, Scyros, in conformity with the detailed plan of campaign which had by now been decided on.

THE GALLIPOLI LANDINGS

Unlike the Grecian Islands and the peninsulas of Italy and Spain, fellow survivors of that prehistoric inundation which buried beneath the Black Sea and the more placid waters of the Marmora, the Aegean and the Mediterranean a once fertile and sunlit Continent, the Gallipoli peninsula has an almost accidental importance. It is no more than a chain of rugged uplands and mountain peaks running down from the Thracian mainland between the Aegean and the Sea of Marmora; a narrow strip of land nearly fifty miles in length, but only a few miles in width, where many nations have passed, many historic events have taken place, and where, for all this, no culture has taken root and no civilization has endured. But beneath the cliffs of its eastern shore, and dominated by its once mountainous peaks, still rising above the level of the sea to a height of seven or eight hundred feet, lies the narrow channel which we know as the Straits of the Dardanelles.

From the first dawn of history the control of the Straits has been the foremost aim of one or more of the great powers of Asia or Europe. Opposite the southern extremity of the peninsula lie buried the seven cities of Troy, and when the control of the Straits was finally wrested from Persia by the Ionian Greeks, the history of Mediterranean civilization begins. With the loss of the control of the Straits by Athens to Sparta at Aegospotami, the power of the Athenian Empire hastened to its premature decline. The assertion of Roman superiority in these same waters was the historic service of Sulla to the cause of Roman imperialism.

On the control of the Straits the Byzantine Empire depended through a thousand years for its amazing stability, amid a world relapsed into barbarism. To her control of these waters, won by her naval supremacy, Venice owed her greatness; and with the defeat of Venice by the Turks off the entrance to the Straits the renascence of Mediterranean civilization came to an end. Through their control of the Straits the Turks had maintained themselves in Europe for more than five hundred years.

And so history was only repeating itself when the seizure of the Gallipoli peninsula became for a little, perhaps for too short a time, an avowed aim of British strategy. But history had no lessons to teach us as to the manner in which we could establish a footing on that inhospitable and barren shore. However old the strategy, new tactics must be brought into play. The greater battles of the past had been fought on the sea; following precedent, we too had attempted a decision at sea, and we had failed. The science of earthwork defences had, as in purely land warfare, so in amphibious warfare, outrun the development of destructive explosives, and, where the wooden hulks of Lysander had been supreme, the *Queen Elizabeth* had proved ineffective.

It was now the turn of the army. The point where the naval operations had broken down was in the reduction of the forts guarding the approaches to the Narrows. The object of the military operations was to succeed where the navy had failed. To this end they had either to reach, and hold for so long as might be necessary, some position on the European or Asiatic shore of the Straits, from which not only these forts but those at Chanak, and Kilid Bahr and beyond, could be dominated and silenced, or so to manoeuvre as to cut off the Turkish garrison in Gallipoli and enforce its surrender.

The alternative plans, discussed at the time and subsequently, were many. Broadly, however, the choice appeared to Sir Ian Hamilton to lie between a landing in Asia to secure the eastern shore of the Straits, a landing on Gallipoli with its objective the Kilid Bahr Plateau, a landing at Bulair, or a landing in the Gulf of Xeros.

★★★★★★

Kilid Bahr Plateau, a dominating feature running inland almost due west from Kilid Bahr for a distance of some four miles, which is at its broadest two miles in length, and from 600 to 800 feet above sea-level throughout.

★★★★★★

The last two projects, particularly popular with amateur strategists, are attractive only on a misreading of the situation and were never very seriously considered.

Looking at the map, we see Bulair to be the narrowest point of the peninsula, and the mistaken impression has prevailed that the seizure of this position would isolate the Turkish forces on the peninsula itself and compel their surrender. But the fact is that the main communications of the Turkish divisions in the peninsula did not run through or anywhere near Bulair, but down and across the Straits to the town of Gallipoli. The most northerly point from which the land communications of the force guarding the Narrows could be threatened was the Sari Bair bridge, south-east of Suvla, and commanding the road from Gallipoli to Maidos. But if this position were aimed at, it would be folly to attack it from Bulair, twenty miles to the north. The distance, in fact, could never be traversed in hostile country, with a large Turkish army in the rear round Adrianople, and the consequent need for a large force not only to maintain communications but to protect the base.

The same objection, with even more force, applies to the proposal to land north of the Bulair lines, in the Gulf of Xeros. From there, only one objective was possible, and that was the main European military centre of the Turks at Adrianople. But such an objective implied warfare on a wide front, with no assistance from the fleet, if it was to be anything more than a futile, if spectacular, diversion. For extensive land operations, we had not the troops: for a diversion, there was no occasion.

The plan for landing in Asia was more attractive, and, in one of its most vital assumptions, it was shown to be justified. A landing at Kum

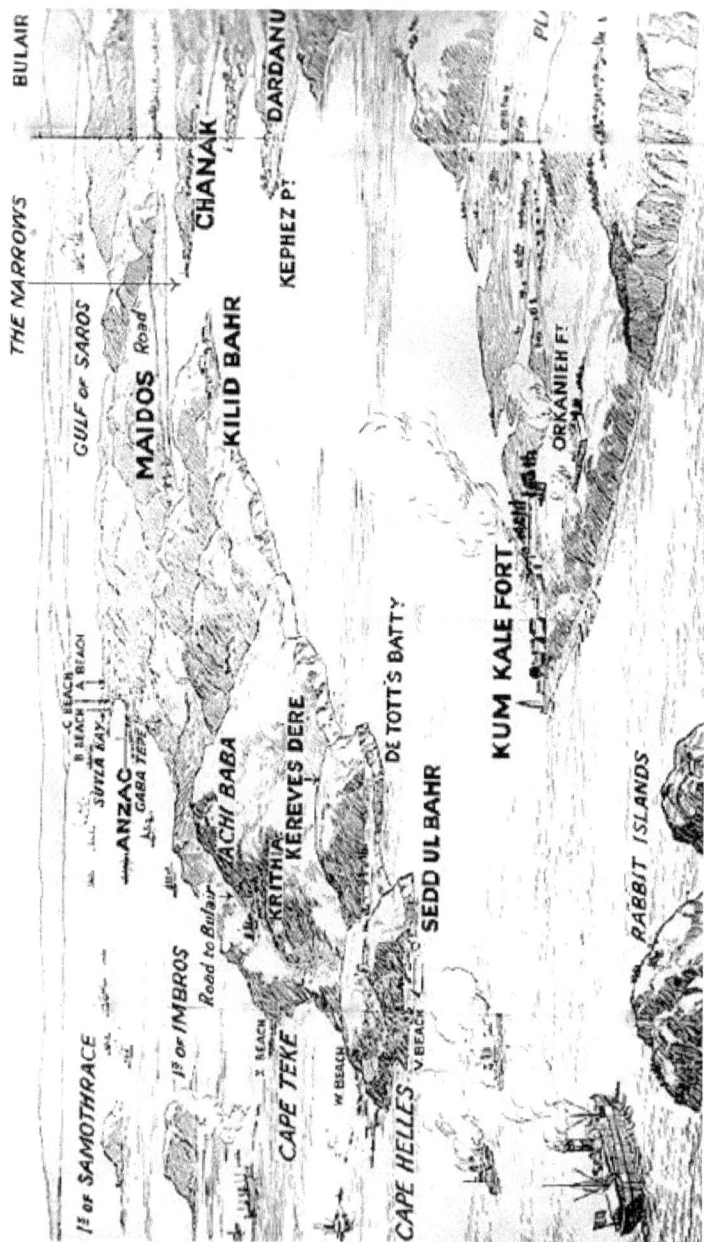

GALLIPOLI

Kale was proved to be a practical, military operation, and the Turks did not expect us to land there. A substantial advance up the Asiatic shore of the Straits might, it was urged, enable the fleet, fired at from one side only, to get through the Narrows. The objection to the plan, and one which, in the light of the gallant and determined character of the Turkish reaction, history will probably regard as decisive, was that we could not, with any certainty, maintain ourselves on the Asiatic shore against a strong enemy attack. The advantages of the narrow front, of the constant support of the guns of the fleet at all stages of an advance, which enabled us to maintain ourselves on the peninsula against the most determined assaults, would not have entered into the situation had we landed on the Asiatic coast. Instead of the guns of the fleet, we should have had the guns of the enemy on our left flank.

The question before Sir Ian Hamilton narrowed itself down to this. Was it possible, with the forces at his disposal, to reach and hold the Kilid Bahr Plateau? The plateau was protected from a force attacking it from the western beaches (Gaba Tepe, or Anzac Cove) by the Sari Bair ridge, and from a force based on the southern beaches by the hill of Achibaba. Both these carefully prepared positions were formidable, if not actually impregnable, should it be necessary to attack them when once the main Turkish forces were concentrated for their defence. The Turks had, so it was correctly thought, four first-line divisions on the peninsula, and they were within easy reach of reinforcements from Asia, where they had another four second-line divisions immediately available. Sir Ian Hamilton had at his disposal only four divisions (with not even a ten *per cent*, margin for casualties in the 29th or Naval Divisions) and the French force, less than two divisions, mainly of African troops. Could we neutralise the overwhelming advantages of the enemy, in position, in preparation, in numbers, by immobilising the bulk of his reserves while we were making good our hold on the shore of the peninsula? Having landed, could we hope to hold the enemy in suspense as to the direction of our main attack sufficiently long for us to concentrate our army before he could concentrate his?

Even if we succeeded so far, were our resources in men, in guns, in ammunition, in equipment, sufficient to enable us to take the offensive with a reasonable chance of immediate success? And, even then, could we maintain ourselves—even on the defensive—with lengthened communications crossing impossible country, without roads, docks, or landing stages, against the full strength of the Turkish reserves?

No man living could have answered these questions with any great degree of conviction in either sense. Yet they had to be faced. The only alternative would have been the abandonment of the whole campaign, in view of its admittedly dubious issue. This course was, indeed, in the first instance definitely recommended by General Hunter Weston, in an "appreciation" written at Malta, and neither General Birdwood nor General Paris definitely excluded this possibility from his consideration. Indeed, as the extracts quoted by Sir Ian Hamilton from the *Memoranda* submitted by these commanders clearly indicate, there was no unreasonable optimism among the higher command in the days immediately preceding the landing. Looking back on these forebodings, in particular on General Hunter Weston's remark that "there is not in present circumstances a reasonable chance of success," and General Paris' less definite but depressing opinion that "To land .. . would be hazardous in the extreme under present conditions," it may seem a matter for regret that their prudent counsels did not prevail.

Although, however, the situation was anxious and obscure, and although no considered estimate of the requirements of an army attempting the seizure of the Gallipoli peninsula had been put before the Cabinet, Sir Ian Hamilton had, nevertheless, been given instructions which he could hardly interpret otherwise than as requiring him to attempt the task with the forces at his disposal. The result was, as it happened, fatal to the success of the operation, for, when the first check occurred, the necessary reinforcements and the still more necessary guns, material and ammunition were not available in time to retrieve the initial failure. By the time we were reinforced, sickness had taken its hold of what had become a beleaguered garrison, and the reinforcements were inadequate. The necessary guns and ammunition were never sent. Here, probably, and not in any tactical mishandling of the forces available, or in any fallacious strategy, was the primary cause of our failure; but it is a cause which redeems the campaign from insignificance as a military achievement. Whatever else may be said, the divisions that fought at Gallipoli (maintained at great expense indeed, but starved of all essential military supplies, denied reinforcements, and forced to fight when, to a man, they would, in France, have been considered medically unfit even for the quietest part of the line), engaged the power of the Turkish armies, and, in the war of armies, if not in the war of positions, they were victorious.

This consideration is relevant not only to an historical verdict on the results of the campaign, but in abatement of any criticism which the legion of those who never fail to be wise after the event may think fit to bring against the undoubted miscalculations which preceded it. To have failed in a great adventure through lack of meticulous estimating of requirements (if, indeed, that was the governing factor) was lamentable. To have let the issue of the war in the Near East go by default would have been an irretrievable disaster. It is with that thought uppermost in his mind, that we must imagine Sir Ian Hamilton to have flung his doubts to the wind in deciding to attempt to seize the peninsula with the slender forces on the spot, and to trust to the military authorities at home for that loyal support which every commander-in-chief has the right to expect.

Having reached his decision, the question was to decide on the best means to give effect to it. The essential problem was to prevent, by a number of simultaneous attacks, whether simulated or actual, the concentration within forty-eight hours of the four Turkish divisions on Gallipoli and their reinforcement from Asia. To do this, it was necessary not only to land in Asia, as well as on the peninsula, but to threaten directly the real objective, the Kilid Bahr Plateau, from more than one side. Any landing or demonstration which did not threaten this position, would, if things went badly for the enemy, be inevitably ignored.

With this object it was decided to make two landings in force—at Gaba Tepe and in the toe of the peninsula—and to detach the French corps for a demonstration in Asia, and the Naval Division for a demonstration at Bulair. This involved a division of forces, but there was no means of avoiding it; on the available beaches only a small covering force and no guns could be landed in the first instance, and subsequent progress must be slow. To land the whole force on either front would have taken longer than it could have taken the enemy to concentrate their own forces, had their reserves not been held to their ground. The only hope was to immobilise their reserves at points as widely separated as possible; and to trust to our fleet to concentrate our forces quicker than the enemy, working across the endless hills and gullies of the peninsula, could concentrate his.

So the plan finally took shape. The main landings were assigned to the Australian and New Zealand Army Corps (in the neighbourhood of Gaba Tepe) and to the 29th Division (south of Achibaba). The Asiatic diversion (to take the form of a temporary landing of at least a brigade) was assigned to General D'Amade's Force, and the bloodless Bulair demonstration to the Naval Division. It was for the purpose of this demonstration that this division, less the Plymouth and Anson

Battalions (attached to the 29th Division for the Southern landings), had been ordered to rendezvous at Scyros.

******

The date first fixed for the landing was April 23rd, and it was on April 21st, after a further conference with the naval commander on the morning of the 21st, that the first operation order of the Naval Division in the campaign was issued. The previous days had been spent in practising landing operations, in case of eventualities, and, with the issue of the detailed orders, nothing but calm weather was now needed for the operations to proceed. Unfortunately on the evening of the 21st a strong wind sprang up, and continued through the following day and night, with the result that the landing was postponed forty-eight hours.

On the 23rd, the day first planned for the landing, Rupert Brooke died; he was buried the same evening in an olive grove, some five thousand yards up the valley that runs northeast from the Beacon on the north shore of Trebuki Bay. There the curious, or the faithful, may find his resting-place marked by fragments of white marble piled above his grave by Charles Lister, Denis Browne, F. S. Kelly, Arthur Asquith, Bernard Freyberg and Patrick Shaw-Stewart. The news of his death was telegraphed to the Admiralty from Lemnos, and Mr. Winston Churchill's tribute in *The Times* of April 26th recalls across the years the position which Rupert Brooke filled in the eyes of thousands of his countrymen at a great crisis of their fate. The lapse of time and the nakedness of the literary horizon have only emphasized the truth of that striking tribute.

> Rupert Brooke is dead. A telegram from the admiral at Lemnos tells us that his life has closed at the moment when it seemed to have reached its springtime. A voice had become audible, a note had been struck, more true, more thrilling, more able to do justice to the nobility of our youth in arms engaged in this present war, than any other—more able to express their thoughts of self-surrender, and with a power to carry comfort to those who watched them so intently from afar. The voice has been swiftly stilled. Only the echoes and the memory remain; but they will linger.
>
> During the last few months of his life, months of preparation in gallant comradeship and open air, the poet-soldier told with all the simple force of genius the sorrow of youth about to die, and

the sure triumphant consolations of a sincere and valiant spirit. He expected to die; he was willing to die for the dear England whose beauty and majesty he knew; and he advanced towards the brink in perfect serenity, with absolute conviction of the rightness of his country's cause, and a heart devoid of hate for fellow men.

The thoughts to which he gave expression in the very few incomparable war-sonnets which he has left behind will be shared by many thousands of young men moving resolutely and blithely forward into this, the hardest, the cruellest, and the least-rewarded of all the wars that men have fought. They are a whole history and revelation of Rupert Brooke himself. Joyous, fearless, versatile, deeply instructed, with classic symmetry of mind and body, he was all that one would wish England's noblest sons to be in days when no sacrifice but the most precious is acceptable, and the most precious is that which is most freely proffered.

While the division was at Scyros, General Paris was asked to supply, for beach duties in connection with the impending landings, a further three hundred ratings with sea experience. These were drawn from the Hood and Howe Battalions, and the party, under Sub-Lieut. (later Lt.-Colonel) J. O. Dodge, R.N.V.R., left for Mudros the same day.

On the evening of the 24th the transports sailed north towards the peninsula. The transports of the 29th Division were at the same time moving out from Mudros Harbour, to the accompaniment of those enthusiastic cheers which echo now with so ironic a significance. With them, and in particular with the Plymouth and Anson Battalions, to whom, as it happened, fell the earlier share in the active operations, went the thoughts of all on board the Naval Division transports, as they steamed north to their solitary but peaceful rendezvous five miles west-south-west of Xeros Island.

The fleet of transports, escorted by H.M.S. *Canopus* (on board which were General Paris and his staff), *Dartmouth* (G.O.C. and the Staff Officer 2nd Naval Brigade), *Jed* and *Kennet,* reached the rendezvous at daylight; at 5.45 a.m. H.M.S. *Dartmouth* and *Doris* began a bombardment of the Bulair lines, which continued throughout the day; two hours later, Colonels Ollivant and Richardson on board H.M.S. *Kennet* carried out a detailed reconnaissance of landing-places on the north shore of the gulf. The *Kennet* was stood in close to shore, and was but once fired on—sustaining no casualties. All this time, the fleet of transports was lying ostentatiously in the background, but there was no evidence that the feint was being taken in any way seriously.

For the same evening, a more realistic enterprise was decided on, and a platoon of the Hood Battalion was ordered to effect a landing under cover of darkness, to light flares upon the beaches and shoot off machine guns and rifles, and, by great activity and in the manner of a stage army, impersonate a force many times their size, and thus to give the threatened invasion the hall-mark of reality. The fact that the fleet of transports had been demonstrating for several hours opposite the point to be invaded insured a warm if not cordial reception, which would in all probability spell disaster to the force involved. This was pointed out by Lt.-Commander Freyberg, who volunteered himself to swim alone to light flares upon the hostile shore. His bold offer was accepted.

The night was dark, with a touch of frost in the air, and there was a slight sea running in the Gulf of Xeros when Freyberg, painted black and greased to keep out the cold, was lowered into the water with a little canvas raft of flares. He was armed with a small revolver, with sheath knife slung round his waist, and wearing a small luminous wrist compass for direction in case the stars became obscured. A start was made at 10 p.m.; it was dark and unattractive, save for the phosphorescent splash from the muffled oars of the ship's boat. By some miscalculation, in the dark, of the distance, two miles had to be swum, and it was midnight before a landing was effected. The raft was hidden while a reconnaissance of the enemy position above the cliff was carried out.

Crawling about, naked, on an open and exposed cliff after two hours' swim on a cold, windy, April night was not a very cheerful occupation, but Freyberg was able, in spite of the noise from his chattering teeth, to get close up to the enemy trenches on the cliffs. After a few minutes of searching, the raft was recovered and the first flare was lighted on the beach. Immediately machine-gun fire was opened from the picket boats all round and the British war ships bombarded the beaches. Freyberg had to take refuge in the water to avoid fire, but swimming in the direction of the Bulair line, was able to light two other flares on the beaches, a quarter of a mile apart. When this had been accomplished the mission was at an end. The stars were all covered by clouds, and so, on a compass bearing due south, he made a start from the inhospitable shore, in the hope of being picked up in the dark by a destroyer or picket boat. The ships, of course, showed

154

no light, and there were no flashes from the guns, which were by now silent. It was a meagre chance; but after two hours' swimming Commander Freyberg was retrieved, cramped and nearly dead with cold.

The effect of these operations was substantial. As we have seen, there were four Turkish divisions on the peninsula; two were allocated to the defence of the Bulair lines, and two to the Southern defence systems hinging on Kilid Bahr and Achibaba. The headquarters of the Southern defensive system was at Maidos, of the Northern at Gallipoli. When the Naval Division feint began, the coast against which they were operating was in truth but lightly held. But no sooner had the transports been sighted, than one of the divisions based on Maidos was moved northwards, another was in held ready to join it, and General Liman van Sanders took up his post of command on a height near the central front of the Bulair lines. Not till nightfall did he even suspect that the operation was a feint—but by this time the landings which the reinforcement of the Southern force might have prevented had been achieved.

The story of these landings (Sir Ian Hamilton had decided on no less than five) must now be told.

★★★★★★

The enemy south of Achibaba held one well-sited line of trenches, strongly wired, which ran across the southern slopes of Achibaba in front of Krithia. This was his line of resistance. His outpost line, known to be held in force, consisted of still more elaborately wired earthwork defences on three small knolls which lay at intervals of about a mile from each other, and not more than 500 yards inland, on a line running roughly parallel with the southern coast of the peninsula from Cape Tekke to Sedd-el-bahr. Linked up with these defences, were advanced posts, guarding the only two beaches on the southern shore at which a landing could be anticipated. The first was the bay below Sedd-el-bahr, where the tall and precipitous cliffs give place for some 350 yards to a green amphitheatre of crumbled and grass-grown slopes, falling away to the sea and ending in undulating ridges of sand. The second was nearer the entrance to the Straits, west of Cape Helles, where the line of cliffs is broken by a small gully, opening on to a strip of beach 40 yards deep at its widest point, and the whole not more than 250 yards long. There were also small detachments watching Morto Bay and Gully Beach.

The main Turkish line on the slopes of Achibaba was our first objective. To enable an attack on this line to be developed effectively, the two main beaches must be stormed. Once the beaches were secured by the covering forces, further troops were to be landed, and the advance was to begin. To ensure the immediate success of this advance, a third landing was to be made at a small cove almost exactly on the left flank of the Turkish position. This force was to join in the pursuit of the Turks as they were dislodged, or in the preliminary attack, should any untoward event make it necessary. The finishing touch to the Turkish *débdcle* was to be given by two flanking parties, landed a couple of miles behind the Turkish position on either flank.

These parties, though small in numbers, were expected to harass the retreating Turk, and prevent anything like an orderly retirement. As the main line advanced, the flanking parties would join in the assault on the main Turkish position. The places selected for the landing of the flanking parties were the north of Morto Bay ("S" beach) in the Straits, an ideal landing-place for a small force, but impracticable for a large one because of its exposure to artillery fire from Asia; and "Y" beach on the Aegean shore. In the case of these two landings there was to be only a covering force: *i.e.,* no more troops were to be landed than those required to carry the position in the face of, what was expected to be, a very slight opposition.

The forces detailed for the five landings were as follows:

Main attack	" V " Beach	1st Dublin Fusiliers
		1st Munster Fusiliers
		2nd Hampshires
		" A " Coy. Anson Battalion
		1 Platoon " D " Coy. Anson Battalion
	" W " Beach	1st Lancashire Fusiliers
		4th Worcesters
		1st Essex
		" B " Coy. Anson Battalion
		Battalion H.Q. Anson Battalion
Subsidiary attack	" X " Beach	2nd Royal Fusiliers
		1st Inniskillings
		1st Border Regiment
		" D " Coy. Anson Battn. (less 1 Platoon)
		" C " Coy. Anson Battalion
Flanking parties	Morto Bay	2nd South Wales Borderers (less 1 Coy.)
	" Y " Beach	Plymouth Battalion R.M.L.I.
		1st K.O.S.B.
		1 Coy. 2nd S. Wales Borderers

BRIGADIER-GENERAL B. C. FREYBERG,
V.C. OF WELLINGTON. (IMPERIAL FORCES.)

The Morto Bay party landed without much opposition, and soon occupied three lines of trenches above de Tott's battery, which was evacuated by a small Turkish detachment. In this they were assisted by sailors and marines from the covering ship. Once safely established on shore, the detachment stood to its ground, waiting till some movement of the enemy should give them an opportunity for effective intervention without risking the loss of touch with their line of supply (and retreat). In this position the detachment was found when the line was finally advanced.

The "Y" Beach party met at first with little opposition; the actual landing was made from trawlers at 5.45 a.m. without covering fire, and the crest of the steep cliffs had been gained without loss by 6.30. Touch with the enemy was shortly obtained about 800 yards to the north, and a defensive flank was formed facing north-east, to the defence of which Lt.-Colonel Matthews, C.B., R.M.L.I., of the Plymouth Battalion (who was in command of the whole force) detailed two companies of the marines. The remainder of the force advanced to the east over a wide front. Crossing the deep Gully Ravine, when a few prisoners were taken, Colonel Matthews took up a position on a ridge running roughly parallel to it, a few hundred yards beyond.

Here, 300 Turkish infantry were seen moving south, and two field guns taking up a position east of Krithia. For two hours the forces remained unmolested and stationary, waiting for signs of the expected advance from the south. There were none. A further advance with this limited force was hardly practicable, if any touch was to be maintained with the left flank, and, as a Turkish attack in some force was expected, failing the success of the Southern landings, it was decided to withdraw to a defensive position covering the original landing-places, with the right flank only thrown forward across the gully, to give immediate support to any advance from the south. By 3 p.m. this withdrawal was completed, and at dusk, when the Turks first began to threaten the position, the right flank also was withdrawn to the shore. The new position was a rough semicircle, with each flank resting on the sea, and the centre thrown forward some five hundred yards. The marines held the flanks, each with two companies, and the K.O.S.B. and South Wales Borderers held the centre.

The decision to remain on the defensive was well-reasoned, and was indeed almost inevitable, having regard to the fact that, although Colonel Matthews had reported the unopposed landing to General Hunter Weston, he had received no acknowledgment and no information of the happenings at the other beaches.

It remains, however, true that a bolder policy would, in all human probability, have had far-reaching results; what those might have been will appear when we turn back to the more splendid, if more tragic, story of the operations which had been going on simultaneously on the southern shore of the peninsula.

As in the case of the other small detachments, the Royal Fusiliers landed at "X" beach without serious opposition. So effective, indeed, was the support afforded to the covering force by H.M.S. *Implacable* that the Turkish infantry lining the cliffs above the beach were driven back on their main position, while the infantry scaled the cliffs without a casualty. Immediately the heights had been made good, Colonel Newenham secured his left and front with half his battalion, and, holding one company in reserve, threw the other forward towards Hill 114, where he hoped to gain touch with the main landing force at "W" beach. He was met, instead, by a heavy and well-directed fire from an enemy clearly still in undisturbed possession.

There was nothing for it but to wait till the whole of his force was ashore, and then, instead of moving forward on Krithia, as he had hoped, to turn south-east to secure his flank. This set-back was, of course, a reaction from the partial check experienced at "W" beach, owing to the dominating position above Sedd-el-bahr being still in the hands of the enemy. The reason for this was that the landing at "V" beach had failed.

"V" beach was of all the beaches selected for landings the most suitable for defence. The beach itself was not more than ten yards wide, and edged by a small but perpendicular bank of sand not above five or six feet high: beyond, was a green amphitheatre rising over a gentle slope of some two hundred yards to a height of two hundred feet above the level of the sea. Not only was the whole beach commanded from Sedd-el-bahr Castle, but these green and peaceful slopes were themselves covered with trenches and dugouts invisible from the shore, and beyond reach of damage from the preliminary bombardment—for the dugouts were cut back in the slopes of the hill, and the trenches themselves so deep as to be immune from any save a plunging fire.

At the first hint of dawn, three companies of the Dublin Fusiliers and the 4th Platoon of the Anson Battalion (Lieutenant Denholm, R.N.V.R.) were disembarked from the sweepers, which had brought them from Mudros, and took their places in the boats, the whole force of six hundred men being borne in six tows (each made up of a pinnace and four cutters) in line abreast. On the right of the line of tows was the *River Clyde,* carrying the remaining company and the headquarters staff of the Dublins, the Munster Fusiliers, half the Hampshire Regiment, and Sub-Lieut. Tisdall's 18th Platoon of the Anson Battalion, accompanied by Lieut.-Commander Smallwood, R.N.V.R., the second in command of the battalion.

The *River Clyde* grounded almost at the same time as the men in the open boats reached the shallow waters, but, owing to the strength of the current, some delay occurred in fixing up the "bridge" of lighters. Meanwhile the Dublins, landing from open boats, had been almost annihilated.

★★★★★★

It was to assist in manning the numerous auxiliary craft (tugs, lighters, etc.), which had to play their part in this unprecedented operation of landing a modern army on a hostile beach from open boats, that the naval ratings from the Hood and Howe battalions had been lent to the navy. These ratings were scattered in small parties and had no independent task assigned to them. Sub-Lieut. Dodge was, however, appointed an assistant Naval Landing Officer at "V" beach and accompanied the Dublin Fusiliers in their first assault. He was wounded before reaching the shore, but remained on the beach throughout the 25th and until the afternoon of the 26th. He was subsequently awarded the D.S.C. for his services at this landing.

★★★★★★

Of three companies of this fine battalion, barely a hundred and fifty men reached the shore alive. A few of these, in the fury of their first attack, climbed the low ridge of sand which edged the lunch, and were seen to disappear into the ruins of Sedd-el-bahr. The rest clung desperately to the slender shelter of the sandbank, waiting.

Where was that tide of men which should have swept before now from the *River Clyde* to overwhelm the enemy by concentrated weight of numbers? Throughout the morning, indeed, the little company of the living below the sandbank, almost on the water's edge, were joined by others from the ship. (Among these was Lieut.-Commander Smallwood, R.N.V.R., who, like Sub-Lieut. Dodge, was wounded coming ashore but remained on the beach till late on the 20th). But they came only in ones and twos, through a hurricane of fire. For every man that stepped ashore from that floating bridge of lighters, six or seven had fallen as they crossed the short fifty yards which lay between the ship and the shore. The wounded fell most often from the lighters as they were hit, and lay in the clear waters, visible but beyond reach of help. The dead lay beside them, or on the lighters or by the water's edge. On that shore, and round the wreckage of those wounded boats, only the living were conspicuous.

Among the foremost of these, were Lieut.-Colonel Doughty Wylie and Captain Walford, who were to lead the desperate and successful assault on the following day, and whose monument, put up by the French in memory of a brilliant feat of arms, still stands, as it stood throughout the campaign, amid the ruins of Sedd-el-bahr. No less conspicuous were those officers and men of the navy who superintended the operations on the *River Clyde*. Keeping the landing parties between decks to avoid useless slaughter, Commander Unwin and his officers worked for continuous hours on the lighters and in the water, in the first instance making fast the bridge of boats, later repairing it, as the connecting hawsers were shot in half; later still, rescuing those of the wounded who had fallen above the water's edge or on to the lighters. Only now and then did their labours cease for a moment, when, in Commander Unwin's judgment, the time had come for another party to attempt the passage ashore. Then, without a moment's delay, the work of repair and rescue would begin again.

In the work of rescue Commander Unwin was assisted not only by all those under his immediate command, but also by Sub-Lieut. Tisdall's detachment of the Anson Battalion. Tisdall's heroism must have been noteworthy even on that day and at that place, for it was noted. The official account exploits, for which later he was awarded the Victoria Cross is as follows:

> During the landing from the S.S. *River Clyde* at 'V' beach in the Gallipoli Peninsula, Sub-Lieut. Tisdall, hearing wounded men on the beach calling for assistance, jumped into the water, and pushing a boat in front of him, went to their rescue. He was, however, obliged to obtain help, and took with him on two trips Leading Seaman Malia, and on other trips Chief Petty Officer Perring and Leading Seamen Curtiss and Parkinson. In all, Sub-Lieut. Tisdall made four or five trips between the ship and the shore, and was thus responsible for rescuing several wounded men under heavy and accurate fire.

> For their share in these gallant exploits C.P.O. Perring, the platoon

"V" BEACH LANDING, SEEN FROM THE "RIVER CLYDE",
11 A.M., APRIL 25TH, 1915

sergeant of Tisdall's platoon (promoted on the field a few days later to commissioned rank), Leading Seaman Malia and Leading Seaman Parkinson were awarded the Good Conduct Medal.

But no amount of individual gallantry could make good the heights of Sedd-el-bahr that day. It was clear that it was only under cover of darkness that sufficient troops could be landed to afford any chance of a successful assault. All that could be done was to keep down the Turkish fire, and prevent the enemy leaving their defences and annihilating the heroic survivors of the ill-fated assault. Even this was only made possible by the machine guns on the *River Clyde*.

"W" beach was longer and less deep than "V" beach, and was no less strongly defended. The two sides of the gully which runs down in the centre of the beach were as deeply entrenched as the amphitheatre at Sedd-el-bahr, and the entanglements actually low down to the water's edge. Moreover, there was no *River Clyde* to hold out the hope (though, as it turned out, a fallacious hope) of instant and overwhelming reinforcement to the detachments landing in open boats.

Nevertheless, the attack on the actual beach was instantly successful. The covering force (the 1st Battalion Lancashire Fusiliers), with whom were Lieut.-Colonel Moorhouse and his adjutant (Lieutenant Newman), with "B" Company of the Anson Battalion, approached the shore in four lines of cutters, eight abreast, towed by eight picket boats. When within a few yards of the beach, the tows were cast off and the boats rowed to the shore. Whether by a happy inspiration or by singular good fortune the boats on the left of the line diverged a little from the direct line of advance, and their occupants landed on a small ledge of rock immediately under the cliff at Tekke Burnu. Here they escaped the cross-fire which was brought to bear on other parts of the beach, and were able in their turn to assist the main assault by flanking fire; the warships also closed in and began an intensive bombardment.

Thus assisted, the main body of the Lancashire Fusiliers cut their way through the wire and collected under the cliffs at either side of the beach. There the companies were hastily reorganised and then led to the assault. By 9.30 a.m. the trenches up the gully were taken, and the beach was in our hands. In all this early fighting, the Anson platoons and the detachments from the Hood and Howe took part, and not until the heights had been gained were they reformed and assigned to their duties as beach parties, when their first tasks were to mount a guard on the Turkish prisoners, to clear the beach of wire, and to collect tools, ammunition and rifles from the casualties. In the course of the first hour's fighting, Sub-Lieut. T. F. Melland, R.N.V.R., was wounded.

The capture of "W" beach gave the army by 9.30 a.m. a temporary security of tenure on the peninsula, for at least the remaining battalions of the 29th Division could be landed; but an advance on Krithia was impossible, for, as things were, it was necessary first to reduce from "W" beach the prepared positions on the Turkish left centre and left, which should, on the original plan, have been penetrated by the forces detailed for the "V" beach landing. Unfortunately, even the gallantry of the Worcester and Essex Regiments, who had arrived to the support of the Lancashire Fusiliers in the firing line by 10 a.m., proved unequal to this task. Though the twin positions of Hill 114 on the left and Hill 138 on the right of "W" beach were in our hands by 4.30 p.m., the heavy fighting had taken a grievous toll of casualties, and, with tired troops, a further advance was judged impossible. In the result the Turks remained in possession of the heights of Sedd-el-bahr.

Thus the night of the 25th found the detachments at Morto Bay and "Y" beach still exposed to independent attack, and the main force in the south still unable to advance from the shore. Daylight, the aimed fire of ships' guns and reinforcements were necessary to any further attempt against Sedd-el-bahr. Could the flanking parties hold their ground no long without support? Could the main body maintain itself where it was until dawn? And what of the heroic survivors of the ill-fated "V" beach landing? Could this small party, crouching still under the shelter of the sand hills only a hundred yards or so from the water's edge, protected only by the naval machine guns on the *River Clyde,* be reinforced during the night, so that they could attack with any hope of success at dawn on the 26th?

On such a scene of tragic anxiety and suffering fell the brief twilight of the Eastern evening. The isolation of the scene was, indeed, a thing for pity. In Egypt were the troops whose presence would have made the landing a sure and swift success. On the *Albion,* with his staff, was the commander-in-chief, held to his post of command, without news, without even a sight of the newly-won positions. And on these stricken shores, where the dead were being buried with that hurried and tremulous silence so much more eloquent of human limitations than any funeral panegyric, the scattered relics of twelve battalions were keeping a ceaseless vigil. Till light came, they were beyond reach of the fleet, with no supports behind them but the Anson beach com-

VIEW FROM THE BRIDGE OF THE "RIVER CLYDE", EARLY AUTUMN, 1915

panies, and in front of them the whole strength of the enemy, able in darkness to mass unobserved and fall perhaps in overwhelming strength on any point which he might choose.

Throughout the whole of the day, the men of the Anson Battalion on "W" beach had been occupied without interval in the unloading of stores, the transport of ammunition and water to the firing line and the burying of the dead. The company which had shared in the first assault had been reinforced during the morning by three more platoons of "A" Company (diverted from "V" beach), under Lt.-Commander Peter McCirdy, and with this party came the Reverend H. C. Foster, the Chaplain to the 2nd Naval Brigade, the first Anglican Chaplain to land on the peninsula. Now when night fell, this small party found themselves the only reserves available on "W" beach in case of a Turkish counter-attack. No less wearing, no less responsible, was the lot of "C" and "D" Companies of the Anson (Lt.-Commander Gordon Grant, D.S.C., and Lieut. Spencer Warwick) at "X" beach.

To attempt to rest within sight of the lights from the firing line, to wake up to a noise of rapid fire only a few hundred yards away, to hear shells passing over you, or dropping round you, and to know nothing, except that your company or battalion may be called at any moment for any duty, and that, unless you rest, you may not be ready when the time comes—that was the everyday experience of the regimental officer for many weeks throughout the campaign. How far more wearing the experience of the beach parties on that first night, when the firing line was barely two hundred yards away, when there were no reserves, when the dead were as yet unburied and the wounded unattended, when there was no place to lie in, which was not under rifle fire, when, through the thinly-held line of shallow trenches, manned by tired men and with but few senior officers surviving, might pour down upon the beach without more than a moment's warning the whole force of the enemy.

It was, indeed, almost a relief when, in the middle of the night, the expected attack took place, and cries for ammunition came down from above. Soon the whole Anson detachments were in the firing line, and the beaches were left to the chaplains, the doctors, the wounded and the dead. The scene in the firing line was less terrifying than the desolation of the beaches. True, the trenches were wide and shallow, there was no wire and no cover; but to troops fighting their first night-battle the risk of death is less alarming than the sense of isolation, the feeling of ignorance, the harassing fear of the unknown.

The Turkish attack was, in fact, not made in force. Skilled beyond all other European armies, except our own, in the art of rapid fire, the Turks attacked more often than not as a measure of defence. Their method throughout the first months of the Gallipoli campaign was to open up and maintain an almost unbelievable volume of fire, generally high, but sufficiently well directed to make close or prolonged observation from the front line a matter of extreme danger. Under cover of what was in effect a formidable barrage, small parties would go forward, and attempt to enter our lines.

The chief damage done by these tactics was in the back areas, where the ceaseless fusillade of "overs" exacted a nightly toll of casualties among working parties, ration parties, and reliefs on the beaches, or, later on, in the cullies. So it was on this first night, and the somewhat alarmist reports which reached the beaches, and from thence no doubt percolated to General Headquarters, were probably due rather to the unexpected nature of the Turkish tactics than to the severity of the actual attacks.

The force at "Y" beach was subjected to much the same tactics, though carried out with greater success. We have seen that Colonel Matthews had completed his retirement to the cliff by 6 p.m. on the 25th. No sooner had he done so than a strong force of Turks came into action against his left and centre, having taken up a position some three hundred yards away from our line in the dense scrub. Heavy rifle fire began at dusk, and, owing to the semicircular position which had to be taken up, the effect was unusually severe, the fire directed from the left of the position at effective range not only taking toll of the marines guarding the left flank, but taking the marine companies on the right in reverse.

As soon as darkness came down, the Turks, under cover of their cross rifle fire, made repeated attempts, as usual in small groups, to break through our line, and the K.O.S.B. in the centre were heavily engaged for some hours. The crowning horror of the scene was the fate of the wounded, who, having been taken to a position half-way down the cliff, were attacked (whether with a calculated disregard of the laws of war and humanity or in the confusion of the night-battle) by a party of Turks, who crawled through the thick scrub on the cliff face and came in behind our lines. Meanwhile, the rifle fire from the main enemy position took constant toll of the front-line troops, who were compelled, by the daring of the Turkish patrols working in and out of the scrub to expose themselves almost continuously. Time and again, these patrols would get into our line, only to be driven out again at the point of the bayonet. Only once, at 5.30 a.m. on the 26th, was a serious breach effected. This, as often happens, was at the junction of two units, the K.O.S.B. and the left-flank companies of the marines, but the line was soon restored by a counter-attack, in which Lieut. F. C. Law, R.M.L.I., took a distinguished part. (In the fighting of this night, Lieut. J. F. May, R.M.L.I., of the Plymouth Battalion, was killed).

This was the final thrust. In the half-light before dawn, the Turks, who had suffered probably nearly as heavily as the invading force, withdrew to a distance, and only the shelling served as a reminder to the tired troops of the horrors of the night. But by now supplies were short, the force had lost a third of their slender effectives (less than two thousand rifles to start with), the K.O.S.B. had lost most of their senior officers, and the experience of the night had made it clear that, failing support from the south, the position could not be maintained without reinforcements, at least not without ammunition and water. Accordingly, at 7.30 a.m., Colonel Matthews signalled his appreciation of the situation to the covering ship, suggesting at the same time a withdrawal, if it should be impossible to replenish his supplies.

It was in answer to this signal that boats at once left for the beach, and simultaneously the right flank and centre, *i.e.,* the K.O.S.B., the company of the South Wales Borderers, and two companies of the marines were ordered to the beach to re-embark. Colonel Matthews, who was on the extreme left at the time, was unaware of what was taking place until the re-embarkation was almost completed. In his judgment, however, a withdrawal was necessary, failing reinforcements and supplies, and having throughout the operations received no message from General Hunter Weston, he withdrew with the remaining companies of marines some two hours later, after collecting and embarking the wounded. By 9.30 a.m. on the 26th, "Y" beach, so gallantly held against the most desperate attacks, was abandoned to a defeated enemy.

Sir Ian Hamilton himself assumed that orders for the retirement, of which he was an irritated eye-witness, had been issued by General Hunter Weston. General Hunter Weston, however, was not responsible for a decision which was defended by Lt.-Colonel Matthews at the time, and subsequently before the Dardanelles Commission.

But if the night of April 25th-26th brought to weary troops at Cape Helles and "Y" beaches their first and, therefore, their most terrifying experience of the Turkish night attack, and if the dawn saw the inexplicable end of the adventure of Colonel Matthews' force, the gathering darkness on the 25th brought a welcome interval of relief to the sorely-tried forces at Sedd-el-bahr, and the dawn of the 26th witnessed their final and amazing triumph.

Under cover of darkness, and perhaps also because the enemy were already preparing for the inevitable retreat, the remaining troops on the *River Clyde* came ashore without loss, and took up a position, marked down during the day as affording the best cover available, under the shattered earthworks of the old castle on the extreme right of the beach. Here they were joined by the survivors of the first landing, who crawled across the enemy's front under cover of the ridge of sand which had sheltered them through the day. At daybreak the force advanced to the assault assisted by a heavy fire from the ships, and, capturing the village, the old castle and the dominating Hill 141 in a succession of brilliant, if costly, open order skirmishes, were in possession of the entire position by 2 p.m. The retreating Turks, retiring through the wooded country round Morto Bay, suffered heavily from the fire of the *Albion,* off Sedd-el-bahr, and of the *Lord Nelson,* keeping watch over the Morto Bay detachment.

Now was the time for an advance. But the beaches behind our line were bare of reinforcements, and, of the slender force which had been landed, nearly half were supplementing the efforts of the Anson beach parties in getting stores, ammunition and water ashore. In these circumstances, it appeared a regrettable necessity to wait for fresh troops and more supplies, and to allow an opportunity for rest to the 29th Division before a further advance. It was decided to devote most of the day to the disembarkation of the French at "V" beach, where Lt.-Colonel Moorhouse and the rest of the Anson Battalion had now landed as a beach party. The commander-in-chief decided at the same time to release, from his slender reserve, the Drake Battalion of the Naval Division. Orders to this effect reached General Paris in the Gulf of Xeros at 1 p.m., and the Drake sailed for Cape Helles at once.

The landing of this battalion, at 8.30 p.m. on April 26th, was in its way as significant as were the heroic landings of the day before. The beaches had been hardly won; even now the line lay only a few hundred yards inland, and it was but thinly held by tired men. But the separate and organised life of the beaches was already beginning. From this night onward, at least until the end of the July battles, the same scene was to repeat itself. The army which was not sufficiently prepared for victory was showing itself as ever impenetrably armed against defeat. The staff, which failed for so long to reduce order out of chaos in the peaceful atmosphere of Mudros, turned the battlefield of the Lancashire landing into a tolerable office while the shells were still falling and the dead were still unburied.

This was the night of the transition. From now onward the nightly scene on "W" beach was one of silent but ceaseless activity. As dusk fell, the sweepers would come in from Mudros, and would be directed by signal from the shore to their allotted anchorage, or, if their draught allowed, to a berth alongside one of the floating piers improvised already from the wreckage of lighters and ships' boats, and strengthened with every unconvincing but effective device which sailors and engineers could concoct without material of any kind. As soon as the sweepers were made fast, staff officers of the different departments would come on board and receive reports of the troops and stores. Then, while any troops would be brought ashore and handed over by the military landing officer to guides from their own formations, beach parties would go on board to unload stores and dispose of them under orders of the different administrative officers.

Meanwhile, it would be bitterly cold for troops called on, within a few hours, to exchange the meretricious comfort of a passenger ship for the sombre desolation of the very edge of a battlefield. It was this sudden change, unparalleled in any other campaign of the present war, a change singularly dramatic, which so heightened the impression left by the first night on the peninsula. For, on the very edge of those indifferent waters, there remained to the end the wreckage of boats and stores; the once green slopes of the gully which closed the view were scarred with trenches and shell holes, and worn to the colour and substance of dust by the ceaseless passage of men. Here and there were gathered in pitiful heaps rifles and equipment, salvage from the wounded and the dead, and amid this wreckage, across the sand still strewn here and there with the remains of rusted entanglements, men moved about with that brisk solemnity which one meets but seldom beyond range of the guns, which contrasts so markedly with the lackadaisical formalism of the base. In the near distance, indeed, could be heard, almost every night for the first four months of the campaign, the ceaseless rifle fire of the Turks, and, occasionally, the sound of artillery bombardment, brought very close by the proximity of our heavy guns.

Of the extent of ground which, in fact, separated the beach from the firing line after the very first days of the campaign, nothing could be guessed by the newly-arrived troops, who could see no further than the sloping walls of the gully, honeycombed with dugouts. No wonder that, at the first glance, the narrow beach seemed the embodiment of desolation, a strange wilderness peopled by flitting figures stumbling against each other sometimes in the darkness, but more usually moving about with the precision of ghosts in a world of shades. And this was no idle fancy, for under the sand and up the sides of the gully many men were buried, and an impalpable atmosphere of death and decay was in the very air men breathed.

THE MAY BATTLES

The situation south of Achibaba on the morning of the 27th April was a curious one. We held the Turkish outpost line, linking up the three small hills overlooking the entrance to the Straits. On the beaches at Cape Helles and Sedd-el-bahr we were busy disembarking not only the stores and guns of the 29th Division but also the French Expeditionary Force, whose operations at Kum Kale, brilliantly executed and maintained for as long as was necessary, were now at an end. For two miles in front of our line was an open plain, clear of the enemy as far as the eye could see; our advance over this plain must moreover be effectively covered from the left flank by the guns of the fleet, and from the right by the flanking force north of Morto Bay. Seeing our troops sitting (or more often standing at their ease) in the shallow trenches overlooking this wide stretch of open and undefended country, an inexperienced observer landing in the peninsula for the first time on this day must have wondered at the stories he had heard of the bitter fighting of the preceding forty-eight hours.

When, at 4 p.m., the French having come into line on the right of the 29th Division, an unopposed advance carried our line forward a distance of no less than two miles, his wonder must have increased. The campaign south of Achibaba, which had threatened throughout the 25th to end in disaster, seemed indeed to have taken an almost miraculous turn for the better. No little wonder that, to the short-sighted, April 28th was expected to see our troops entrenched on our first objective. Little less is it to be wondered at that critics who look back on this period of the campaign in the light of subsequent events have actually been found to suggest that the Turks were anxious for us to consolidate our position, and land our guns, stores and reinforcements, if only to ensure that we thus committed ourselves to wasting our strength in a subsequently fruitless struggle,

The explanation of the dramatic advance of the 27th is, however, simple. The Turks had planned two positions south of Achibaba. The first was on the lower slopes of the hill covering Krithia, with their left resting on the Kereves Dere (a deep ravine running, roughly, across our front, inland from a point on the shore of the Straits a mile and a half north of Morto Bay). The second was the line commanding the beaches, a line which we had finally captured at dawn on the 26th. The average distance between the two lines was about four and a half miles. There is no valid reason for thinking that our capture of the first position was anything but a great military victory, the truth being that the enemy was thus committed to a defensive campaign in barren and inhospitable country which must last as long as we wished, and which must, while it lasted, prove a disastrous drain on those resources which he had hoped to employ in a decisive offensive. In these circumstances, our initial success decided the enemy to retire as soon as might be on to his second prepared position at Krithia, rather than risk his as yet slender forces by standing on an intermediate position, the defence of which might prove more costly.

This was only elementary military commonsense. But there was a further consideration, equally important to the enemy: this was time. He had been perilously delayed in his concentration by the Bulair and the Kum Kale demonstrations. The forces ultimately available for garrisoning the Krithia defences were not as yet south of Achibaba. Moreover, the Krithia defences were incomplete. It was necessary accordingly to delay our advance as far as possible with a skeleton force. For this, the country for nearly two miles in front of our line of the 26th was unsuitable, and so our advance on the 27th was unopposed; the remainder of the ground might, on the contrary, have been designed for delaying actions.

A line drawn from Gully beach to de Tott's Battery would show roughly our position on the morning of April 28th. Behind us was open plain, unsuitable for our communications. In front of us, the country up to the lower slopes of Achibaba was far less open and was split by three gullies down which mountain streams flowed in winter from the heights of Achibaba; of these gullies, the widest and deepest, known as Gully Ravine, runs down parallel to the western coast of the peninsula, till it opens out abruptly to the sea at Gully beach, midway between "X" and "Y" beaches. The others, known as the Krithia and Achibaba Nullahs, divide the rest of the peninsula into three roughly equal sectors, until they open out into the plain, at the point reached by us on the evening of the 27th. These gullies were the key to the Turkish tactics. They provided covered communications through which their rearguards, undetected by our infantry, unassailable by the fleet, could harass any further daylight advance.

The unexpected ease of our progress on the 27th, might have been expected to give, and perhaps gave, a clue to the enemy plans. The country in front of us should certainly have confirmed our suspicions if we had had any. The forces opposed to us must moreover be slender; the strength of the Turks at Anzac and other information from prisoners told us that. Yet in spite of all we rested on our gains on the early evening of the 27th, and prepared an elaborately staged "attack" for 8 a.m. on the 28th. The argument for a daylight advance of a formal character was that the losses in officers made a night advance unsafe. If, however, there was a chance of reaching Achibaba before the enemy's reserves were concentrated, we must get in touch with his main body at once, and defeat it. The question was whether a frontal attack in daylight, across country perfectly adapted for a delaying action conducted with the minimum of force, was the most likely method of achieving this result.

The course of the battle (in which the Drake Battalion attached to the 87th Brigade was the only battalion of the Naval Division to be engaged), suggests only one answer. The attacking force consisted from left to right of the 87th Brigade, the 88th Brigade and five French battalions. In reserve was the 86th Brigade. At 8 a.m. the battle opened.

As on a-field day, the front battalions advanced in open order by short rushes, their bayonets glistening in the sun. The supporting battalions followed in artillery formation. The Turks offered, at first, no resolute resistance to that part of the advance which lay over open ground, covered by the ships' guns, and the left flank advanced at the outset for a mile or so, over the high, hilly ground on either side of Gully Ravine. In the centre, however, the 88th Brigade made slower progress on a front which included the narrower Krithia and Achibaba Nullahs, and on the right, the French, trying to fight up the steepish slope that leads to the Kereves Dere, were checked at the start. Even on the left, the Turks advanced more than once to counter-attack, and elsewhere their rearguards took a heavy toll of our troops, from positions mostly concealed in the long grass and scrub.

The defence is brilliantly organised. In and out of the gullies are little concealed trenches, cunningly sited. We take one; it is commanded by another. Where are the men to take the next? Another company comes up, and takes it, only to find it empty; but the rifle and machine-gun fire still takes its toll, the performance has to be repeated again and again, and yet, in as costly a battle as many first-class engagements on the Western front, many in the centre and on the right never see a Turk. All this time we have been advancing on the left, but the line has become thin, and now the Turks, heartened by their success in the centre, come on again.

Then orders come to Commander Campbell to take the Drake through the 87th Brigade, with the South Wales Borderers, and reinforce the firing line. This much they do, but the advance is at a standstill. In the centre the line is thinning, and the 86th Brigade, the shattered but still heroic battalions of the landing, have been thrown in. Scattered parties of the Munster Fusiliers even come up against the Krithia defences, but a fighting patrol is not a match for an army corps in prepared, albeit incomplete, positions; the isolated units fall back, and when they retreat the Drake and the South Wales Borderers can do no more than stand fast. For there are no reserves. One fresh division at least, almost certainly two, are wanted.

We dug in on the night of the 28th-29th on a line nearly a mile beyond the gully on the left, but bending back to our original position in the centre and on the left. It was the first of those "tomorrows" which were to see us entrenched on Achibaba. It was the most hopeless and the least successful. No sooner, indeed, were we dug in, than the Turks drove back the French on the right almost to Sedd-el-bahr, and two Drake companies had to be withdrawn from the firing line to guard General Hunter Weston's headquarters above "W" beach. So little had we broken the Turkish resistance.

★★★★★★

With them went Commander Campbell; Major Barker, R.M.L.I, (the adjutant), was left in command in the front line. This fine officer was unfortunately killed by a shell during the night.

★★★★★★

While the battle of the 28th was in progress, the remainder of the R.N.D. transports were ordered to Gaba Tepe to disembark the Marine Brigade (Brigadier-General C. Trotman, R.M.L.I.) and the 1st Naval Brigade (Brigadier-General D. Mercer, R.M.L.I.). These brigades, each only two battalions strong (for the Plymouth and Drake Battalions remained with the Anson attached to the 29th Division), were to reinforce the Australian and New Zealand Army Corps. (The story of the early days at Anzac and the doings of these brigades is told in the next chapter).

The losses at Cape Helles in the attack of the 28th made the reinforcements of that front no less imperative; and as soon as the disembarkations at Anzac were completed (by about 3 p.m. on the 29th) the transports were ordered back to Cape Helles for the disembarkation there of the Divisional and 2nd Brigade Headquarters, and the Hood and Howe Battalions. At the same time was disembarked the bearer sub-division of 3rd Field Ambulance under Surgeon Rivers, R.N. The 2nd Brigade was now concentrated under Commodore Backhouse, R.N., and was placed in corps reserve under General Hunter Weston; the Drake and Plymouth Battalions were assigned to beach duties, and General Paris temporarily had no executive responsibilities. This was a disappointment for the division. It was also the deliberate, though inevitable, throwing away of a fighting organisation, which, had circumstances allowed of its employment as a whole on the southern front immediately after the first landing, might possibly have helped to achieve an historic success.

The fighting value of the division for subsequent operations was inevitably weakened by the decisions taken on April 28th and 29th. By the time it was re-formed, many officers, many men, had become casualties, yet the sacrifices made had gone but a little way to the formation of a fighting tradition. The tradition came in time, but if it is asked why the Naval Division never in Gallipoli achieved the same reputation which it held later in France, the answer is, not that it was better trained in 1916 than in 1915 (it was, but not relatively to other new divisions), but that the fruits of its first period of training at Blandford were never gathered,

but scattered to the winds at the bidding of an imperious necessity which was imposed on the Dardanelles army by the superior tactics of the enemy. He had succeeded in countering our strategy by fighting south of Achibaba a series of brilliantly effective rearguard actions, and so preventing the junction of the two halves of our force. Our failure in this respect carried with it the division of our slender, and therefore indivisible, reserve.

The release of the remaining battalions of this reserve to reinforce General Hunter Weston had not been premature, for on the night of May lst-2nd the great Turkish counter-attack against our southern line was launched. Abandoning their usual tactics, presumably because of the failure of our advance on the 28th and the consequent easing off of our pressure, the Turks came on with determination, their first line without ammunition that they should rely solely on the bayonet.

The 2nd Naval Brigade were bivouacking at this time among the derelict trenches taken from the Turks in the first advance from "W" beach. This was the corps reserve line. The Turkish attack broke out at 10.30 p.m., and the brigade, called out by the brigade-major, Lt.-Colonel Maxwell, at once moved off. The Anson Battalion was sent up independently to support the French on the extreme right of the line, and the Hood and Howe Battalions went into support trenches across the Achibaba Nullah. Thus it was, on this night, that Commodore Backhouse established his headquarters for the first time at (or at least near) the point in the *nullah* known throughout the campaign as Backhouse Post, and that the men of the Naval Division for the first time set their feet in that strange valley, which was to be the scene of so many of their more laborious exploits, of so much tragedy and suffering, of sacrifices so freely exacted.

Along that mile and a half of scrub and heather was already formed the dusty track which runs from Skew Bridge, when the bed of the mountain stream turns north to Achibaba, past Backhouse Post, and into the glade beyond. Across the glade, not halfway up, and on the higher ground to the left, where the 86th Brigade was standing fast against the Turkish attack, the front line now lay. The shelling and the rifle and machine-gun fire was heavy still, the trenches afforded but little cover, and the casualties were considerable. By dawn, however, the front was quiet, and only small bodies of the enemy could be seen falling back on a wide stretch of front. With the exception of Cox's Indian Brigade, just landed, all the reserves had been drawn into the line, which even then was but thinly held; but it was decided to counter-attack, and at 10 a.m. the whole line moved forward.

The essential conditions of success were lacking, and the Hood and Howe Battalions found themselves engaged in a futile and hopeless task. Advancing up the gully, and on the left, with the greatest resolution, their casualties made it essential to dig in, if at all, not more than four hundred yards in advance of the old position. Seeing them halt and not knowing the reason, a general some distance behind the line sent up reinforcements. These were the 2nd Hampshire Regiment, and this fine battalion came up under heavy fire with a smartness and precision which was a remarkable example, not lost on the Naval battalions, of the power of discipline and training to rise superior to the most disastrous conditions.

As they came up, however, the enemy artillery not unnaturally increased their activity, and Lt.-Colonel Quilter had no alternative but to order the Hood to fall back. The Hampshires retired at the same time and for the same reason. The Howe Battalion conformed. What such an order means to men fighting their first fight in the open is not hard to imagine. It is pleasant to recall that Charles Lister, who was wounded in this unfortunate engagement, was able to write home that the men in his brigade "showed great steadiness for raw troops." Much good work was done also by the bearer subdivision of the 3rd Field Ambulance, and by Surgeon Shaw and Sergeant Roberts (C section) in particular, in withdrawing the wounded from the advanced position. But Sir Ian Hamilton has written the true epitaph of this operation, which came to an inconclusive end along the whole British front, when he says it "was half heroic, half lamentable."

In the evening of the 2nd, the naval battalions were withdrawn to their bivouacs on "W" beach, near the Drake Battalion; but on the night of the 3rd the Turks renewed their attack on the French, and the Anson was again called on to go to the support of their extreme left flank. In this position they stayed throughout the 3rd and 4th, fighting continuously and doing much to restore the confidence of the French native troops, who had not as yet got acclimatised to the strange conditions. For their fine work with the Anson at this time, Lieut. Davidson and Lieut. Warwick were awarded the D.S.C. The part played by the Anson Battalion in the first days of the campaign has not received due recognition. They had been fighting at this time almost continuously since the landings, in three of which they had taken part, and in the intervals had been employed on fatigue duties. If their share in the heavy fighting of April 25th had been less arduous than that of the 29th Division, their intervals of leisure since then had been even fewer.

On the 5th, the Anson was withdrawn from the front line trenches, but neither for this nor for the other naval battalions was there any rest in store. After the fruitless attacks of May 2nd, 3rd and 4th,[3] General Liman von Sanders decided to revert to the defensive, and the result was soon evident in numerous working parties busily strengthening the Krithia line throughout the 4th and 5th. (It was during the fighting on this day that Lieutenant M. D. Campbell, R.N.V.R., of the Howe Battalion, was killed). In these circumstances, it was decided to make one more effort to reach and engage the main body of the enemy before they were finally secure in their defences. To reinforce the British troops, seriously depleted by casualties, an Australian and

177

a New Zealand Brigade were brought from Anzac to Cape Helles. These two Brigades, and a Composite Brigade consisting of the Drake and Plymouth Battalions of the Naval Division and the 1st Lancashire Fusiliers, under the command of Lt.-Colonel Casson, C.M.G., were formed into a Composite Division operated by the Naval Division staff and under the command of General Paris: a brigade of the 42nd Division (arriving from Egypt, but not yet concentrated) was attached to the 29th Division, and the 2nd Naval Brigade, under Commodore Backhouse, was lent to General D'Amade. The Composite Division, less the Composite Naval Brigade, and Cox's Indian Brigade were placed in reserve; the troops for the attack were the 29th Division (with the Brigade of the 42nd Division attached) on the left, the Composite Naval Brigade in the centre, and the French Expeditionary Corps (with the 2nd R. N. Brigade attached) on the right.

This was a stronger attacking line with more adequate reserves than on April 28th. But it must have been expected that the enemy would be reinforced to an equal extent, and they were known to have strengthened their defences. Moreover, the problem which faced us on the 28th, the problem, of dealing with the scattered enemy rearguards without exposing our whole force to merciless fire from concealed machine guns, still remained for solution; although we had now a few more guns, we had not sufficient to put down anything in the nature of an intensive bombardment in depth. Nevertheless, the orders for the battle as planned for May 6th, gave the main enemy position in front of Krithia as the first objective only, and actually contemplated two further phases. In the second, the 29th Division on the left was to push forward to two hills to the west and north-west of Krithia, and so enforce a Turkish retreat from Krithia itself. In the third, the whole force was to close in on Achibaba from west, south-west and south simultaneously.

We read these orders with a certain surprise.

Sir Ian Hamilton had suggested (as before the battle of the 28th) that the advance should be made at night, or, at any rate, that the troops should be led to assembly positions in advance of the line held by them, with a view to an attack at dawn. The corps commander was determined, however, on a daylight operation, though half an hour's spasmodic bombardment from some fifty eighteen-pounders was all that could be afforded: the plea was the shortage of regular officers and of trained troops. The plea was perhaps hardly adequate, for, if it was impossible to make even a local advance by night because of the inexperience of the troops, why should daylight (with its accompaniment of aimed fire) enable the same officers and men to achieve the spectacular success which the orders foreshadowed ?

The battle opened at 11 a.m., the first advance being made by the French on the right and the 29th Division on the left, and in the centre, up the Achibaba (right centre) and Krithia (left centre) Nullahs, by the Composite Naval Brigade, under General Paris's orders, and the 2nd R. N. Brigade, under the orders of General D'Amade. The 2nd Brigade was originally intended to advance merely in support of the French, but, at the last minute, a change was made, and on the French left the Hood and Anson Battalions (with which was one platoon of "A" Company Howe, under Lt.-Commander Waller, who did excellent work throughout the day) and the French infantry advanced in alternate lines. On the Composite Brigade front, the advance was carried out by the 1st Lancashire Fusiliers (attached from the 29th Division), the orders being for the Drake (and, if necessary, the Plymouth Marines) to follow up any advance, and consolidate the ground gained.

By 12.30, the Hood and Anson Battalions reported an advance of 600 yards, and had passed the Turkish advanced trenches by the White House; the Lancashire Fusiliers had made slower progress, owing to shrapnel fire and the necessity for keeping in touch, not only with the 2nd Naval Brigade, but with the 88th Brigade. On the extreme left of our line little or no progress had been made, and the French advance was also disappointing. By 8 p.m. the advance, which at no point had got near the Turkish main positions, seemed to be everywhere held, and at 3.30 p.m. the Hood and Anson were definitely ordered by General D'Amade not to advance further, as the rest of the force could make no progress along the Kereves Dere ridge. An hour and a half later the whole line received the same orders, and the Drake went forward to dig in on a line joining the Hood left with the 29th Division right.

This was done and a gap which had existed for some hours between the Lancashire Fusiliers and the 88th Brigade was reported as filled by the Drake at 8 p.m. Fighting between the French and the 29th Division, the Naval Battalions, in their first serious engagement, had actually achieved the most substantial advance recorded, and could look forward with confidence to the renewal of the battle. But from a wider standpoint the day's fighting was disappointing. An Army Corps had been easily held by the Turkish outposts, and we were not yet within striking distance of their main position. The Naval Brigade had encountered plenty of opposition at long range, but each position when reached had been found to be empty, and no connected position had been captured or even approached.

And yet, though the losses had been heavy and the strain severe, the attack must continue.

The next day, the advance began on the left only and, after fluctuating fortunes, looked like failing definitely by 8 p.m. In these circumstances, a general attack was ordered, the New Zealand Brigade being detached for the purpose from the Composite Division and sent over to the extreme left, where our failure had been most complete. The 2nd Naval Brigade under General D'Amade and the Composite Naval Brigade under General Paris had each the same task in this attack, to keep in touch with each other and with the flanks. The Composite Brigade had had this task before it all day, and, with the object of rendering it simpler, had been reorganised with the 1st Lancashire Fusiliers next to the 88th Brigade and the Drake on the right next to Commodore Backhouse's Brigade (who now held their front with the Howe and Anson, the Hood being in reserve). Commander Campbell was in charge of the Composite Brigade front line.

The new attack opened at 4.45 and, except again on the extreme left, met with some success. The French progress, however, along the Kereves Dere ridge was slow, and no substantial advance was possible for the Naval or Composite Brigades. The Lancashire Fusiliers' front was indeed, in the end, 300 yards in rear of that of the 88th Brigade when the fighting died down at sunset; the gap was covered by machine guns. The net result of the day's fighting was a slight advance by the French and the 2nd Naval Brigade, and a gain of some 300 yards by the right and centre of the 29th Division: between that Division and the Naval Brigade was the Composite Brigade. Throughout a long and trying day, Commander Campbell had been responsible for maintaining communication between the two forces advancing unequal distances at different times, and, for his successful conduct of this inconspicuous but essential operation he was awarded the D.S.O. on the recommendation of the Composite Brigade commander.

The dawn of May 8th saw yet another advance attempted, and repulsed on our left. The outlook was dark, especially as the French professed themselves for tactical reasons unable to undertake a further attack until the British had achieved a distinct advance; but the battle thus launched was not to be allowed to close with so signal a defeat.

To offer battle may have been premature; but once offered it must be fought to a finish, and Sir Ian Hamilton determined to throw in the last of his reserves, the Australian Brigade, so as to help the French. If the left flank could not advance (though one further effort was to be made, this time by the 87th Brigade), the right must be securely lodged on the Kereves Dere ridge before the troops could rest on their gains.

The final assault was ordered for 5 p.m., the main attack to be delivered by the comparatively fresh Australian Brigade of General Paris's Division in the centre, with the 29th Division and the New Zealand Brigade on the left, and the French on the right. This time only a quarter of an hour's bombardment was possible, but at last the pertinacity of the commander and the finer endurance of the troops met with their reward. Well might the Turks, called on to resist four general attacks in two days, presume that they had broken their enemy's will to victory. But they presumed in vain. As ever the allied armies were as irresistible in the face of defeat as they were ineffective in the organisation of victory.

The chief honour of the fight went to the Australians and the French, the former advancing, with an impetuous courage which recalled and explained the "Anzac" landing, for a distance of at least 600 yards, while the latter swarmed up the southern face of the Kereves Dere ridge, capturing the redoubt which had held them up for nearly three days and consolidating the position on which (though it would have cheered few to realise it at the time) our right flank was to rest throughout the campaign. But the Naval and Composite Brigades had their part to play. The Hood and Howe Battalions, advancing behind the French, came up into line with and prolonged their left, and two companies of the Drake Battalion, under Lieut. Cherry, R.N.V.R., closed the gap between them and the Australians at a critical moment when at 8.15 p.m., the Turks were breaking through in force. At 1.15 a.m., the Plymouth Marines were moved up and came into line between the Drake Battalion and the Australians.

Throughout the night and the next day, the work of consolidation, the evacuation of the wounded, many of whom were in, or in front of, our first line, and the replenishment of supplies, had to be carried out under heavy fire and over ground wholly exposed to view.

★★★★★★

In this work Surgeon Rivers (3rd Field Ambulance), Surgeon Ballance (Anson), Surgeon Schlesinger (Howe) and Surgeon

McCracken (Hood) did most brilliant and gallant service.

✶✶✶✶✶✶

On the morning of the 9th, the 2nd Brigade suffered a severe loss through the death of Lt.-Colonel Maxwell, the brigade major, who was killed from close range while reconnoitring the Turkish positions in front of our line. To his experience and enthusiasm, this brigade, during their months of training as well as in their first engagements, owed incalculably much.

Even now, though we were consolidating our line, the Turks had no continuous positions within 500 yards of our front, and to harass us in our work (which they did with never-failing effect until we had the whole organisation of trench warfare in working order) relied chiefly on concealed machine-guns and snipers, and on shelling the back areas and our still open communications. Some of these snipers had actually been found behind our lines, but by this time generally they were a little in front of it. The accuracy of their aim, even at long range, was amazing. Many fantastic stories were told of these men, but no very supernatural skill, though the most undoubted courage, was required for a sniper to conceal himself in the long grass and scrub which still covered the face of the peninsula.

"Sniper drives" became in these circumstances an essential form of warfare, and many fine exploits, spoken of at the time, must be omitted here only because in the confusion and constant anxiety of those days no written reports of such minor operations were submitted. Particularly fine work of this kind was done, however, by Lieut. Magrath, R.N.V.R., and Sub-Lieut. McHardy, of the Drake Battalion; and Petty Officer W. Mason of the same battalion was mentioned in despatches for his gallantry on May 9th in bringing in two men of his battalion wounded in an operation of this character.

✶✶✶✶✶✶

Distinguished service was also rendered in the May operations by Lt.-Commander Boissier, R.N.V.R. (Howe Battalion), who received the D.S.C. C.P.O. Toy, of the same battalion, was awarded the Good Conduct Medal at the same time

✶✶✶✶✶✶

At dawn on May 10th a counter-attack of exceptional vigour was delivered by the Turks against the French and the Naval Battalion on their left. For a time the situation was critical, but in the end the position was restored, on the Composite Brigade front, largely through the initiative of Captain Tetley (Plymouth Marines), who led his company in a counter-attack when the enemy were on the point of breaking through.

So ended the first engagement in which the Naval Division took a substantial and determining part on the peninsula. The quality of the services rendered by these inexperienced battalions can best be gauged from the tribute paid to the 2nd Naval Brigade by General D'Amade, in a letter to Sir Ian Hamilton, written on the receipt of the commander-in-chief's orders on May 10th that the brigade was to revert to General Paris's command. General D'Amade himself read his letter to the brigade when he inspected them in their rest camp a few days later. It ran as follows:—

In accordance with your orders I am returning the 2nd Naval Brigade to the Composite Division. It is my pleasant duty to place on record how much I have appreciated the brilliant military qualities, the devotion to duty, the courage and the intrepidity of the three valiant battalions—Anson, Howe and Hood—of which it is composed. It is a great honour and a great satisfaction to me to have had during the 6th, 7th, 8th and 9th of May the devoted, active and ever-ready collaboration of Commodore Backhouse, an officer who has inspired his troops with those noble qualities to which every French soldier who has seen them at work renders homage.

Allowing for all the requirements of international courtesy, it is reasonable to assume that the battalions to whom such a tribute was paid, had at the least, shown themselves fully competent to engage in active operations of a character more trying than is even at this date readily appreciated. And the Drake and Plymouth Battalions, fighting side by side with Commodore Backhouse's Brigade, had made almost identical progress under the same conditions.

The evening of May 10th marked our firm establishment on the peninsula, not only south of Achibaba but, as we shall see in the next chapter, at Anzac; it marked also, and equally definitely, the end of the first phase of the Gallipoli Campaign, and the definite failure of the plan for concentrating the entire force against the Kilid Bahr plateau before either part of it was pinned to its ground by the Turkish reserves.

In these circumstances, a reconsideration by the government of the chances of the campaign was essential, and Sir Ian Hamilton at once submitted to the War Office a revised estimate of his requirements in men, guns, stores and ammunition. Any precise calculation of our chances of success, had these reinforcements been immediately forth-coming, is merely guesswork, but it is certain that they would have been at least more favourable than at the beginning of August, when the reinforcements ultimately arrived. Before that time in the costly war of positions, which could not, it was felt, be allowed entirely to die down (though some argue that this would have been wiser), and still more from climatic disease which inactivity might only have made worse, our original landing force had been irremediably depleted. At the time, however, prospects seemed less dubious, for our victory had at least, though at a heavy cost, won for us a sort of security failing which we must, without a doubt, have withdrawn.

It would have been impossible to keep an army corps indefinitely in an area so exposed as that occupied by us on the 28th April. Now, though our advance had been at the most three quarters of a mile and in places less, we had got astride of the different *nullahs*, and had won a considerable belt of country, whose occasional trees provided a substantial measure of protection. The result was cover from view for our infantry and guns and reasonably safe communication with our front line positions.

To reach even thus far, the Naval Division, though less hotly en-gaged than the 29th, had lost heavily. Colonel Quilter of the Hood Battalion, one of the most distinguished and popular officers in the Division, and, of the Anson Battalion, Lieut.-Commander Anderson (who had led the beach party at *Implacable* landing), Lieutenant Dun-can, Sub-Lieut. Bryan Melland and Sub-Lieut. Tisdall (whose heroism at the "V" beach landing yet awaited recognition) had been killed early on May 6th, in the first advance of the Naval Division up the Achibaba Nullah. Later, in the same engagement, Lieut.-Commander Waller of the Howe Battalion, Lieutenant M. D. Cherry and Lieu-tenant Edgar of the Drake and Captain B. Andrews and Lieutenant Barnes of the Plymouth Battalion had fallen, the last two in the Turk-ish counter-attack on May 10th.

The losses in non-commissioned officers and men were also se-vere, and the five battalions south of Achibaba had been reduced to an average strength of barely 500 officers and men when, on May 10th (the 2nd Naval Brigade being then withdrawn from General D'Amade's command), they came once more under General Paris's command. The battalions could not, however, yet be withdrawn from the line, and with the Cyclist Company and some Motor Machine Gun detachments they were formed, during May 10th, into a new

Composite Brigade and put into the line between the Australians and the French left which had been withdrawn. This Brigade and the Australian Brigade remained as a composite division under General Paris till the whole was relieved by the 42nd Division on the 12th, and the Naval battalions withdrew to bivouacs southwest of Achibaba Nullah.

There, with battalions already so dangerously weakened, General Paris waited for the long-delayed concentration of his division, to be completed by the return of his two brigades from Anzac, and the arrival of the Hawke, Benbow and Collingwood Battalions and the third field company of engineers now on their way from England.

The narrow plain shut in between the sea, the Straits and the curved lines of Achibaba, which was all that we had won at the price of so much blood and treasure, was to be the home of the Naval Division for many months, and the scene of all the fighting it was to see on the Eastern front.

Recalling the scene in memory, as it appeared from the line of the rest camps, which now grew up between Morto Bay and Gully beach, the chief feature was the distinctness with which all the prominent features of our own and the enemy position could be noted, in the course of an hour's walk across the peninsula.

Standing to the north of Morto Bay, a little way inland, you see only an expanse of rocky plain, broken here and there by a small patch of cultivated ground leading up to the skyline, which is the ridge overlooking the Kereves Dere. On the side of the Straits, the view was bounded, as everywhere on the peninsula, by the cliff line, so that you could not see the Straits or Asia—unless you stood on the very edge (a fact which saved many lives during the campaign); and on the other side, by a belt of wood beyond a valley of shrub and fruit trees, narrowing gradually to form the Achibaba Nullah. Between the cliffs and the valley (less than a mile) was the French sector.

Turning to the left to walk across the peninsula, you struck the end of the valley, where, by the side of the small stream which runs down from the *nullah*, the Naval Division made their first advance on May 2nd, and advanced again, and with greater success, in the battles of the 6th to the 8th. In the later days of the campaign, the men of the division came up and down the valley daily, going between the rest camps and the trenches. The way from the rest camps was marked for them by a line of ruined towers, ruined before the war, more ruinous now, but which still challenged the assaults of time and the violence of man with mighty memories. For these towers were the ruins of a Roman aqueduct, which had carried the waters of the uplands from the same Achibaba to an earlier Sedd-el-bahr.

Coming up roughly along the line of the aqueduct into the green valley, the battalions followed the course of the stream till it wound into the small glade, overhung with trees and memorable for the incessant croaking of frogs, across which lay our front line before the advance on May 6th. Beyond the glade, the earliest regular trench system began; further on was the White House, and further again the line reached by the division on May 9th. You could see nothing of these trench lines from the entrance to the valley, but only the sloping uplands beyond, leading, as ever, to the inevitable symmetry of Achibaba. On these slopes lay the main Turkish defences.

Continuing westwards across the peninsula, you reached higher ground, but for nearly half a mile beyond Achibaba Nullah the country was more thickly wooded, clusters of olive trees shutting out your view on all sides. Among these trees were the first settled bivouacs of the Naval Division, and, under the largest clump, General Paris's Divisional Headquarters. So small, however, was the area sheltered by these trees that those battalions which arrived last inevitably bivouacked beyond the sheltered zone, in full view of the enemy on the edge of the open plain. Here the scene changes, and you can look across almost unbroken ground to the coast-line of the Aegean sea, two and a half miles ahead. Not only this, but the country is open to the north to Achibaba (except for some trees bordering Gully Ravine), and to the south to Sedd-el-bahr. Down the middle of the plain runs the main road from Krithia, the village which can be seen for the first time on the southwest slope of Achibaba, to Sedd-el-bahr on the sky-line in the extreme south.

Walking on a little and then turning to face Achibaba, you could follow the line of the main enemy position along the southern slopes of the hill, through Krithia, and then, turning back again with the curve of the hill, to the coast-line in the western distance. Across that expanse of level and unsheltered country, broken only by the Krithia Nullah and Gully Ravine, the army had to advance if it was to turn the Turkish position from the left.

At this time in May the plain was still green and smiling in the sun, as when it first burst on English eyes on April 25th. Later, except for the trees and shrubs, the peninsula, worn down by the passing of thousands of men, and the endless coming and going of transport from the beaches to the camps, became a bare sandy waste. In time it was worse than that. On three sides the plain rises slightly towards the coast; on the fourth side it culminates in the domed height of Achibaba. In this there came to be realised a certain symbolism. The army was indeed caught between the hill and sea; it could go neither backward nor forward. The plain, for all its openness, was a prison, which became a tomb.

The Defence of Anzac

We must now turn to the northern zone, where the Australian and New Zealand Army Corps, reinforced, as we have seen, by two weak brigades of the Naval Division, had been fighting as desperately to maintain a bare foothold on the peninsula, as had the forces south of Achibaba to extend their gains. The casualties of two Australian Divisions, during the first two days' fighting, amounted to more than 5,000 officers and men. And withal, the generals on the spot were not confident of their ability to retain their hold on the position. They held it, but the result was due only to the fighting capacity of the individual officers and men. For all their gallantry, the Australians and New Zealanders had, even by April 28th, reached no naturally defensible position, and the only alternative to evacuation was to set about the systematic construction, under fire, and in face of continuous attacks, of an impromptu fortress, the garrison of which would have to maintain, in effect, a siege, until they were substantially reinforced; or until such time as the encircling enemy might be diverted by pressure from our forces in the south or elsewhere.

Seeing that it was necessary in any event to remain temporarily on the defensive, it may be thought that the slender reserves available from the Naval Division would have been better employed somewhere else, but the conditions of the first three days' fighting on this front had in fact led to such a measure of confusion, that it had become urgently necessary to rest and reorganise the Dominion divisions unit by unit. Till this had been done there could be no security, and security was essential, at least while we were still fighting for elbow room south of Achibaba.

The position held by the Australians and New Zealanders, on the evening of the 28th, consisted of a strip of beach (known to history as Anzac cove) more than half a mile south of the intended landing-place at Gaba Tepe, of the ridge dominating it (named Maclagan's Ridge, after the leader of the first assault which had carried it), and of the inland heights on either side of Deep Gully, running north-west

187

from the coast, immediately south of Maclagan's Ridge for a distance of a mile and a half.

The heights on the left of the gully (known as the Sphinx, Walker's Ridge and Russell Top) were in our hands, and between these and the Turkish positions further to the northwest was a wide valley. The left of our position was thus already reasonably secure. Not so our centre and our right. The heights east of the gully, divided by innumerable narrow, but often precipitous, ravines into as many separate features, had been fiercely contested, and on the different plateaux, covered with tangled undergrowth and rock, the Turks and Australians still lay face to face actually within bombing range. Not here, as on the left, had our foothold on the heights forced the enemy to retreat, nor throughout the campaign did we ever appreciably loosen his hold of these, his first positions.

In the centre, at the head of the gully, the position was even worse. About a mile from the coast, the gully is split in two by a spur (known as Pope's Hill), running out from the line of hills, which, facing Maclagan's Ridge, formed the northern defensive position of the Turks. On the eastern edge of Pope's Hill the Turks were entrenched, and they thus commanded the heights on either side of the eastern arm of the ravine as well as the high ground at its head. Only on the western edge of the spur had the Australians a foothold, and even here we had no defensive position covering the head of the ravine, and no cover, even from view, from the enemy position on the heights to the north-west.

The first Naval Division units to land were the Marine Brigade, (*i.e.,* the Portsmouth and Chatham Battalions, the Plymouth Battalion was still attached to the 20th Division), the 1st Field Ambulance (Staff Surgeon Fleming, R.N.), and No. 1 Field Company of the Divisional Engineers (Major Morgans, R.M.). The engineers distinguished themselves in their first nine hours under fire by constructing the main road from the beach to the reserve position on Maclagan's Ridge. The Portsmouth and Chatham Battalions moved at once into the front-line trenches on the right of the gully. The position allotted comprised the posts which afterwards became famous under the names of Quinn's and Courtney's Posts, and covered the approach to the gully from the east.

The intention was to relieve the 4th Australian Brigade, but the sector was greater than could be defended by two battalions, even under normal conditions; and all that could be done was to occupy parts of it, and enable a tentative beginning to be made with the Australian reorganisation. The next day (the 29th) more progress was made, for General Mercer's 1st Brigade was landed, (this brigade also comprised only two battalions. The Drake Battalion was already engaged at Cape Helles), and the Deal Battalion was brought into the line on General Trotman's left. The Nelson Battalion remained in reserve.

The general conditions were very different from those which the organising capacity of the trained Staff of the 29th Division had brought about at Cape Helles. On the beach the crowd and confusion had been astonishing. So great, indeed, was the intermixture of units, and the number of men moving about independently on errands of which they alone knew the nature, that it was extremely difficult to assemble even a platoon and march it off. The difficulty in assembling a battalion, landed in open boats, was correspondingly greater.

When it had been surmounted, it was necessary to climb the steep hills leading from the beach to the south of Maclagan's Ridge, and cross the main gully. Here were no organised lines of reinforcement or supply, no resting-places for the reserve formations; but every possible piece of level ground had been appropriated by individuals of different units, many of them resting where they had fallen asleep involuntarily after the exertions of three days' continuous fighting. In the darkness it was impossible to tell what places were fully exposed to the view of the enemy. The result to the Nelson Battalion—the only battalion not in the firing line from the start—was that their labours on the construction of dugouts during the night of the 29th-30th proved in the morning to be fruitless.

The sides of the gully were rocky, and what, in the wet season, was the bed of a mountain stream, was now the only path which the landscape offered. On the upper slopes, thickly covered with arbutus, dwarf oaks, and other shrubs, the passage of men had, indeed, worn narrow tracks, but these were not serviceable, and merely showed the least dangerous line of approach for individuals to the firing line.

This was nothing but a series of hastily-dug posts, untraversed, unwired, broken with the wreckage of battle, scarred with the marks of intensive bombardment, just a series of footholds on the edge of the plateau, but defending the life-line of the Anzac position. The ground in front of the trenches was covered with thick scrub, broken by small depressions and ravines. Beyond it was another gorge, similar to the gully which formed the centre of the Anzac position. Here were the Turkish reserves, and from here on to and across the plateau there was a constant movement of the enemy. Even when the utmost energy and skill had been spent on the fortification of our trenches, the situation at this point remained dangerous, and this key position could only be maintained throughout the campaign by hand-to-hand fighting of a desperate character.

The three marine battalions remained in these trenches till May 2nd, fighting being more or less continuous the whole time. The novelty of the conditions, and the entire lack of a disciplined organisation of the defences, imposed a strain on raw troops which led inevitably to one or two unfortunate incidents. There is no room for doubt, however, that in general great resolution and a very high degree of gallantry distinguished the defence of the posts by the marine battalions during these days, when the first V.C. was won from the ranks of the division (by Lance-Corporal Parker, of the Portsmouth Battalion), and very severe losses were incurred. The official record of Lance-Corporal Parker's exploits gives an indication of the character of the fighting on a day when, according to Mr. Philip Schuler, "a comparative calm stole over Anzac." One must presume that it stole so quietly as to be unobserved.

> On the night of April 30th–May 1st, 1915, a message asking for ammunition, water and medical stores was received from an isolated fire trench at Gaba Tepe. A party of non-commissioned officers and men were detailed to carry water and ammunition, and, in response to a call for a volunteer from among the stretcher-bearers, Parker at once came forward; he had, during the previous three days, displayed conspicuous bravery and energy under fire, whilst in charge of the battalion stretcher-bearers. Several men had already been killed in a previous attempt to bring assistance to the men holding the fire trench. To reach this trench, it was necessary to traverse an area at least four hundred yards wide, which was completely exposed, and swept by rifle fire.
>
> It was already daylight when the party emerged from shelter, and at once one of the men was wounded. Parker organised a stretcher-party, and then, going on alone, succeeded in reaching the fire trench, all the water and ammunition carriers being either killed or wounded. After his arrival, he rendered assistance to the wounded in the trench, displaying extreme courage, and remaining cool and collected in very trying circumstances. The trench had finally to be evacuated, and Parker helped to re-

move and attend the casualties, though he himself was seriously wounded during the operation.

Of the two officers in charge of this trench, Lieutenant Empson was killed, and Lieutenant Alcock conducted a fine defence for four nights and three days (during which period no adequate supplies could be brought up), before he was forced to withdraw, owing to shortage of ammunition. For this, and other services, this officer was mentioned in Sir Ian Hamilton's dispatch of 12th June, 1915, and was awarded the D.S.O. The same dispatch contains the names of Lt.-Colonel Luard, Major J. A. M. Clark, Major H. G. B. Armstrong, Captain D. J. Gowney, D.S.C., and Lieutenant W. R. Sanders, of the Portsmouth Battalion, all of whom did fine work in these operations. (Major Armstrong was killed in action on May 6th when his battalion was again in the line on this front). Surgeon Playne, of this battalion, also rendered the most conspicuous service, and was awarded the D.S.O.

On the night of April 30th, an attack was carried out by "B" Company of the Chatham Battalion, who had been driven out of a portion of their line a little earlier. The position lost was retaken, though with considerable loss. Lieutenant Herford, who had succeeded to the command of the company, was killed, and Lieutenant Watts (Battalion Machine Gun Officer) was wounded.

The next day (May 1st) the Turks came back to the attack, but were repulsed. (In the defence of this position Lieutenant J. Cheetham, R.M.L.I., was conspicuous, and, for his courage and initiative, was awarded the D.S.O.) In this fighting the marines suffered a severe loss in the death of Sergeant-Major Hayward, the regimental sergeant-major of the Chatham Battalion.

The marines were relieved on May 2nd. The reorganisation of the Australian and New Zealand Corps was now completed, and the position was appreciably more secure. This was due less, perhaps, to Mr. Schuler's "inexplicable calm" during the period from the 28th to the 1st, than to the relief which the arrival of the two Naval Brigades gave to the main force, at a time when the resistance of the Turks was by no means broken, and when the position, so bravely won, could only be maintained by equally soldierly qualities.[5]

★★★★★★

In this early righting, In addition to those previously mentioned, Lt.-Colonel R. N. Bendyshe, R.M.L.I., Major G. F. Muller, R.M.L.I., Lieutenant J. F. Moxham, R.M. and Lieutenant K. A. Higgins, R.M. of the Deal Battalion, and Captain J. C. Teague, R.M.L.I., Lieutenant C. J. Black, R.M. and 2nd Lieut. D. M. G. Ferguson, R.M. of the Portsmouth Battalion, were killed. The death of so many experienced officers at the outset of the campaign was a grievous loss to the Marine Brigade. Major Tupman, R.M.L.I. (so well known later as Brigade Major to the 1st R.N. Brigade), succeeded now to the command of the Deal Battalion.

★★★★★★

On May 2nd, after a series of misunderstandings had led to the postponement of a larger scheme, it was arranged to attempt the capture of the heights overlooking the head of the gully. The Naval Division troops were held in reserve for this attack, but were called on early in the operations.

The precise objectives were Pope's Hill and the high ground on either side of it. Two columns were formed for the attack of this position. On the left, the Otago (New Zealand) Battalion was to attempt the high ground at the head of the left arm of the gully, immediately to the west of Pope's Hill. On the right, the 16th Battalion was to scale the two ridges commanding the head of the right arm of the gully. The 13th Battalion, coming up in their rear (there was no possible line of approach up the hillside to the left of that to be taken by the 16th Battalion), was to extend the line to the left, and join up with the centre, where the 15th (Australian) Battalion, garrisoning Pope's Hill, was to make a sortie and push forward mi advance line in touch with the Otago Battalion.

In general support in the gully, were the three marine battalions under General Trotman. Two companies of the Nelson Battalion were in brigade reserve to Colonel Monash, who was in command of the Australian and New Zealand troops detailed for the operation.

The assaulting columns were timed to reach the fringe of the hills to the right and left of Pope's Hill at, approximately, 8 p.m. From thence, they were to move forward to the assault of the Turkish trenches on the forward slopes.

The shades of night, always so confidently and justly reckoned on to bring relief to troops acting on the defensive, were particularly helpful to the Turks on this occasion, for the position attacked was in the form of a semicircle, with the Australians attacking from the centre. The columns necessarily advanced by routes separated by nearly half a mile, and they found themselves, when they had got within striking distance of the enemy, isolated from each other. The 16th Battalion passed through a line of trenches dug by the Turks on the very edge of the ravine, and took up a position a little way beyond, to enable the 13th Battalion to move to their left and join up with the troops in the centre. The 13th Battalion, late in starting, were late in arriving in position, and appear never to have made touch, either with the 16th Battalion or with the troops on their left. But, without hesitation, the battalions each endeavoured to advance.

We must not imagine the scene as an orderly and well-appointed battle, with the opposing positions clearly defined. On this rugged hill top, thickly covered with scrub and dotted with rock, Turks and Australians, losing all organisation, fought a running fight for some hours. But neither the Australians nor the New Zealanders seem ever to have reached the main enemy position, and their hold on the plateau's edge was but precarious by midnight, when a huge bonfire lit by the Turks revealed the most complete and hopeless confusion in the ranks of the assaulting troops on the right of Pope's Hill.

Two hundred yards or so from the edge of the gully, officers had set to work constructing a support line, and this appears to have been manned with some degree of method. Ahead, some hundreds of yards nearer the Turkish position, the assaulting troops, beaten to the ground by a murderous fire, formed what was alternatively a firing line or a covering, force for the main body behind. Between the two lines were a confused mass of leaderless men—men from the firing line driven back, reinforcements coming up from the gully, stragglers looking for their units, perhaps a Turk or two caught up in the confusion of the night battle, officers looking for orders, or for men to obey them. The attack had failed, and in the prevailing excitement the failure seems to have passed unnoticed.

When the confusion was at its height, at 2 a.m., the two companies of the Nelson Battalion came up under orders from Colonel Monash to support the 13th Battalion. While the rear platoons of the force were still in the gully, an ill-supported local advance was in progress, and the leading platoons of the Nelson became involved. The attack was unsuccessful, but when the two companies were at last concentrated, no attempt seems to have been made to make use of these fresh troops, or of the very numerous army of leaderless Australians wandering between the lines, for a final assault on the main positions.

Instead, the Nelson Battalion was ordered, by the senior officer on the right of the 13th Battalion front, to move to the left and cover the New Zealanders (Otago Battalion), if and when they could be found. Later, however, the Nelson were ordered to prepare a position in rear of the 13th Battalion, the New Zealanders not being in evidence, and no one having any knowledge of their whereabouts (they were actually digging in a quarter of a mile further to the left). This was approximately at 2.30 a.m., and the Nelson companies remained, accordingly, till dawn fruitlessly digging in with entrenching tools in rear of the thinly-held Australian support line. In front, the Australian firing line began to dig themselves in at the same time. On the right of the front of attack no greater success had been won. The position was, indeed, ominously similar. Gallant attacks had been made, but they had failed, and the losses among the men and also, perhaps, to some extent the inadequate preparations, had prevented the construction of any strong defensive line.

The over-riding weakness of the position as a whole was the isolation of the three assaulting battalions from each other. When dawn broke, this, and the superiority of ground still enjoyed by the enemy, made the situation desperate. In these circumstances the Portsmouth Battalion of Marines, in reserve in the gully, were asked to go forward. Owing to a misunderstanding, the request was not addressed to General Trotman, under whose orders the battalion had remained, and, while the matter was under discussion, the left flank of the 16th Battalion were pushed back into the gully, spreading confusion as they retreated. In the half-light of dawn, amid a hail of bullets coming from every direction (for the trenches in the gully itself were under fire from both flanks, from the front, and in places even from the rear), with an uncertain battle raging on the very edge of the plateau above, the rumour that the Turks were pouring into the gully might have had disastrous results.

The men were, however, promptly rallied by the staff of General Trotman's brigade, and those who had been the first to turn were among the first to regain their self-control and to assist in stemming the dangerous panic. Nothing, however, could save the position on the plateau itself but the capture even at this eleventh hour of the main Turkish trenches; and, in the belief apparently that these trenches had, in fact, been captured elsewhere on the battle front, and were still in our hands, the Chatham Battalion were sent forward to attack those opposite the sorely pressed 16th Battalion. Almost at the same time, an ill-fated order was given, in the centre of the battle front, for the Nelson Battalion companies to attempt, by attacking to a flank, to protect the 13th Battalion.

The attack of the Chatham Battalion, brilliantly led by the Adjutant, Captain Richards, R.M.L.I., was extremely successful, and in the face of a very heavy, but not devastating, fire, two lines of trenches were taken and, in the first instance, held. Unfortunately, no support was now forthcoming on either flank, and after a gallant defence of some six hours, during which Quartermaster-Sergeant White and Sergeant Oakey specially distinguished themselves, the position, so finely won, had to be abandoned. With it, went our hold on the improvised trenches dug by the Australians on the edge of the plateau at this point.

The fate of the attack on the other sectors was in the end the same: the Nelson Battalion companies had failed to drive home their flanking attack (directed against an advanced machine-gun position), and were ordered by the Australian commander to retire. Unfortunately, here, as on the 16th Battalion front, the terrors of the night battle had led to a good deal of disorganisation, and here, too, something in the nature of a temporary panic broke out. The position was, however, restored, and the Nelson companies, rallied in the gully by Sub-Lieut. Sowerby, returned to the 13th Australians' trenches. Here from 6 a.m. till dusk a memorable stand was made.

By the afternoon, when our positions on the right had been abandoned, it became clear that it was only a useless waste of life to cling on in the centre to a position which could not possibly be held against a determined assault such as its importance to the enemy would certainly produce. But before the position could be surrendered, countless wounded, and stores and ammunition had to be cleared. Under constant harassing from the enemy, this was successfully achieved, and, at 5.30, the garrison were able to begin an exceedingly cool and well-planned retreat, so well-planned, indeed, as to be carried out almost without loss, although it was daylight and the enemy were closing in on all sides.

On the extreme right of the battlefield, the Otago Battalion had, it was learnt later, achieved much the same measure of success and failure as the 18th Australians; in the end they too, though some hours later, had to retreat.

In this unfortunate engagement, the division suffered many serious losses. The Chatham Marines lost nearly three hundred officers and men, killed and wounded, among the killed being their Adjutant (Capt. Richards, whose services since the early days of the Antwerp expedition to this last assault had been so uniformly distinguished) and Lieutenant Grinling. In the Portsmouth battalion, Lieutenant Sanders, 2nd Lieutenant T. A. D. Deane and 2nd Lieutenant T. H. C. Fulton were killed while the battalion was in support on the gully. In the Nelson Battalion the losses, in proportion to those engaged, were even more serious. Lt.-Commander Gibson (commanding "B" Company), Lieut. P. C. Garnham, R.N.V.R., and Sub-Lieuts. Paton, Bookless, Whitaker and Cooke were killed or mortally wounded, and Lt.-Commander Primrose (second in command) and Lt.-Commander T. L. Price (commanding "A" Company), wounded. The losses in petty officers and men were nearly two hundred.

The local results of this costly and unfortunate affair were intangible. Heavy losses were inflicted, but they were sustained, and the same factors that turned against us the balance of advantage in the indecisive assaults at Cape Helles later in the campaign, turned it against us here. The Turks could relieve their tired troops and replenish their casualties, while we could not. As at Cape Helles, however, the immediate results were good. The Turks were put on the defensive, and our men got breathing space for the all-important work of consolidation and organisation.

The next day a definite scheme of defence was drawn up, under which the three main posts covering the front of the position, on the safety of which, in view of our failure to secure the high ground dominating the heads of the gully, our security still depended absolutely, were placed under a united command and organised for mutual support. The responsibility for these historic strongholds (which came to be known as Courtney's, Quinn's and Pope's Posts, after the officers who had garrisoned them in the earliest days), fell, for so long as his Brigade remained on this front (till May 12th), to Brigadier-General Trotman, R.M.L.I., who had under his command the Portsmouth and Chatham Battalions and the 4th Australian Infantry Brigade.

As Mr. Schuler tells us:

> It was on the holding of these precarious and well-nigh impossible positions in the early days of the occupation that the whole Australian line depended.

Of the part which the Marine Battalions took in their defence, during these critical days, at the very beginning of the campaign, the records tell little, and published history even less. (The Australian sources rightly concentrate on the assistance, invariably forthcoming,

196

which Australian units rendered to the Marine Battalions on more than one occasion). But it is a sufficient commentary on the part which they had played in the earlier days of active fighting, that they were allocated to the defence of positions of such importance.

The history of these posts throughout the campaign is a history of desperate conflicts, sustained with equal tenacity by the enemy and by the Australian infantrymen and the (dismounted) Light Horse Brigade. It was a style of warfare in which individual gallantry and resource told more than scientific training. Yet gallantry and resource could not do more than just hold out. From Quinn's Post, indeed, a series of abortive assaults were made, often with disastrous losses, and the first of them took place while the Marine Brigade was still at Anzac, on the evening of the 10th May. Like so many which followed it, it failed, owing to the failure to join up of the assaulting parties, each of which gained a lodgement in the enemy trenches. Each party in turn was enfiladed, and forced to withdraw down the communication trenches, newly dug from our own to the temporarily captured position.

Two days after this unsuccessful effort, the Marine Brigade was relieved by the Light Horse Brigade, and sailed at once for Cape Helles.

★★★★★★

The period from May 3rd to May 12th was one of severe, if discontinuous, fighting, and the Marine Battalions suffered further losses. Among the officers killed during this period were Major A. C. H. Hoskyns, R.M.L.L, Lieutenant J. F. Hyland and 2nd Lieut. F. A. Erskine of the Portsmouth Battalion, and Lieutenant M. Curtin and Lieutenant A. F. Hayward of the Chatham Battalion.

★★★★★★

The lot of General Mercer's Brigade was less arduous and responsible. This brigade had seen little or no actual fighting, save the two companies of the Nelson Battalion on May 2nd and 3rd; and they were sent, immediately on the conclusion of that engagement, to relieve Australian and New Zealand troops on the left of the position. Here, owing to the lie of the land, the lighting was infinitely less severe; the main enemy positions were some hundreds of yards off, and only in the many saps, which ran out from the opposing lines, did the forces come to close quarters.

The sector first allotted to General Mercer's Brigade was on the extreme flank, partly covered from direct assault by the Australian trenches, slightly to the north on Walker's Ridge. The enemy position was centred on a ridge still further to the north, and the flat ground, immediately off the shore, was held only by rival outposts and wire entanglements. Looking north, indeed, from the shore at this point the whole view was open as far as Salt Lake, and beyond Suvla Point the mainland of Turkey and Bulgaria was visible on a clear day in faint outline across the Gulf of Xeros. If they turned their backs on this view of the promised land, the men of the Nelson and Deal Battalions could see, to the south, the whole western coast of the peninsula and the ships off Cape Helles. To the west, set in the placid water of the Aegean, could be seen Imbros and Samothrace, behind which the setting sun would throw a brilliant glow over the rugged outlines of their purple peaks.

The trenches on the extreme left held by the Nelson Battalion backed on to a sandy gorge opening out to the sea. The sides of the cliffs were precipitous, and cut by the wind and rain of the unequal climate into sharp edges, bare of all vegetation; only birds and in-sects seemed to abound, and at one and the same time could be seen vultures, pigeons, shrikes, martins, swallows and small greyish hawks; while the trenches abounded in yellow centipedes, caterpillars, lizards, and brown and blue butterflies.

The firing line was manned throughout by a composite force of the Nelson and Deal Battalions, under the command of Lt.-Colonel Eveleigh, R.M.L.I. No incidents of moment mark this period, though the line taken over had to be considerably extended to release the whole of the New Zealand Brigade, who normally garrisoned the sector, for service in the general engagement at Cape Helles on May 6th to 8th. The Naval Brigade remained in the line till the 13th, when they also re-embarked for the southern front. The 1st Field Ambu-lance, whose work had won high tributes from all sides, left at the same time. (For Particularly gallant work during these operations Sur-geon Pratt, of this Field Ambulance, was awarded the D.S.C.)

By this time, the situation had immensely improved. Most notice-able of all, was the order which had been won from the earlier chaos of the beaches, and the regular system of trench reliefs, which had been worked out in the face of such appalling difficulties. In this trans-formation, as well as in the offensive of the 2nd and 3rd, the Naval Di-vision brigades (raw as they were) had played a small but honourable part, and had vindicated their courage and their training.

By May 13th, when the units which had been sent to Anzac had returned to the Achibaba front, the Naval Division (Save for the Hawke, Benbow and Collingwood Battalions, by now on the high seas) was concentrated under General Paris's command. The campaign developed very rapidly into trench warfare. In three brief weeks, the order and method imposed by the necessities of a siege came over a scene which heretofore had been expanding, changing, taking fresh colour almost every hour, under the stress of active warfare, its cruel losses, its alternating moods of exultation and depression, the knowledge of triumph or the tacit admission of defeat.

The first salient change was the allocation to different formations of the responsibility for certain sectors of defence. No longer was there to exist that camaraderie of the battlefield, when even divisions cease to exist as distinct units, and the reserves, the supports, and the front-line troops develop, almost, an *esprit de corps* of their own. Now each division found its own supports, its own reserves, and each looked askance on its neighbour. In one sector, sniping and bombing had become a science; in another, sapping and digging in at night ("straightening out the line") was the order of the day, a third excelled in the discipline of its sentries, a fourth in the excellence of its field engineering. And each came to regard the other with a peculiar mixture of admiration and dislike, bred by differences of character and ambition and training.

On the right of the line, standing fast to their finely won position on the ridge of the Kereves Dere, were the French, whose sector was a monument of field engineering, of effective organisation of all things material. Next came the Naval Division, with their front stretching from the French left across the Achibaba Nullah to the right of the Krithia Nullah: this was the front to which the naval battalions of the 2nd and the Composite Brigade had fought in the earlier battles. On the left came the 42nd Division, and on their left again, the 29th Division and Cox's Indian Brigade, stretching across the main gully to the sea.

With the organised sectors of defence, came the rest camps. Whether a battalion was out of the line for rest and reorganisation, or in corps reserve, or in divisional or brigade reserve, the only place for it except actually on days of battle was the rest camp. There were its household gods, in the shape of its quartermaster's stores and transport, and there, more important, the laborious dugouts, which alone offered cover from view of the enemy and a possibility of shelter from the more than occasional shells.

The Naval Division rest camps were directly behind their trench sector, on the broken ground to the left of the lower reaches of the Achibaba Nullah. Without timber or corrugated iron of any kind, neither comfort nor safety could be immediately attempted. Only through long weeks of scheming and contrivance and loot could the former be approached. The latter remained beyond reach.

The early camps suffered in another way: they were never meant to be permanent; and the Naval Division camps were dug by young men who still cherished the illusion that what generals did not intend would not occur. And so the camps were carelessly planned, unnecessarily cramped, avoidably uncomfortable in their layout.

For these reasons, among others, it would be wrong to suppose that the reversion to trench warfare carried with it intervals of rest and that generally peaceful atmosphere which we ordinarily associate with it. Every square yard of the peninsula was under fire; and in a situation where the safety of the fighting troops depended absolutely on constant artillery support and a plentiful supply of engineering materials and labour for extensive digging, there were none of these essentials. The days following on the May battles were, in the circumstances, days of unremitting anxiety and hard work, in which every man who could be spared had during the brief hours of darkness to be employed on digging communication trenches, or in pushing forward our front line to within striking distance of the enemy. Only, it was felt, by renewing the offensive very soon and driving the enemy north of Achibaba could we gain sufficient ground and protection to concentrate the expected reinforcements for a decisive victory.

In pursuance of the prescribed policy, the Naval Division, in addition to providing innumerable digging parties all over the peninsula, carried out no less than four night advances before the end of May. These operations, on the 18th, 23rd, 24th and 27th, the first two of which were carried out by the 2nd Naval Brigade, and the next by the 1st and Marine Brigades respectively, took our front line forward nearly half a mile at a cost of less than fifty casualties, and brought the division within from two hundred to four hundred yards of the main defensive position across the Achibaba and Krithia Nullahs. Incidentally, these operations gained for us almost as much ground as had those of May 6th-8th, without giving any unnecessary chances to the enemy to reduce our strength still further before our next assault.

Howe Battalion Rest Camp, Gallipoli, June 1915

If, however, the losses in specific operations were miraculously few, the daily rate of wastage from shells in the camps and trenches, and overhead rifle fire in the gullies and communication trenches, was high. The 1st Brigade suffered a particularly grievous loss when their brigade major, Major Frank Wilson, R.M.L.I., was killed by a sniper only a few days after the 2nd Brigade had lost Lt.-Colonel Maxwell in the same way. Among other fine officers killed at this time were Lt.-Commander P. McCirdy, R.N.V.R., of the Anson Battalion, Sub-Lieut. E. Rennie, of the Drake Battalion, Lieut. Treves, R.N.V.R., and Sub-Lieut. Gilbert, of the Nelson Battalion, Lieut. R. O. Tollast and Lieut. A. M. Oakden, of the Divisional Engineers, and Lieut. White, R.M., of the Chatham Battalion. Major Wilson's place was filled by Lt.-Colonel Moorhouse, and Major Huberts, R.A., took over the Anson Battalion.

On May 28th and 29th, under conditions safer, but more dispiriting, than those which their fellows had faced on April 25th, the three remaining battalions landed on the peninsula. The division was at once reorganised on the original plan. The Hawke and Benbow joined the Drake and Nelson in the 1st Brigade, the Collingwood joined the Howe, Hood and Anson in the 2nd Brigade, and the Deal with the Plymouth, Portsmouth and Chatham battalions formed a complete Marine Brigade.

For all this, the division was weaker than on April 25th. Then, the effective strength was 10,500 men. At the end of May, before the arrival of the reinforcements, it was less than half; and the arrival of three fresh, but wholly inexperienced, battalions was, as far as the immediate future was concerned, a very moderate compensation. What was needed were not fresh units who had to buy their experience, but drafts for the more seasoned battalions. The urgency arose from the decision to make the next attack on June 4th.

It is easy now to say that this attack was foredoomed to failure. Yet such is the buoyancy of temperament of inexperienced soldiers that to many, at least in the Naval Division, this fateful day seemed to hold the promise of a long-awaited opportunity. Never since Antwerp had the whole been concentrated under the hand of their commander. Then they had been raw troops, untrained and unequipped; now, save for three battalions, they had had the finest of all training, worth how many years of peace-time manoeuvres, fighting continuously for a month, side by side, with some of the finest regular battalions. Even the inexperienced Collingwood, Hawke and Benbow were by no means untrained, were well equipped and well commanded. The more seasoned battalions were indeed thinned by losses, weakened by illness, handicapped by reorganisations under trying conditions. But in the excitement of a concerted advance might not tired troops regain their enthusiasm? Might not the Naval Division, now for the first time united under the orders of their own commander, set the final seal on their reputation?

★★★★★★★

The new attack, like those of May 6th and 8th, was to be a direct frontal assault on the whole Turkish forward position. We started, moreover, with three advantages, which we had not previously enjoyed. We were now right up against our objective, not vainly groping for it; we had limited the objectives of the first waves of the attack, and, finally, our troops, though not fresh, were infinitely more rested than they had been early in May. To this extent, the modified optimism which prevailed was justified; but there was another side to the picture. The Turks had been strongly reinforced and were deeply entrenched, and their left flank (against the French; that is, on the right of the Allied line) rested on the Kereves Dere Ridge. This position was unassailable, except to an advance along the line of the ridge. Such an advance the French had attempted on May 6th and 8th, but had only pushed forward for a distance of two or three hundred yards along the crest.

Seeing that the ridge ran diagonally to our front, it was clear that any failure to advance further along the crest and the upper slopes in the forthcoming attack must prejudice our chances on the lower slopes, where were the Naval Division. Equally, failure there might imperil any gains in the centre, and must, in any event, reduce their tactical value. On this view the success of the operations as a whole must depend largely—far too largely, considering to what extent we were committing all our resources to the uncertain issue—on the success of the French attack. This made the attack from the outset an incalculable gamble.

On the British front the attack was to be carried out by the 29th, 42nd and Naval Divisions, each attacking the Turkish trenches opposite to their own. The Naval Division, which had the shortest sector (less than a thousand yards of front), had to supply two brigades, less one battalion, to the Corps as a general reserve, and were left, for their share in the battle, only the 2nd Naval Brigade and the Drake Battalion. Holding the last-named in reserve, General Paris arranged with

203

Commodore Backhouse for the Howe, Hood and Anson to attack the first two front-line trenches and the redoubt on the right of the brigade boundary, and for the assault of the Turkish third line to be carried out by "A," "B" and "D" Companies of Commander Spearman's Collingwood Battalion. The remainder of the Collingwood were held in Brigade reserve, under Lt.-Commander West, R.N.V.R.

Next to the Anson (on the right of the Brigade) were French Colonial troops, and next to the Howe (on the left) the Manchester Brigade of the 42nd Division.

At 2.30 a.m. on the 4th the battle may be said to have opened with the departure of the 2nd Brigade from the rest camps. Stumbling across the broken ground into the valley of the Achibaba Nullah, the leading battalion walked up the dusty road, past Backhouse Post, where Colonel Quilter and Major Maxwell were buried, into the communication trench alongside the stream. Behind them could have been seen an endless number of small groups of heavily-laden tired men, ten or a dozen in each group, or sometimes less, walking almost as though in their sleep, so well did they know the road, or so little did they care to awake the memories which it held for them. These groups were the platoons of three battalions. Very different must have been the appearance of the Collingwood Battalion, at full strength, confidently going forward to the unknown event. The Turks were very quiet that night, and, save for the frogs croaking, there was scarcely a sound.

After the attacking groups had gone forward, the 1st Brigade Battalions came down from the trenches, the Drake to those round Backhouse Post, and the Nelson and Hawke Battalions to the rest camp.

The attack was timed for noon, and the hours of waiting, from dawn to midday, added a new chapter to the horrors of war. To move with a light heart to the assault in the grey half-light of dawn is difficult enough, but at least there is a shadow over the sun to veil the shadow in men's hearts. Here, hour by hour, the sun beats down more pitilessly. Towards ten o'clock the air grows fetid, and the flies begin to swarm on the filth of the parapets, and maggots crawl over the bodies of the dead but a foot or two below the ground. Even the small comforts of garrison duties in the line seem strangely remote. Everything is still, expectant, uncomfortable.

With curiosity, officers and men watch the bombardment, on which their chance of survival so greatly depends. In the rest camps, and near the headquarters of generals, the noise is terrific, and the impression one of a vastly efficient destruction. In the trenches the noise is immeasurably less, and the passage of the occasional shells tells the true tale.

A desultory bombardment had begun at 8 a.m., and at 10.30 a.m. the rate of fire was increased, but the results were negligible. We now know that the proportion of guns to rifles was only a third of that allowed in France, and the number of rounds per gun immeasurably less. No statistics were needed to reveal, at 11.20 a.m. on June 4th, the full measure of the weakness of our artillery, for at that moment the first intensive bombardment ceased, and a feint of attack was made along the whole line. In an instant the whole enemy line burst into rapid fire, machine guns swept the parapets of our trenches from end to end, and the Turkish artillery searched our reserve trenches and our communications. The bombardment, which should have disorganised the Turkish defences, driven their riflemen in cover, and destroyed their machine-gun emplacements, had done—just nothing.

At 11.30 the bombardment was resumed, and at 12 noon the Howe, Hood and Anson advanced to the assault. Once again, the Turkish rifle and machine-gun fire swept our parapets. This time they found a target. In the first seconds of the attack more than half the officers of the 2nd Naval Brigade (including Major Roberts, R.A., of the Anson, Major Sparling, R.M.L.I., of the Howe (who were both killed), and Lt.-Colonel Crauford-Stuart, of the Hood) were hit. Once the whole of the men were over the parapet and in the open, the law of averages came into play, and of the few officers, who still found themselves standing, about half, with about half their men, reached the Turkish front line. It was unoccupied, save by the dead, the dying and the wounded.

Without a moment's delay, the Anson went on, led by Lieut. Stuart Jones, R.N.V.R., the senior surviving officer, and stormed the redoubt in the Turkish second line, (with him was C.P.O. Stear; later promoted to Lieut., R.N.V.R., who, for fine work in this attack, was given the D.S.M.); the Hood and Howe came up on the flank. Seen through field-glasses, it was an orderly and dashing advance, particularly on the right, where the Anson were described by Sir Ian Hamilton as fighting in the best style of the Regular Army. But in the captured trenches the impression was different. There was an ominous inactivity on the right of the line, where the Turks could be seen in force in their original trenches: there was a still more ominous volume of fire pouring in on the trenches which had been captured. To hold the eight hundred yards of line which had been their objective, and which they had reached, there were left of the attacking force only some twenty officers and three hundred men. Every minute took its toll of the slender garrison. Would the Collingwood come up in time?

Punctually the Collingwood began their advance. But the success of their comrades helped them in no way. From the Turkish left, on the Kereves Dere Ridge, there broke out the same tornado of fire on a target as impossible to miss as the first. The Collingwood, afterwards supposed to have suffered their losses almost wholly in their retreat, actually suffered more than half of them in their advance, among those to fall being Commander Spearman, R.N., and his adjutant, Lt.-Commander Annand, R.N.V.R., both of whom were killed in the first moments of the attack. The Turkish positions on the upper slopes of the ridge were still intact, and our attempt to retain our hold on the lower slopes of the ridge was foredoomed to failure. Not more than three hundred of the Collingwood reached the advanced trenches, where by now the scene was one of indescribable confusion.

On the right, the enemy could be seen in full command of their second- and third-line trenches, while parties were coming back even into the front line, where the French had once been. The Naval Battalions were still in the enemy's second-line trenches on the Anson and Hood front; but on the Howe Battalion front, where there was no dead ground between our lines and those of the enemy, only a few of the Howe, and none of the Collingwood, had reached the enemy's line; and here also the Turks were now beginning to come back.

★★★★★★

Among the Howe were Lieut. P. H. Edwards, R.N.V.R. (wounded), and C.P.O. Homer, P.O. Smith and A.B. Pierce. These N.C.O.'s displayed the greatest gallantry and resolution, and each received the D.S.M.

★★★★★★

With great gallantry, the Anson and Hood and Collingwood Battalions actually attempted a further advance, at 12.30 p.m., but the situation was impossible. With the exception of Lieutenant Stuart Jones, of the Anson, and Sub-Lieut. Cockey, of the Hood, all the surviving officers were hit before the enemy's third line was reached.

With the Turks converging on the captured positions, a retirement became imperative. This was hardly less costly than the advance, partly because of a brave but useless attempt to hold on to a position half between the Turkish and our own original line. It was at this point that "B" Company of the Collingwood, who had advanced at 12.30 to dig a communication trench across the captured ground, were almost annihilated. No more now at the eleventh hour than earlier, in the first fury of the assault, could gallantry and self-sacrifice prevail against the enemy's machine guns on the flank. Any attempt to hold a position in advance of our front line was, in the prevailing circumstances, merely quixotic; and after sustaining cruel losses the surviving officers rightly decided on completing the retirement.

They were only just in time. At 12 noon the assaulting force had consisted roughly (excluding details left in the transport lines, at the Field Ambulance, or at the rest camp) of 1,900 men and 70 officers, almost half the men and a third of the officers being in the Collingwood battalion. Now, at 12.45, there returned to our lines 5 officers and 950 men. But of these not all could now be relied on, for many were of the Collingwood, who in this hour of horror had been deprived of all their officers, save one, and of all stability, and there were none to rally and organise the survivors of this fine, but ill-fated, battalion. (The battalion was actually brought out of the line by C.P.O. Carnall (later promoted to Sub-Lieut. R.N.V.H., and posted to the Hood Battalion). For his services on June 4th he received the D.S.M.)

The situation, if a counter-attack had developed, must have been critical, for, in the audacious hope of a crushing victory, the divisional commander had been left with but one reserve battalion. The Drake Battalion were ordered up at once to the front line, and General Paris was forced to ask for a battalion from the corps reserve to take their place as a reserve to the division. The request was granted, and the Benbow Battalion left the rest camp at 2.30 p.m. and moved up into the gully.

Every effort was made to secure French co-operation for a renewal of the attack. The first intention was for an attack by the R.N.D. alone at 2.15, with artillery support from the French. This support was not, however, forthcoming, for the commander-in-chief was at the same time organising and attempting to arrange for a joint operation by the French and the Naval Division. All his endeavours failed. The French commander found himself wholly unable to co-operate, and an unsupported attack by the Naval Division was rightly judged impossible. The issue of the battle had depended from the start on the success of the first assault, and this in turn had depended, for the reasons given, on the advance of the French Colonial troops along the ridge. The gamble had failed.

The failure was unfortunately conspicuous. In the centre of the line, the 42nd Division had achieved a memorable advance, and had captured and held three lines of Turkish trenches. Their casualties throughout the day had been serious, but not overwhelming, and they had been able to hold on, though with steadily increasing losses, in the hope of enabling the attack on the right to be renewed. Now their right had to be withdrawn. Here only the first line of captured trenches could be safely consolidated so long as our left remained where it was. Even then the front line held by the 42nd Division to the west of the Achibaba Nullah was nearly 350 yards ahead of the old front line on the east, to which the Naval Division had fallen back. This gap had to be filled, or the last of the morning's gains had to be surrendered.

The Manchester Brigade were still heavily engaged, and could find no troops for what must be not only a difficult but an expensive task. In the circumstances, the Nelson Battalion were sent forward to get their first experience of active operations south of Achibaba.

It was apparently first thought that an attack would have to be made on the Turks who still held on to their old front line on the immediate right of the Manchesters; but Colonel Eveleigh, after discussing the position with the brigadier on the spot, hit on a wiser, though still hazardous, plan, the execution of which was entrusted to "D" Company of his battalion (Lt.-Commander H. C. Evans, R.N.V.R.). This plan was to construct a number of separate entrenchments covering the gap between the two front lines, and so sited as to afford the maximum protection for the exposed flank. Protected by covering parties, these posts could be completed before dawn, and could then be joined up during the day into a continuous line.

Throughout the night the Turkish fire was continuous, and casualties were heavy, but the plan was so far successful that digging was able to continue, which would almost certainly not have been possible had the Turks been led to realise our intentions by a formal attack on their flank. When dawn broke, the fire, aimed from close range by the enemy in the front line to the right of the Manchesters, became intense, but enough cover had been won during the night to enable the posts to be not only held but steadily strengthened and extended throughout the day. By four o'clock (when "C" Company of the Hawke Battalion relieved the Nelson Company to carry on the work of consolidation), the trench, though shallow, was almost continuous.

With the safeguarding of the captured line the main battle of June 4th–5th was at an end.

★★★★★★

Hard fighting continued, however, on the left front of the 42nd Division throughout the 6th and 7th of June, and the Chatham Battalion was detached from the corps reserve to assist General Firth's Brigade in their efforts to safeguard the most advanced of the captured trenches. Owing to lack of artillery support the full scheme of consolidation (which necessitated two small advances) was not carried out, but the position was substantially maintained.

★★★★★★

It only remained for General Paris to relieve the remnants of the Howe, Hood and Collingwood Battalions, and this was done without delay, the Hawke Battalion taking over from the left of the Drake (who had relieved the Anson some hours before), and filling the gap between them and the Nelson Battalion.

This left as an effective divisional reserve only the Benbow Battalion, who remained in the neighbourhood of Backhouse Post.

Having regard to the disastrous reverse suffered by the French and the Naval Division on the morning of the 4th, the result was not wholly unsatisfactory. The fine pertinacity of the 42nd Division during the afternoon of the 4th and the work of the Nelson Battalion the next night had at least prevented the enemy from exploiting his earlier success and had preserved for us some substantial gains.

The price paid by the Naval Division for this very negative success was, unfortunately, out of all reckoning. More than sixty officers and 1,300 men became casualties, and, of these, nearly half were killed. The losses in senior officers and in Company Commanders impaired the fighting efficiency of the Division for some time to come. In the 2nd Brigade, one battalion commander (Lt.-Colonel Collins), one second in command (Major Myburg, of the Hood) and one company commander (Lieut. the Hon. K. Dundas) remained. The loss of the few regular officers of experience was particularly grievous. A drastic reorganisation was necessary, if those battalions who had already won for themselves a first-class fighting reputation (the Hood, Howe and Anson Battalions) were to retain a separate existence, and it was in these tragic circumstances that General Paris found it necessary to disband, not only the Benbow, but the ill-fated Collingwood Battalion, whose cruel losses were due in no way to lack of gallantry or skill. Under this arrangement, the Hood, Howe and Anson absorbed the officers and men of these battalions, and the Naval Brigades were reduced to three battalions apiece.

The veteran Colonel Oldfield, of the Benbow, had been wounded on June 5th, and it was thus his second in command, Major Bridges, R.M.L.I., who took command of the Anson Battalion, with Lt.-Commander Stuart Jones, the senior surviving officer of the old battalion, as his second in command. Major Myburg succeeded to the Hood, and Commander West was appointed second in command of the Howe. Among other officers transferred to the Anson Battalion were Lt.-Commander Bernard Ellis and Lt.-Commander Gilliland (both from the Benbow), who were to serve this battalion with such distinction in France.

The disaster of June 4th raised wider issues than the organisation of the division which had been most signally involved in it. The battle had been watched from first to last with alternate hope and disappointment by the commander-in-chief, and when it was over his mind was made up. He would not seek for another decision at Cape Helles. The strong reinforcements for which he had already asked would be thrown in on a new front. The campaign at Cape Helles would be for the future directed towards the gradual demoralisation of the enemy by minor operations, with a view to exhausting his manpower, drawing his reserves, and diverting his attention from other points. To enable this policy to be carried out, one fresh division, and one only, would be landed at Cape Helles.

With this decision the campaign south of Achibaba entered on a new phase, lasting till the middle of July, during which active fighting was always in progress somewhere or another, but the routine of trench warfare was also continuous, and attention was ever increasingly concentrated on the strengthening of our defences.

★★★★★★

And brought its toll of casualties: Surgeon Stewart, R.N., Sub-Lieut. C. E. C. Flood, Captain C. G. Bulling, R.M. (Deal Battalion), Sub-Lieut. T. E. Love (Hood), Sub-Lieut. A. C. Iliff (Nelson) and Surgeon F. H. Reas, R.N. (Drake) were among those killed in the last three weeks of this month while on ordinary trench duties.

★★★★★★

The local offensives of this period were not unimportant; if nothing else, they forestalled an attack by the enemy and enforced his respect. But, proceeding continuously, and side by side with the more spectacular happenings, we find constant work on saps, on the deepening and traversing of old trenches, and the making of new ones, on wiring, on the construction of strong points and machine-gun

Inspection of the 2nd R.N. Brigade by
General Sir Ian Hamilton, G.C.B., at Imbros, June 1915

emplacements, which was at least equally important. At this time, too, trench mortars and catapults (barbaric weapons, manufactured by some effort of inherited memory by—so it was said—Messrs. Gamage) appeared for the first time, to give a superficial touch of science to the primitive Eastern scene.

The reorganised Naval Division maintained throughout this period their old sector astride the Achibaba Nullah, slightly extended by taking over a small stretch of line from the French. The sector was held alternately by the Marine and the 1st Naval Brigade, and Commodore Backhouse's brigade were taken to Imbros for an essential rest. A use was found at this time for the Divisional Cyclist Company (Major N. O. Burge, R.M.L.I.), who were trained in bombing and attached to the different battalions to assist them, as far as might be humanly possible, to master the constant and untimely vagaries of these peculiar instruments. Later, when all battalions had developed a section of trained bombers of their own, the experts returned to Divisional Headquarters, to form the nucleus of the first bombing school founded on the peninsula.

★★★★★★

The metaphor is not without point. From now onward, till the end of 1917, the army was subjected to continual epidemics, the first symptom of which was almost invariably the formation of a new section of specialists attached to Battalion Headquarters. When the epidemic died down, the specialists would either cease to specialise or be distributed among the companies—according to the severity of the onset of the particular disease.

★★★★★★

After the battle of June 4th-5th the attention of the divisional commander was also directed to the construction of a more advanced firing-line, with a view to the renewal of the attack, should occasion arise, under conditions more favourable than those prevailing on June 4th. It was clear that the line could be pushed forward, without great hazard, to a distance of nearly 100 yards, but, opposite the centre section of the divisional front, was an advanced Turkish trench which it was felt ought to be at once easy to capture and useful to hold, and which, had it been either, would have assured an even more substantial advance. This trench it was decided to attack with the Hawke Battalion on June 19th. A daylight assault was out of the question, since every rifle and machinegun on the slopes of Achibaba and the Kereves Dere commanded the ground, and Colonel Wilson was left with no alternative to a night attack.

This was carried out by "A" Company (Lieutenant Morgan, R.N.V.R.). The first assault, for which the Turks did not seem unprepared, was met by a very heavy fire; Lieutenant Morgan and a number of men were killed round the enemy trench, and a large number were wounded. Rallied, however, by Lieutenant Horsfield, R.N.V.R., the company went forward again, quickly made good their hold on the trench, and began consolidating. Till day broke, the position looked secure, though our losses, both in the original attack, and from rifle and machine-gun fire in the later stage of the operation, were very high, having regard to the comparative unimportance of the objective. At dawn, the situation took on a very different aspect. The captured trench was discovered to have no adequate field of fire, and to be so sited as to be subject to direct enfilade from the main Turkish position. This was not all. In the darkness, the Turks had pushed down a small party of bombers, who were able from an old communication trench which lay in dead ground to the garrison of the captured trench, to inflict the most severe losses on them.

Had the bombing attack developed during the night, the position might have been retrieved by a sortie. By day, this was impossible. Already, moreover, the garrison was dangerously reduced. Lieutenant Horsfield, wounded in the first assault, had been wounded again, this time mortally. Sub-Lieut. Tremayne, the battalion machine-gun officer, had been killed. Of the original assaulting party not more than twenty were unwounded. These survivors had been relieved about 6 a.m. by a platoon of "C" Company, but within ten minutes of entering the trench half of this platoon also had become casualties. In these circumstances, it was decided to evacuate the position, as the only alternative to further and useless losses. In addition to Lieutenant Morgan, Lieutenant Horsfield and Sub-Lieutenant Tremayne, Sub-Lieutenant Little had been killed on his way back to the line after "A" Company had been relieved, and Sub-Lieutenant Milvaine had been seriously wounded while in charge of a working party engaged on a communication trench; he died of wounds a few days later. Of the petty officers and men, fourteen were killed and seventy-four wounded.

The next day but one, the French carried out a brilliant advance along the ridge of the Kereves Dere, and captured the key positions which they had failed to secure on June 4th. The Marine Brigade was in reserve for this operation.

On June 22nd, the Marine Brigade relieved General Mercer's Brigade in the trenches, and were called upon to attempt once again the capture of the trench which the Hawke Battalion had, three days before, held for six hours and then been obliged to abandon. This time the attempt was made by "A" Company of the Portsmouth Battalion, under Major Grover, R.M.L.I. The attack again succeeded, but the retribution came even more swiftly; the utmost gallantry and skill could not prevail against the facts, and the position was rightly given up within an hour and a half. In this operation the marines suffered seriously, Major Grover and 2nd Lieut. P. L. L. Jermain being among the killed. On this day the Drake also lost a fine officer in Lieutenant P. W. Magrath, R.N.V.R.

After these set-backs, the division reverted to its older and wiser policy of sapping by day and digging in in the open and wiring by night. In these operations the Chatham Battalion (Lt.-Colonel R. McN. Parsons, R.M.L.I.) did fine work, which was carried on by the Drake Battalion (now under Lt.-Commander H. D. King, R.N.V.R., Commander Campbell having been invalided a few days after June 4th).

On July 5th the monotony was relieved by an episode which the available records have dignified by the name of a Turkish attack. This was directed against the French lines, but, despite the blandishments of two extremely smart German officers who were seen urging the Turks to go forward, it never developed. Some twenty Turks, however, impelled perhaps more by curiosity than by zeal for battle, entered the Anson Battalion lines. (The Anson, having returned from Imbros, were attached at this time to the 1st Naval Brigade). A counter-attack was immediately organised by Major Bridges, and the battalion returned to their line. The enemy meanwhile had taken advantage of our timely retreat to return to their own lines, and the officer commanding the Anson Company in charge of the front line had finished his breakfast and had come out of his dug-out. This fantastic episode made an amusing tale in the mouths of the division's enemies in the peninsula (who were not all Turks). The more important thing was that the main attacking force of the enemy had been suitably handled on the parapets of their own trenches by the machine guns of the Hawke and Drake Battalions. Altogether at least a hundred casualties were inflicted by the Naval Battalions alone, and the French undoubtedly accounted for more. Our losses were negligible.

The day following, the Naval Division were relieved by the newly-arrived 52nd Division, who were to undertake our divisional attack.

Behind the scenes, the last act in the drama was being rehearsed; and it was felt to be essential that the attention of the Turks should be effectually diverted from other fields.

The decision to renew the offensive south of Achibaba on any considerable scale in advance of the larger operations now pending was nevertheless unexpected. A resolute defensive, designed to improve the health of the troops and to lead up to a general attack to be made simultaneously with the major operations, would have been a policy more easily understood. The fact was, however, that the general staff felt for some reason convinced that we could not risk a purely defensive policy throughout July. The result was a compromise between the need for an offensive as it presented itself to General Headquarters, and the still more urgent need for rest as represented by the authorities on the spot.

The compromise took the only possible form of an attack by the only fresh division, but its results were not fortunate. The attack was the most bloody engagement (in proportion to the number engaged and the nature of the objective) of any fought south of Achibaba, and it led indirectly to the spread of sickness on this front, on a scale which cannot have been without influence on the final issue of the campaign. (It should be explained that dysentery was already rife on the peninsula in June, 1915. The wastage, however, was only gradual. After the July battles the wastage became very rapid).

During the days preceding the attack (which was planned for July 12th) the Naval Division, already so severely depleted, and having now an establishment of only ten infantry battalions, was ordered to furnish a battalion at full strength, to be trained in pack mule work in connection with the new landing. The Anson Battalion, reinforced by details from other battalions and from the divisional troops, were detached for this duty, and the Deal Battalion of Marines had to take their turn on fatigue duties at "W" beach. The strength of the division on the eve of the attack consisted thus of eight weak infantry battalions. General Paris had proceeded to Mudros on leave, on July 8th. Brigadier-General Trotman, R.M.L.I., was temporarily in command.

The objectives of the 52nd Division were the same as of the Naval Division on June 4th, and the French were to co-operate on the right, in so far as was necessary. The Turkish positions on the right, which had then made it impossible for Commodore Backhouse's brigade to retain the trenches which they captured, had, however, been already taken by the French, on June 21st; and to make assurance against enfilade fire from the right doubly sure it was decided that the 52nd Division should themselves attack in the first instance only on the right. An advance from the left of their front was to be attempted only if the attack on the right succeeded.

The first attack (by the French, and the 155th Brigade of the 52nd Division, from the right of Parsons Road) began at 7.30 a.m., after an eighty-minutes' "intensive" bombardment, and was generally successful. The second stage of the operations, when the 157th Brigade were to advance from the left of their line, was also carried out according to plan later in the day, although the situation in the centre was not altogether clear. By the evening the position was that on the left the attack had succeeded completely, as also on the extreme right of the French line; that in the centre the attack had not got beyond the front two enemy lines, and that parties of Turks were holding out even here in communication trenches and shell holes. The day's fighting had been exceptionally severe, and the whole of the 52nd Division reserves had somehow become involved in the attack. In these circumstances, the Chatham, Portsmouth, Plymouth and Drake Battalions of the Naval Division had unexpectedly been called up to take the place of the original divisional reserve, and the Howe, Hood, Nelson and Hawke Battalions were under orders to move at ten minutes' notice.

During the night of the 12th-13th the position remained unchanged (though the Nelson Battalion moved forward to Backhouse Post), but on the morning of the 13th the communication between the 157th Brigade in the advanced trenches by the Achibaba Nullah and the remainder of their division, was still extremely precarious; and it appears that an attempt made by this brigade, by working back along old communication trenches, to establish touch between themselves and the right of the position in the enemy's old second line led to a temporary retirement. Major Sketchley, R.M.L.I., who was on a reconnaissance when the retirement took place, had no difficulty in restoring the situation, and the Turks, who had followed up the retreat, were soon driven back.

★★★★★★

G.S.O.2 of the R.N. Division, for his forceful intervention on this occasion Major Sketchley was awarded the D.S.O., and Lance-Corporal Way, his orderly, who assisted him in organising the counter-attack, gained the G.C.M.

★★★★★★

But the advanced position, so restored, remained isolated, and the

FIRING LINE IN R.N.D. SECTOR, MID SUMMER, 1915

Turks, still in possession of most of their third-line trenches, and consequently of covered approaches to the forward positions of the 52nd Division on the left, appear to have remained masters of the situation.

It seemed certain, from the grievous losses which were being sustained, and from the entire breakdown in communications, that we must either advance further or withdraw. In these circumstances, Brigadier-General Trotman (temporarily commanding the R.N. Division) was asked to clear up the position, and he determined on a general attack on those third-line positions of the Turks which had so far defied capture. This attack, the orders for which were issued at 3.20 p.m., was to be carried out by the Chatham, Portsmouth and Nelson Battalions at 4.30 p.m. The Nelson Battalion was to attack on the left, the Portsmouth in the centre, and the Chatham, in co-operation with the French, on the right. The Drake and Plymouth Battalions remained in divisional reserve.

Owing to an inexplicable congestion in the trenches, the orders did not reach the Chatham Battalion (Lt.-Colonel Godfrey, R.M.L.I.) till 3.55 p.m., and the thirty-five minutes left before the attack were quite inadequate to the necessary preparation; more particularly as it was impossible to get any news of the movements of the French. (Lt.-Colonel R. McN. Parsons, R.M.L.I., had been wounded on June 28th. For his services with the R.N. Division he was later awarded the C.B.)

The attack, therefore, was actually carried out only by the Nelson and Portsmouth Battalions, though Colonel Godfrey worked forward into the two lines of previously captured trenches on the Chatham Battalion front, which were held by scattered details of the 52nd Division. The Nelson and Portsmouth Battalions, on the other hand, advanced with the greatest gallantry. Colonel Eveleigh's battalion had no difficulty in capturing and consolidating the left of the objective, where they found themselves in touch with the 5th Battalion H.L.I., still clinging on to the gains of the previous afternoon in the neighbourhood of the Achibaba Nullah.

The Portsmouth Battalion, like the 5th K.O.S.B. before them, found that the enemy third line, further to the right, did not exist in recognisable form (the dispatch puts it, perhaps, less clearly, when it says that the Portsmouth Battalion fell into the same error as the K.O.S.B. at the same place), and they advanced too far. Losing almost all their officers, they had to fall back, but, even then, they dug in on a line in advance of the narrow ditch (not more than eighteen inches deep) which was all that there was of the enemy's third line at this point. One platoon of this battalion (under Lieutenant Murdoch Browne, R.M.L.I.) remained isolated from the rest of the battalion in a still more advanced position. (Lieutenant Browne, R.M.L.I., was awarded the D.S.C. for his services in the Gallipoli campaign. By his death in France, November 13th, 1916, the Corps lost an officer of exceptional promise).

Only those who actually witnessed the unbelievable confusion of the battle, the sickness of the troops, intensified a hundredfold by local conditions, and the tenacity of the Turkish resistance at this time, can appreciate the brilliant character of these advances, which were, in terms of the operations of these two days, decisive.

The losses in the Nelson and Portsmouth Battalions had, however, been disastrous. Lt.-Colonel Eveleigh and Lt.-Colonel Luard and ten other officers had been killed.

★★★★★★

Lieutenants Wilmot-Sitwell and Dougherty, of the Portsmouth Battalion, Lieut. Baldwin, R.N.V.R., and Sub-Lieutenants J. M. F. Dickson, W. H. Edwards, W. Lintott, E. V. Rice, B. W. Smyth and F. H. J. Startin, of the Nelson Battalion, Sub-Lieut. Weaver, of the Howe Battalion, and Assistant Paymaster H. Biles, R.N.V.R., of the 2nd Brigade Staff.

★★★★★★

Five other officers and 278 other ranks had become casualties in the Nelson Battalion alone, and in the Portsmouth Battalion Captain Gowney, D.S.C., was the only unwounded officer. For the survivors, moreover, clinging desperately to their gains as night came on, the conditions were well-nigh unendurable. Some of the worst scenes ever experienced on the battlefields of France or Mesopotamia were crowded into this narrow front of half a mile, over which fighting had been continuous for nearly forty-eight hours, where many hundreds of men lay dead or dying, where a burning sun had turned the bodies of the slain to a premature corruption, where there was no resting-place free from physical contamination, where the air, the surface of the ground, and the soil beneath the surface were alike poisonous, fetid, corrupt.

The Nelson Battalion were the best off, in tolerably deep and traversed trenches, but they had no safe communications either with our old line or with the Portsmouth Battalion, whose scattered relics were digging in on an undefined line, running back from the right of the Nelson to a point some two hundred yards in advance of the left of the Chatham Battalion. With the Chatham Marines in the old Turkish second line were the confused elements of many units of the 52nd Division, facing gallantly the almost impossible task of organising the defence of what may have been a trench, but had become a graveyard. Even from here, there were no safe communications with our old front line.

If the brilliant success of the afternoon were not to be thrown away, prompt and energetic measures were needed. They were taken. The Drake Battalion was sent up to take over the whole disputed ground between the entrenchments of the Nelson on the left and the Chatham on the right. Though the battalion came up for the first time in the dark, the correct line was found, held, and consolidated, and by dawn lateral communication had been established along the whole front. For this fine piece of work Lt.-Commander King, R.N.V.B. was to a large extent responsible.

★★★★★★

Lieut.-Commander (now Captain) H. D. King, R.N.V.R., was soon after this engagement awarded the D.S.O. and promoted to the rank of Commander. His fine work with the Drake Battalion was a feature of the campaign.15. The general had returned from Mudros on the evening of the 13th.

★★★★★★

The losses of the Drake Battalion were not inconsiderable. In particular the two senior Company Commanders in the battalion, Lt.-Commander N. Wells and Lt.-Commander Sir J. H. Campbell, both survivors of all the earlier battles, were wounded.

The line now held was still short of our objective, for a portion of the enemy's third line, which had been the objective of the right of the 115th Brigade and of the French left on the morning of the 12th, had, owing to the inability of the Chatham Battalion and the French to co-ordinate an advance on the afternoon of the 18th, not been again attacked. The new line was, however, in General Paris's view[15] the best from a purely military point of view which his division had as yet been called on to hold, and it was wisely decided to be content with it. General Paris was thus able to devote his unfailing energies to the extremely difficult task of reorganisation and consolidation. The first move was to withdraw from the overcrowded, insanitary and dangerously exposed trenches as many men as possible of the gallant 52nd Division (the whole sector had now been handed over to the

Naval Division. All, save one battalion on the extreme left of the sector, were withdrawn on the 14th from the forward trenches. The new sector was then divided into two brigade sub-sectors, with the Marine Brigade on the left and the 1st Naval Brigade on the right.

Here, for ten days, hardly less anxious and no less unpleasant than the actual days of battle, the division laboured on the essential tasks of burying the dead, reconstructing the trenches and pushing forward barricades along the trenches communicating between our own lines and those of the enemy. The strain on the troops must have been almost unprecedented in the annals of defensive warfare, but the work proceeded: battalions worked at high pressure for short spells in front line, and within less than a fortnight conditions reverted to normal. The Hood Battalion carried out a highly successful operation during this period, when they rushed a Turkish barricade, which had been established too close to our line, and won another thirty yards of trench. In this operation Lieut. Charles Lister played a very prominent part, and was wounded, leading the attack with a characteristic distinction. Lt.-Commander Freyberg, D.S.O., who had taken over command of the Hood Battalion from Major Myburg (sick) earlier in the month, was on this occasion wounded for the second time. He was temporarily succeeded in command by Lt.-Commander E. W. Nelson, R.N.V.R.

On July 25th the responsibilities of the infantry, so often incomparably the heaviest, were at last lightened, the garrisoning of the trenches being taken over, under Naval Divisional arrangements, by the 33rd Brigade. This was the beginning of the long promised rest, and on August 1st the Naval Division handed over the line for a definite period to the 42nd Division and the French. The long deferred time of rest had come, but it had come too late. The strength of the division, even after the June disaster, had been 208 officers and 7,141 other ranks. On August 1st, it was shown as 129 officers and 5,038 other ranks.

The strain of the July battles and of the subsequent fortnight in the line had definitely broken not the fighting spirit but the physical health of the men. Even of the five thousand officers and men remaining at the beginning of August, not 10 *per cent*, would have been considered fit in France for duty in the quietest part of the line. In Gallipoli at this time all officers and men who could actually walk to the trenches were reckoned as fit. On any other classification the campaign must have been abandoned. The plain fact was that the capacity of the troops to stand the strain of continuous fighting under unhealthy conditions had been overestimated.

The only relief which the infantry could find was in bathing when out of the line. This was not merely pleasant but safe, since a wise discrimination in the choice of bathing places ensured the protection of the cliffs against shell fire. The test of morale at this time was the ability to face the walk to the beaches for the pleasure of bathing on arriving there. Samuel Butler says somewhere that the essence of morality is that the pain precedes the pleasure. On this view, bathing in July was a highly meritorious achievement. It was certainly the only thing which enabled even the hardiest to survive, though not to escape, dysentery and jaundice and the other effects of living on tinned food (shared with swarms of flies), in an almost tropical climate for a period of months.

The Naval Division had at this difficult time their own peculiar difficulties to contend with. No sooner had the division reached their bivouacs and begun the first tentative reorganisation than an order was received that 300 fleet reserve stokers were to be transferred for fleet service. The first thought was that the division was being broken up. It was not far wrong. The Naval Battalions were being deprived of their backbone of trained and disciplined veterans, and the task of reorganisation had assumed serious proportions. So severe had been the losses experienced by the Anson, Howe, Hood, Nelson and Drake Battalions, that the withdrawal of 300 stokers meant, practically, the withdrawal of every regular rating from the battalions.

The needs of the fleet were no doubt urgent; but it is probable that the stokers would have been allowed to remain if adequate reinforcements could have been provided to bring the division up to full strength. The strongest representations, personal and official, had been made to the authorities at home, pointing out the urgent need for reinforcing the Naval Division after the battle of June 4th, mid again after the battle of July 12th-13th. Before this date Sir Ian Hamilton, in a personal letter to Mr. Winston Churchill, wrote that:

> The Naval Division have really done superbly. They have . . . suffered proportionately heavy losses. . . . The particular brigade I spoke of (the 2nd Naval Brigade) will, if it receive reinforcements within a fairly short time, be second to none as a fighting machine in the service. If, on the other hand, I am forced by circumstances to shove it into another severe fight before reinforcements come, then it will be so pulled down in strength

that there will not be enough of the old soldiers remaining to leaven the new drafts.

The First Lord of the Admiralty received at the same time the most urgent official representations, and the Army Council were formally requested to assist in the provision of reinforcements on the very grounds so forcibly urged by Sir Ian Hamilton. The War Office were unable, however, to assist in any way, and indeed, stated that they proposed to telegraph to Sir Ian Hamilton giving him *carte blanche,* after consultation with Sir John de Robeck, to make any necessary reductions in the establishment of the division. The fact that a division was at the Dardanelles had appeared before now to be a sufficient reason for starving it of the ordinary reinforcements, and, in any case, it is arguable that the War Office could not have been expected to go out of its way to help the Naval Division. The fact remains that their decision meant that the division could be fit for little more than garrison duty for the remainder of the campaign, and that the fighting strength of the whole force was thus avoidably diminished.

With the stokers, went Commodore Backhouse and his staff, and the 2nd Naval Brigade ceased to exist. So also did the Marine Brigade. For the marines, too, there were no adequate reinforcements, and the Portsmouth, Plymouth, Chatham and Deal Battalions were amalgamated into two battalions under Lt.-Colonel Matthews, C.B., R.M.L.I. (succeeded a little later by Lt.-Colonel Hutchison, R.M.L.I.) and Captain F. N. White (temporary, pending the arrival from England of Lt.-Colonel Stroud, C.B., R.M.L.I.). With the Marine Battalions were brigaded the Anson (still on detached duty) and the Howe Battalions. This now became the 2nd Naval Brigade. The 1st Brigade consisted of the Drake, Nelson, Hawke and Hood Battalions. Lt.-Commander H. D. King and Lt.-Commander B. C. Freyberg were confirmed in the command of the Drake and Hood Battalions and were promoted to the rank of Commander. Major Burge (from the Divisional Cyclist Company) was appointed to command the Nelson with Lt.-Commander Nelson, R.N.V.R. as Second in Command; and Lt.-Colonel L. O. Wilson, D.S.O., M.P. continued in command of the Hawke Battalion.

With this reorganisation our detailed narrative of the events on the Gallipoli peninsula must close. The remaining four months of the campaign surpass perhaps in historic importance, though assuredly not in dramatic interest, the days of the earlier struggles. But neither

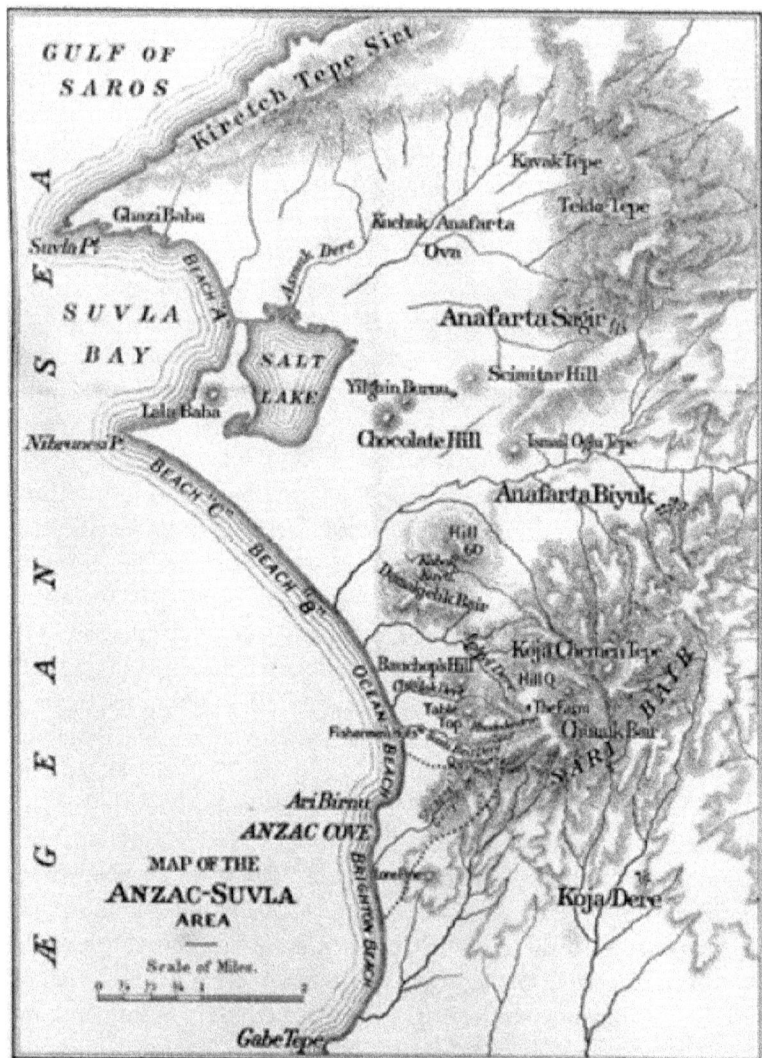

GULF OF
SAROS

Kiretch Tepe Sirt

Kavak Tepe

Teke Tepe

Ghazi Baba

Suvla Pt.

BEACH "A"

Kuchuk Anafarta
Ovn

Anafarta Sagir

SUVLA
BAY

Asmak Dere

SALT
LAKE

Yilghin Burnu

Scimitar Hill

Lala Baba

Nibrunesi P.

Chocolate Hill

Ismail Oglu Tepe

BEACH "C"

BEACH "B"

Anafarta Biyuk

Hill
60

Kidney
Knoll

Damakjelik Bair

OCEAN BEACH

Koja Chemen Tepe

Baychops Hill

Chailak Dere

Hill Q

The Farm

Table
Top

Chunuk Bair

Fisherman's Hut

Quinns Post

SARI BAIR

Ari Birnu

ANZAC COVE

BRIGHTON BEACH

MAP OF THE
ANZAC-SUVLA
AREA

Lonesome Pine

Koja Dere

Scale of Miles.

0   ¼   ½   ¾   1   2

Gabe Tepe

Stanford's Geog Estab London

SEA

AEGEAN

Dotted Line .... represents roughly the boundary of Anzac Area
on Aug. 4, 1915.

in the great events at Anzac and Suvla in August and September nor in the heroic local assaults delivered at Cape Helles in August and September by the 29th, the 42nd and the 52nd Divisions, did the Naval Division play a part. Sir Ian Hamilton's prophecy had been fulfilled at any rate to the extent that the division was numerically too weak to be thrown into any severe engagement. How it was that so much had been sacrificed for so little can never be wholly accounted for in a single page, or even in a single volume.

But it is hardly possible to doubt that, as things turned out, in the light of the unexpected resistance by the Turks to the attack from Anzac, and of the unexpected breakdown in our offensive at Suvla, the battles of June and July on the peninsula cost more than they were worth. For they cost much more than the equivalent of the aggregate of our casualties. The Naval Division in August, 1915, was something very different in numbers, in experience and in their capacity for endurance from the Naval Division in May. The same was true of the other divisions on the peninsula throughout the same time.

And so the only thing that remains to tell about the Naval Division in Gallipoli is the story of an anticlimax rising almost, in the end, to the dramatic level. Yet at the same time we shall be able to trace the Naval Division developing, reorganising, even under the most depressing conditions, finding within itself and in its reinforcements unexpected sources of strength, and in the end needing but little more than rest and a change of diet before it was ready to take its place in the line once more as a fighting division trained and equipped for the offensive. New personalities had come and were coming to the front under provocation of the urgent opportunity.

Commander King more than upheld the reputation of those officers of the regular R.N.V.R. who had formed the majority of the original officers of the division, and of whom so few were now left, and the new adjutant of the Drake, Lieut. Sterndale Bennett, R.N.V.R. was gaining that experience which alone was necessary to make him an equally outstanding figure. Commander Freyberg had enhanced the reputation which he had won by his dashing exploit in the Gulf of Xeros and was showing himself not only a fine soldier but a distinguished leader of men, and Lt.-Commander Asquith, Lt.-Commander W. M. Egerton and Lieut. F. S. Kelly shared with Commander Freyberg the credit for bringing the reorganised Hood Battalion in the ensuing months to that brilliant standard of efficiency which was later to assist the division to an historic success. Lt.-Commander Stuart Jones,

GULLY RAVINE GALLIPOLI

Lt.-Commander Ellis and Lt.-Commander Gilliland were creating at the same time a new Anson tradition, and Lt.-Commander C. S. West and Lt.-Commander P. H. Edwards were setting an inspiring example to the Howe Battalion, which had its own difficulties to contend with.

The new Nelson Battalion under Lt.-Colonel Burge, the Hawke Battalion still under the courageous leadership of Lt.-Colonel Leslie Wilson and Commander Ramsay Fairfax, R.N., and the reorganised Marine Battalions (as finely officered as ever before) were also to show themselves fully capable of profiting by the example of their commanders. In short, the Naval Division as it had sailed for Gallipoli was passing away, but a successor was growing up whose achievements, when the time came, were to challenge, if not to surpass, those of its predecessors. The time, however, was not yet. The force south of Achibaba was no better in its present situation than a beleaguered garrison, and the wind from Suvla bore on its wings no rumour of relief.

ANTICLIMAX

Neither in the landing at Suvla and in the general offensive from Anzac to which that landing was subsidiary, nor in the diversions at Cape Helles early in August, had the Naval Division, as such, any share. Only the Anson Battalion and the 2nd Field Ambulance were detached for special duty at Suvla, the former in charge of pack transport, the latter as corps troops. Amid the constant fluctuations of the new front these two units carried out their essential if inconspicuous task and won high praise from those in authority, but no account can be written here of the scenes amid which they moved, of the nature of the fighting, and of the day-to-day incidents which marked the different stages of the campaign.

******

There is a fairly full account in that excellent work, *On Four Fronts with the Royal Naval Division*, by Surgeons Sparrow and McBean Ross (this is also republished by Leonaur). Lieut. the Hon. K. Dundas, R.N.V.R. (Anson), was killed at Suvla on August 7th by a chance shot. As is known, the landing was virtually unopposed.

******

The Naval Division remained south of Achibaba, and it is only in its effect on that front that we can treat, of the August and September fighting further north.

Considering all things, the secret of the date and place of the new landing was fairly well kept, but towards the end of July the excitement grew, for all knew that somewhere, and soon, a new attempt was to be made to break through the Turkish cordon and set our armies once more on the move. For those divisions who, with the bitter experience of more than three months' continuous fighting behind them, were called on to suffer the inevitable losses entailed by a demonstration against entrenched positions, or who waited, as did the Naval Division, as spectators, for the news which might restore to them their freedom of action, the early days of August were memorable. The initial disappointment, when it came, was severe.

The partial failure of the operations of August 6th-11th not, however, fully realised as involving the final breakdown of the campaign.

From a purely military point of view, the delay at Suvla is fatal as the delay at Cape Helles in April; but it was not more so. Just as we had had to take Achibaba within forty-eight hours or fail even to threaten our real objective, so, in August, we had to carry Ismail Oghi Tepe and threaten the flank of the enemy position centred on the historic hills of Chunak Bair and Koja Chemen Tepe, if these vital positions from which our guns would command Maidos and the Narrows were to fall to the assault of what was now the main force operating from Anzac. But the breakdown of this plan was not in itself the ultimate disaster. There was still a chance of victory. New formations were available, and could have been sent to Gallipoli early in September, to exploit the inadequate, but still remarkable, success gained in August. Why they were not; how they were first held up till the perhaps premature offensive at Loos had petered out, and how then they were diverted to Salonica, is told in full detail in Sir Ian Hamilton's Diary. It was for the news of these reinforcements that every soldier on Gallipoli waited during the days following the inconclusive close of the first northern battle.

Slowly the hope of reinforcements faded. Rumour—truly the swiftest of military as of other disasters—spoke of doubts and hesitations at home. Troops returning from hospital in Egypt brought news of the indifference with which their great if unavailing sacrifices were regarded by the hierarchy of conservative opinion which ruled the councils at that rather Capuan base. It was then that the spectre of doubt, which had loomed up first when the authentic news from Suvla came to hand, began to cast a lengthening shadow. As things happened, the failure at Suvla, inexplicable perhaps, perhaps merely' unexplained, was indeed the cause of the untimely ending of the campaign. But it was not simply the decent charity of one soldier towards another which made common men hesitate, and in the end refuse, to place the whole blame on the staffs, generals and battalions whose several responsibility for the defeat it is still so difficult to determine. Others, who had intrigued against the expedition almost from the start and who now abandoned it, not in favour of the French front, but in favour of Salonica, must share the ultimate responsibility for the decisive failure, for "a disaster," as Mr. H. W. Nevinson rightly says, "leaving its lamentable mark upon the world's history."

The immediate result of the admission of defeat on the northern front was that, south of Achibaba, the resistance of the sorely tried infantry divisions to physical ills and hardships long endured was weakened by the subconscious realisation that the campaign was at a standstill. During the September and October, the war-weary divisions at Cape Helles melted like snow in the noonday sun. By the middle of October, the effective strength of the division had sunk to 3,200. Since April 25th, out of more than 16,500 men of unmatched physique and still unimpaired determination, over 13,000 had become casualties, killed, wounded, or evacuated sick. But for the splendid work of the naval surgeons throughout the whole period, these figures—appalling as they are—would have been far higher.

It was when this wave of sickness was at its height that it became known that Sir Ian Hamilton was handing over the Supreme Command. Only a few days before he had visited the Naval Division trenches with General Paris and General Mercer, and spoken to very many officers and men. It was no surprise when this visit became, in retrospect, a visit of farewell. And it was no coincidence that his resignation came at a time when the strength of the division was at its ebb. For the change in command was no more than the logical and expected result of the change in the opinions of the government at home. It is one of the ineradicable misfortunes of modern war that the fighting soldier can never get to know his commander-in-chief, but it was generally felt that, with Sir Ian Hamilton, went the last hope of an energetic prosecution of the campaign. His departure, in fact, summed up the situation, crystallized it. What everyone had feared, was now to happen.

From mid-August onward, the division were in the front line, and often actively engaged in the modified offensives peculiar to stationary warfare. The new divisional sector which they took over from the 29th Division on August 15th lay between Gully ravine and the

BATHING FROM THE BEACH BETWEEN CAPE HELLES AND SEDD-EL-BAHR

Krithia Nullah. The sector, sadly damaged in the costly demonstrations of August 6th and 7th (carried out on this front by the 29th Division), was neither healthy nor secure. The front line was a part of the old Turkish trench system, and was joined to the present Turkish line by numerous communication trenches, watched from barricades, generally within hand-bombing distance of the enemy. These barricades marked almost invariably the scene of the most bitter hand-to-hand fighting.

The bodies of English and Turks alike were built into the walls of these rough-and-ready fortifications, and others were buried only a few inches below the ground. In the rest of the front-line trenches the conditions were only a little less unhealthy. These conditions accentuated the sickness which was due primarily, as has been said, to other causes. The numbers available for duty in the trenches fell constantly, while the length of the divisional sector could not be correspondingly Induced. In the result, the hours of duty were lengthened, the reliefs were less frequent, the fatigues were more arduous.

If active fighting was at an end, the strain of the defensive war carried on under these difficulties was considerable. Moreover, in face of the possibility of a winter campaign, communications had improved; a trench drainage system had to be prepared, and a new front-line trench had to be dug and wired. Our trenches were so sited as to be extremely open to effective bombardment, and the work of reconstructing the sector was dangerous, as well as irksome, to the depleted garrisons. (And to the Engineers, whose energies were unfailing. It is certain that no division was ever better served by its field companies than was the Naval Division).

Throughout this period, a semblance of an offensive war also had to be maintained, if only to forestall any possible Turkish attack. To this end, saps were pushed out, barricades pushed forward, and intensive trench-mortar bombardments added to the horrors of war.

The incidents of this eventful but unromantic period call for little mention. On August 27th we read of a daring reconnaissance of the Turkish front line by Lt.-Commander Asquith (Hood) and Lieut. Blyth (Drake); two days later, of a Turkish reconnaissance of our own trenches in the neighbourhood of the Northern barricade, which was beaten off with loss by the Hawke Battalion. Again, two days later, we read of the advancement of one of the barricades by Lt.-Commander Isgar, of the Howe Battalion, in a cool and successful operation. During September and October episodes of this character, so vivid in experience, so drab in retrospect, follow one another almost monotonously. By October 6th, the new firing line was completed, and the rest of the month was occupied with the almost more dangerous and uninspiring task of wiring it. Later in the same month, Lt.-Commander Isgar, assisted by C.P.O. Gray, P.O. Conway and L.S.Townes, pushed forward the Worcester barricade. Early in November, Sub-Lieut. Hancock's platoon of "C" Company of the Hawke Battalion carried out the same operation at the Southern barricade with equal success.

The value of these operations, entailing as they did a constant stream of minor casualties, and aggravating if possible the prevailing sickness, was sometimes called in question. We had, however, to hold on this front a very superior force, fully conscious of the victory which they had won on the Northern front in August. On other grounds, too, the policy of the divisional commander had much to recommend it. In these operations, the newly-joined reinforcements, put into the line as they arrived, were able to learn something of war, and to retain something of discipline. The tactics afforded, in fact, the only solution of the most serious domestic problem with which the division was confronted, the absorption of reinforcements under conditions so circumscribed, that it was actually impossible to parade even a platoon.

Difficulties of organisation and discipline were heightened by the heavy losses of officers from sickness in August and September. Brigadier-General Trotman was away ill for the whole of September, and Lt.-Colonel Stroud, R.M.L.I., temporarily assumed command of the Brigade. Lt.-Colonel Matthews, R.M.L.I., was invalided permanently from the peninsula at the same time. Lt.-Colonel Wilson (Hawke Battalion), was invalided on October 7th, and was succeeded temporarily by Commander W. G. Ramsay Fairfax, R.N. Lt.-Colonel Burge, R.M.L.I. (Nelson Battalion), was invalided in October, and was succeeded temporarily by Lt.-Commander E. W. Nelson, R.N.V.R.

The rate of sickness among junior officers was correspondingly high. During the period August 15th to November 30th the 1st Naval Brigade alone, in addition to losing four officers killed (Sub-Lieut. Farrow of the Hawke, Sub-Lieut. Bligh of the Drake, and Lieutenant the Hon. Charles Lister and Sub-Lieut. E. H. Gibson of the Hood) and two wounded, lost sixty-three officers evacuated sick. Among those who left the division during this period were three chaplains, the Rev. H. C. Foster, the Rev. B. Failes and the Rev. F. Pierce, and the medical officers of the Nelson (Surgeon Parker, R.N.) and of the Hawke (Surgeon W. Bradbury, R.N.), all of whom had done magnificent work throughout the campaign.

★★★★★★

In the 2nd Brigade Captain E. B. Carpenter, R.M. (Plymouth), Lieut. G. S. Perkins, R.M. (Deal) and Sub-Lieut. Massey (Howe) were killed during this period.

Among them were Surgeon D. R. Bedell Sivright, M.B., R.N. (best known, perhaps, as a Rugby international) and Lt.-Commander W. S. Miall Green (Benbow), both of whom died a short time after.

For his services in the peninsula Staff-Surgeon Bradbury was later awarded the D.S.O. and Surgeon Parker the D S.C.

★★★★★★

If the health of the officers was bad, that of the men was no better, and the constant fatigues made their existence infinitely more burdensome. The result was that in September and October the division lost well over four thousand men (though they received reinforcements which made the net loss a little less), and even in November, when the colder weather made the conditions in the trenches more bearable, the loss was over a thousand.

That work continued without cessation, and that the sector was very materially strengthened, was to the credit of the men of the infantry and the officers and men of the engineers. Their work was not materially lighter whether they were in or out of the line. In preparation for winter, and to make room for the 2/2nd and 2/4th Battalions of the London Regiment, who came to reinforce the division in October, the R.N.D. rest camp was moved during October to the extreme left of the peninsula, behind the new divisional sector. The new camp was systematically planned to afford the maximum protection against the shell-fire, but there was no available timber, and only a little corrugated iron. Safety and comfort, therefore, alike, depended on digging.

The idea was to build rows of oblong dugouts, five feet deep at the back and six feet in front, each draining into a narrow communicating trench, at least seven feet deep, along which officers and men could move round the camp entirely unobserved. In the event of a heavy bombardment it was thought that these deep and narrow trenches would themselves afford fairly effective protection. The chances of prolonged bombardment of the rest camp were, however, serious, and it was decided to ensure against its effects still further by linking up the rest camp with the cliffs, by a prolongation of two or more of the internal communicating trenches. The camp could then be evacuated, if necessary, under cover.

This elaborate scheme, necessary though it might have proved itself, entailed an almost heartbreaking task for the infantry battalions. Yet this task, too, was well on the road to completion by the end of November, and the division was experiencing the nearest approach to comfort which had yet been encountered on active service when the weather broke. The first sign was a torrential downpour of rain on the night of November 26th-27th. The next night it turned to snow, and throughout the next two days a northerly gale blew, while the frost, which had set in on the 27th-28th, lasted for the best part of three days, reaching its height on the morning of the 30th, when the thermometer stood at 18° Fahrenheit. For three days it had not risen above 22°, and the effect of this sudden cold on men who were still suffering from the effects of an almost tropical summer was extremely bad.

Only one dugout per company was roofed. The remainder (four-fifths) of the men were in the open, or at best under a covering of worn-out waterproof sheets; and the supplies of blankets, fuel and oil were wholly inadequate to the emergency. Had the cold continued, the situation must have become as serious at Cape Helles as it did at Suvla and Anzac, when two hundred died of cold in three days, and ten thousand men were evacuated sick. Even as it was, there were many cases of frost-bite among the troops whose ill luck it was to be in the line at this time. Twenty-four occurred in the 1st Marine Battalion alone.

To the general surprise, for the Army Corps at Cape Helles had learnt to expect but little from fortune, the weather improved (though only for a week or *so)* on December 1st, and, though the trenches were temporarily flooded by the thaw which came as suddenly as the frost, things were normal again by the end of the first week in December. In one all-important respect they were actually better. The frost, unbearable while it lasted, put an end at once to the lingering summer sickness.

On December 5th, the division, just as it was nearing the completion of the rest camp, received orders to take over a new sector on the left of the line, from the right of the 42nd Division to the left of the French sector, which was now to be shortened. This relief was carried out by General Trotman's brigade on December 11th. On the 17th, the rest camp was given over to the 87th Brigade, and the Naval Division moved into French billets on the coast above Morto Bay.

The first thought of the division, on learning that they had to take over part of the French line and a French camp, was one of dismay. The French artillery and the French wine were universally admired, but the fact that the new sector would be supported by a group of "75's" was regarded as the one consolation. It was assumed that the French trenches would be more primitive, less clean, and less well organised than our own, and that the French camp would be a poor substitute for that which the division had built up at so great an expenditure of energy. No assumption could have been more incorrect. Though the ground on which the camp and the reserve lines stood was rocky to a depth of some feet, the trenches and dugouts were both deeper than our own. They were also weather-proof, built round with stones, and roofed with corrugated iron.

The officers' quarters were as comfortable as could be, with tables and chairs, wooden floors, firmly constructed stone walls, and doors and windows complete with everything but glass. This was not Sybaritic luxury. It merely meant that the French War Office had sent out to Gallipoli supplies of stores essential to the health and comfort, and so to the fighting efficiency, of the troops, in quantities which were proportioned to the numbers of their expeditionary force. For English troops, corresponding supplies had never been available.

In the trenches, also, was much that the British Army had lacked through the campaign. Particularly striking was the abundance of strong corrugated iron (very different from the flimsy material of the same name which was doled out in yards to the British) which formed the material for most of the dugouts, and was in itself almost splinter-proof, being more than a quarter of an inch thick. The whole of this corrugated iron was of English manufacture.

From a military point of view, the most striking feature of the French organisation was the artillery liaison system. The arrangements were no better (at least in theory) than those universally adopted a little later by all formations, but they were in advance of anything yet experienced by the Naval Division.

It was, however, no period of rest or comfort which awaited the division in this sector. All that can be said is that the arrangements made by the French made it just practicable for the trenches to be maintained in reasonable security by a numerically weak division, under conditions which were extremely unfavourable. Two new factors made a profound change in the military situation in December, 1915.

In the first place, the weather settled down by the second week in December to definite winter conditions, which meant heavy, though not continuous, rain. In the second place, the Turks, for the first time, began a systematic and effective bombardment of our front-line trenches with heavy guns. (Captain C. F. Mead, R.M.L.I. , Deal Battalion, Sub-Lieut. C. Bridgland, R.N.V.R., Drake, and Sub-Lieut. B. W. Kenny, R.N.V.R., Nelson, were among those killed in these closing days of the campaign).

Both these adverse factors were such as could be, and were, overcome on other fronts. By an army starved of supplies, starved of rest, under-officered, suffering from continual disappointment, hopelessly under-gunned, they could only be endured.

★★★★★★

I do not intend to suggest that the morale of the division was on the ebb. It was not. The truth is that it was only the morale of the troops which enabled a resolute defence to be maintained under almost impossible conditions. The mere physical strain, however, made a renewal of the offensive, unless reinforcements could be supplied, impossible.

★★★★★★

To offset the obvious hardships and increasing dangers to which the force was exposed there was little but the improved health of the troops, which clearly would not be maintained indefinitely through a winter campaign, and the return to all battalions of not a few tried officers and men who had been evacuated sick earlier in the campaign.

It was in these circumstances that official news came of the evacuation of Suvla and Anzac. The official announcement naturally did not forecast—rather, it definitely denied—the possibility of the evacuation of the southern beaches, but, from the point of view of the linesmen, this was immaterial. Whatever happened, the relief of the Naval Division for a period of rest, if only on the adjacent islands, could not now be long delayed.

Few military histories, which record so proudly and so truly the enthusiasm of all ranks of an army at the beginning of a campaign, give equal prominence to the no less fervent longing of all soldiers for a period of rest after months of continuous fighting. To live on the Gallipoli peninsula was to be continuously, not merely within effective range, but under fire. Not a day passed but that some camp was shelled, and all the beaches; while the daily fatigues were as often as not carried out under indirect rifle fire. The prospect of a temporary change from these conditions could have been nothing less than joyous in any circumstances. As it happened, the prospect first dawned on the men in the front-line trenches during a week of exceptionally persistent bombardment, when the casualties were severe. Austrian heavy artillery, moreover, was reported to be coming into position.

The first hint of relief for the Naval Division was the announcement, made on December 29th, before the policy of evacuation was definitely decided on, that the 8th Corps would be relieved by the 9th Corps. (It is not universally known that among those in high command on the peninsula and in the Eastern Mediterranean were many vigorous opponents of evacuation). This was the alternative scheme which would have been adopted had it been decided to remain at Cape Helles; but the purpose of the announcement was wider. On December 24th, Sir William Birdwood, now commanding the Dardanelles Army under the supreme command of Sir Charles Monro, had received orders to make all "preliminary preparations for immediate evacuation in the event of orders to this effect being received," and it was essential to make some public explanation of the withdrawal of certain surplus stores, etc., which had to be put in hand without delay. The situation soon resolved itself, and on the next day (December 30th) General Paris received orders to prepare for early evacuation.

Immediately on receipt of his instructions to make preliminary preparations, General Birdwood had ordered silence to be maintained at stated intervals each night from the 25th onward, and, as far as the front line was concerned, nothing was required in the way of definitive preparations but to continue in the same way. But much elaborate organisation remained to be carried out behind the lines. The first thing was to complete the relief of the French troops from the right of the line, and to relieve the 42nd Division from the sector to the left of the Naval Division, the object in each place being to reduce the number of separate formations to the minimum. In place of these, the 13th Division and the remainder of the 29th Division, now at last strongly reinforced, returned to Cape Helles.

The necessary trench reliefs were carried out on the nights of December 31st and January 1st, and the lines from sea to Straits were held thereafter by only four divisions, the 13th on the left, the 29th and the 52nd in the centre and the Royal Naval Division on the right. In support of the last named, there remained some French artillery, which the French commander readily agreed should come under our orders for the remaining few days of the campaign, to "escape the disadvantages of divided command in the final stage" of the evacuation.

The Naval Division sector, which had previously consisted of some two thousand yards of line between the restricted French sector overlooking the Straits and the 42nd Division, now ran, roughly, from the centre of the old sector to the coast. General Mercer's brigade remained where it was before, and General Trotman's brigade moved across to the new sub-sector on the left, the 52nd Division taking over the old sub-sector on the right. The Hood and Drake Battalions of the 1st Brigade and the 1st R.M. and Howe Battalions of the 2nd Brigade were now in the front lines, the Hawke Battalion and the 2nd R.M. in the reserve (Eski) line, and in bivouac the Nelson and Anson Battalions and the 2/2nd and 2/4th Battalions of the London Regiment.

The date of the evacuation had been fixed for January 8th, and the final plans, modelled on those so supremely successful at Anzac and Suvla, had been made. The task before the corps commander was, indeed, more arduous than had been the case on the other front. The accumulation of stores was more considerable, the front deeper and the communications more exposed. But the problem was still essentially a simple one. During the days immediately following the reorganisation of the sectors of defence, all troops not required for front line or support duty, and all stores not needed for the maintenance of this smaller force had to be withdrawn.

As soon as this was done the final withdrawal, accompanied inevitably by an increasing, but still a very limited, measure of risk, could begin. For the purpose of the final orders issued to the troops concerned, this stage of the operation was defined as beginning on "X" day, "Z" day being, of course, the day on the evening of which our positions on the peninsula would be surrendered. The date of "X" day was necessarily determined by the progress made with the withdrawal of stores, guns and reserve troops.

For this the arrangements were in charge of Major-General the Hon. H. A. Lawrence, then commanding the 52nd Division (later Chief of Staff to Sir Douglas Haig in France).

Progress was, on the whole, as good as could have been expected. The first units to leave were, as has been stated, the French infantry and 42nd Division. Next came the bulk of the artillery, the horses, and the surplus transport of the remaining troops. Then, in the last days, the baggage of the Divisional and Brigade Headquarters, the battalion records and the regimental stores of the units in the line.

By "X" day, first announced as January 5th and then postponed till

January 6th, all this had been accomplished, and there was nothing to show that our movements had aroused the enemy's suspicion. On this day the period of calculable risk began. The front line trenches and the reserve (Eski) line were still held in full strength, but the artillery was now reduced to a minimum, and the reserve infantry were preparing for embarkation. Thus, on the night of January 6th-7th, the two battalions of the London Regiment attached to the Naval Division were embarked, and by the morning of January 7th the total strength of the division (all arms) was reduced to some 4,400.

Assuming other divisions to have been similarly thinned, there were not many more than 16,000 men on the peninsula on January 7th, when the Turks opened a terrific bombardment at 2 p.m. The shelling on the left was the heaviest ever experienced on the peninsula; on the right, where the Naval Division were, it was less severe than the bombardments of December 23rd, 24th and 25th. This was extremely opportune, since an effective counter-bombardment could be maintained on the left flank by the guns of the supporting squadron (Captain Dent, R.N.), but on that flank only. As it was, the attempted attack was broken by the help of the navy, and the whole front was quiet again by 5 p.m.

After this episode, the execution of the plan went on uninterruptedly, and during the night of January 7th-8th the support battalions (Hawke and 2nd R.M.) of the Naval Division left the trenches for the last time. They were relieved in the Eski line by detachments of the front-line garrison The final allocation of troops for the divisional sector of the firing, support and Eski lines was 845 all ranks and 8 machine guns to the firing line, 300 all ranks and 2 machine guns in immediate support, and 460 all ranks and 3 machine guns in the third line, all drawn from the Hood, Drake, 1st R.M. and Howe battalions. Simultaneously, all other arms of the division in the defensive zone were reduced proportionately, except the medical personnel, which was fixed at the proportionately high figure of 210 all ranks.

The dangers of leaving the defence of a position 2,000 yards in extent to be defended in depth by nearly 2,000 men were obvious; but they were not overwhelming. In bivouac, were approximately another 2,000 men (the Hawke Battalion, two companies of the 2nd R.M. Battalion and details of engineers, medical personnel and the other infantry battalions), and a new line covering the beaches had been organised by the G.O.C. embarkation. To this line had been allotted (from the Naval Division) 400 officers and men of the 2nd R.M. Battalion. Even the absence of artillery, though it must have meant very heavy losses had an infantry engagement developed, could hardly have meant disaster. The real danger was of a storm at sea, which would cut off the slender garrison for a period of days. But against this risk no staff work could prevail.

By now it was "Z" day. The day's programme was mapped out in detail. Ammunition had to be buried, control posts had to be manned; officers in charge of the different parties had to familiarize themselves for the last time with the exact route of their departure, with the posts to which they must report. The burden of work fell, however, to the staffs of battalions and brigades. Strengths of platoons and companies, which are usually left to the computation of clerks in orderly rooms, were the key to the whole operation. No margin of error was permissible. The route from the front line to the beach was picketed, and, at stated points, control posts in charge of officers and signallers had to be furnished with exact numbers of the parties which would pass them at different times, each scheduled to the minute. As the parties passed, the figures were to be telephoned to the next post, and so on till the beach was reached. If the strengths were inaccurate, or the parties not up to scheduled time, the embarkation arrangements must break down, for each boat had to be loaded to capacity, and as it became available. There was no margin for men, expected at one time, arriving at another.

The computation of a battalion state is at all times one of the minor horrors of war. In a campaign where it is impossible by parading a battalion to exercise the only real check on the figures supplied, it verges on the major category. Where the state has to be exact, the balance goes over. And so, for many of the officers, this last day on the peninsula, which should have been charged with so many poignant and dramatic memories, was spent in feverishly tracing bombers, signallers, transport men or batmen, detached some months before for some special duty, but electing to appear or disappear at this eleventh hour with a quiet modesty which may have indicated a high degree of personal charm, but which accounted for a regrettable absence of that quality in brigade majors, staff captains, colonels and adjutants. Besides these trifling but urgent anxieties, was the disinclination to be wounded at this last moment of an historic campaign.

The afternoon of January 8th wore on, and as the bright sun faded from the winter sky to sink beneath the still placid waters of the Aegean, a silence fell upon the peninsula. Faded now were those dreams of

Horses picketed on the road made between Cape Helles
and Sedd-el-Bahr

suffering, of ambition, or of victory, which each man, however humble, or however noble, holds in the secrecy of a mind dominated by trustful humility, or ambition, or the inspiration of patriotism. Beneath the soil of that dedicated peninsula, were many who had experienced all these things; and by these, who had experienced none, those others were to be abandoned. No longing for rest, for the joys of decent and homely comforts, for the society of friends, could quite remove the impression. The trenches were to be surrendered, and the graves of friends were to be abandoned to the enemy. Nearer home, in battles more vast, and in their material issue more important, something of what had been lost was to be regained. But what was saved, was saved by the material victory of superior force. The chance of a victory against odds, and so of an earlier and a wiser peace, had gone for ever.

Probably the judgment of the rank and file was on the whole a merciful one. Perhaps it was too merciful. But, at any rate, it was amid a silence which it needed no discipline to enforce, that at 6.15 in the gathering dusk of that fateful but uneventful day, the troops in bivouac were paraded for the last time on the peninsula, and marched off along the familiar roads worn by the feet of so many men of their own race now dead or broken in battle. With no more than a look, men passed by landmark after landmark familiar in earlier battles, till they reached those beaches, so nobly won, which it was now so important to abandon with quickness and precision. Hardly a shell came from Asia, and those that did, fell mercifully. Each party, as they arrived, were marched along one or other of the piers, packed into lighters or destroyers, so many, methodically counted, into each, and moved off to the larger transports waiting off the coast.

All this time, the front line garrison remained; it was no use their leaving till the destroyers and lighters, having taken all the reserve troops, were ready to make their second journey. Then only, between 9 and 10 p.m., did the critical hours begin. For at this time the strength of the trench garrisons was to move off, leaving only a skeleton force capable of a resistance long enough, so it was planned, to enable the main garrison to be recalled, or to be embarked, as the situation might dictate. At 11.45 p.m., as soon as the main garrison had been embarked, the skeleton force was itself withdrawn, and the line was left open to the assault of the enemy.

Even now the victory would not have been a bloodless one. As the force withdrew, special parties of engineers and others connected mines previously laid, and closed up barricades and entanglements, before they, too, passed down to the beaches. With them passed the control posts. So, stage by stage, the procession moved on. The period of extreme hazard seemed over. The bulk of the garrison was already embarked, and no Turkish patrols could have got through the mined and barricaded trenches, in time to worry the slender rearguard on the open road between the trenches and the last line of defence above the beaches.

Here, however, the situation was more disquieting. Ever since seven o'clock the wind had been rising, and though the first and second trips were well up to time, the arrangements for the 11.30 embarkations had had to be altered at the last minute, and the prospects for the final trip were anxious. The last troops were expected between 2 and 3 a.m. By 2.30 a.m. all had arrived, but a heavy surf was dashing upon the shore, and it was only under conditions of great stress and peril that the embarkations were effected. The last of the Naval Division to embark were General Paris and his staff, who left soon after 3 a.m. The last of all were Corps and General Headquarters staff and the Naval and Military embarkation officers.

By 3.30 a.m. the inevitable step had been taken. Never again, till peace had been signed, would British troops revisit the peninsula which they had conquered and held against all assaults of the acknowledged enemy.